SPRING IS THE ONLY SEASON

SPRING IS THE ONLY SEASON

How it Works, What it Does and Why it Matters

SIMON BARNES

BLOOMSBURY PUBLISHING
LONDON · OXFORD · NEW YORK · NEW DELHI · SYDNEY

BLOOMSBURY PUBLISHING
Bloomsbury Publishing Plc
50 Bedford Square, London, WC1B 3DP, UK
Bloomsbury Publishing Ireland Limited,
29 Earlsfort Terrace, Dublin 2, D02 AY28, Ireland

BLOOMSBURY, BLOOMSBURY PUBLISHING and the Diana logo are
trademarks of Bloomsbury Publishing Plc

First published in Great Britain 2025

Copyright © Simon Barnes, 2025
Illustrations © Cindy Lee Wright, 2025

Simon Barnes is identified as the author of this work in accordance with the
Copyright, Designs and Patents Act 1988.

Excerpts of *The Waste Land*, by T.S. Eliot reproduced with permission from Faber
and Faber Ltd; excerpt of 'The Vatican Rag' by Tom Lehrer reproduced with
permission from the author; excerpt from *The Lion, the Witch and the Wardrobe* by
C.S. Lewis © copyright 1950 C.S. Lewis Pte Ltd. Extract used with permission

Every reasonable effort has been made to trace copyright holders of material
reproduced in this book, but if any have been inadvertently overlooked
the publishers would be glad to hear from them. For legal purposes, the
Acknowledgements on p. 411 constitute an extension of this copyright page

All rights reserved. No part of this publication may be: i) reproduced or transmitted
in any form, electronic or mechanical, including photocopying, recording or by
means of any information storage or retrieval system without prior permission in
writing from the publishers; or ii) used or reproduced in any way for the training,
development or operation of artificial intelligence (AI) technologies, including
generative AI technologies. The rights holders expressly reserve this publication
from the text and data mining exception as per Article 4(3) of the Digital Single
Market Directive (EU) 2019/790

A catalogue record for this book is available from the British Library

ISBN: HB: 978-1-5266-6737-3; EBOOK: 978-1-5266-6732-8;
EPDF: 978-1-5266-6733-5

2 4 6 8 10 9 7 5 3 1

Typeset by Newgen KnowledgeWorks Pvt. Ltd., Chennai, India
Printed and bound in Great Britain by CPI Group (UK) Ltd, Croydon CR0 4YY

To find out more about our authors and books visit www.bloomsbury.com
and sign up for our newsletters

For product safety related questions contact
productsafety@bloomsbury.com

CLW
for all seasons

Hope springs eternal in the human breast
>Alexander Pope, *Essay on Man*

'In the spring, Jeeves, a livelier iris gleams upon the burnish'd dove.'
'So I have been informed, sir.'
'Right ho! Then bring me my whangee, my yellowest shoes, and the old green Homburg. I'm going into the park to do pastoral dances.'
>P.G. Wodehouse, *The Inimitable Jeeves*

CONTENTS

	Foreword	xi
1	Astronomical spring	1
2	Botanical spring	17
3	Spring comes to Streatham	37
4	Mythological spring	55
5	The song of spring	75
6	Poetic spring	93
7	Spring on the wing	113
8	Feasting in spring	131
9	Springtime travellers	149
10	Sporting spring	167
11	Sweet spring	183
12	Lady Chatterley's spring	199
13	The dark side of spring	217
14	Portraits of spring	233

CONTENTS

15	Spring awakenings	251
16	Love in the spring	269
17	Oological spring	285
18	Agricultural spring	301
19	Spring at sea	317
20	Agribusiness in spring	333
21	Phenological spring	351
22	Subversive spring	367
23	Spring in the time of climate change	385
23.5	Spring comes to Holkham	403
	Acknowledgements	411
	Index	413
	Image credits	429

FOREWORD

The meaning of life is 23.5.

In Douglas Adams's *The Hitchhiker's Guide to the Galaxy* the computer Deep Thought concludes that the meaning of life is 42. Nice try, but wrong. No one who lives in the temperate parts of the world could ever doubt that the correct answer is 23.5.

This is the angle at which the earth wobbles as it makes its annual journey around the sun. During half of the year the top bit is inclined away from the sun and it's winter in the north. But then – glory be! – it starts to wobble back the other way. And that means spring.

If you live above the Tropic of Cancer or below the Tropic of Capricorn – 23.5 degrees north and 23.5 degrees south – you live with the seasons. That means that every single bloody year you get spring. I have slept in rainforest, patted a great whale and walked with lions; I have heard the B Minor Mass, read *Ulysses* and strolled round the Van Gogh Museum in Amsterdam – and spring is more miraculous than them all.

Every year the time of cold, dark, hopelessness and death gives way to light, life, hope and joy. Could anything be more remarkable? Spring determines the growth pattern of trees, the life cycle of butterflies, the song of birds, the sex life of mammals and the way every non-tropical human understands life.

Most of us who experience spring live with hope as an ever-present certainty. We base our lives on the premise that things will get better. From the December solstice to the solstice of June, every day has more light than the one before: so let us define spring as the time when every today is longer than yesterday: a six-month season of enlightenment.

We associate light with every good thing in our lives. We turn to virtue when we have seen the light, good people are a shining light or a beacon of light, in bad times we look for the light at the end of the tunnel and my beloved is, indeed, the light of my life. But those who turn bad go over to the Dark Side, have a dark side to their character, perhaps indulging in murky business deals, while those who taste despair are in a dark place going through a dark time. Horror and evil come from the darkness, but we can live through the dark times of the year because we know that in the end the light will return.

In winter very little grows, but then spring starts to advance. It marches – strolls – the length of mainland Britain south to north, from Lizard Point to Dunnet Head, at 1.9mph: a three-week journey that brings light to the land and the sea. Plants use the light to make food for themselves and by doing so they power the plant-eaters, they power the eaters of plant-eaters and they power those who eat the eaters of the eaters of plants. Every food chain[1] begins with plants — with the sun — with light.

Winter is the time for holding on, when the only aim in life is not dying. But in spring everything changes. That's because for most living things it's the only time they can fulfil their destinies and become ancestors. In spring life lives to make life.

The glorious restlessness of spring hits us humans even in the heart of our cities. We have all welcomed the blessed day when spring seems to arrive in a single mighty leap and in the springtime streets people bare their arms or wear their jackets on their thumbs, everyone is more pretty or more handsome than yesterday, the pubs spread out across the pavement and the air buzzes with the love of company and a little light flirtation.

> In springtime, the only pretty ring time,
> When birds do sing, hey ding a ding ding;
> Sweet lovers love the spring

as they sing in *As You Like It*. At the beginning of Ovid's *Metamorphoses* we are taken back to the Golden Age, the time when everything was infinitely better.

> Spring was the only season. Flowers which had never been planted

---

[1] Not counting oddities like the ecosystems that exist around hydrothermal vents in the deep oceans.

were kissed into life by the warming breath of the
  gentle zephyrs ...²

Or as Harry Secombe sang:

If I ruled the world
Every day would be the first day of spring ...³

Spring is our closest contact point with nature. In spring we are more alive and so more aware of non-human life than at any other time in the year, and more inclined to take joy in it. So let us celebrate spring: the glorious six-month-long awakening that stretches from one solstice to the next, from December through to June. Let's look at how it works, what it does, what we have done with it and how it dictates the way we live and think and understand the world. Let us look at spring by way of butterflies, birds, bees and bats, by way of great artists and poets, by way of major religions and undying mythologies. Let us try and understand what spring has always been, how it has shaped us and what it will become in a changing world.

As is my habit, I have just paused in writing these words to look from my window in search of the next line. It's February: a bright spring day on the edge of the Broads in Norfolk. The buds are starting to burst on

---

² Translation David Raeburn, Penguin Classics, London, 2004.
³ Written by Leslie Bricusse and Cyril Ornadel for the 1963 musical *Pickwick*.

the elder. I can hear two song thrushes singing combatively. Two oystercatchers have just flown over calling hard, only one thing on their minds. It's nice and warm in the sun, bloody freezing when it goes behind a cloud.

Let us celebrate spring by trying to understand it. Let us attempt to do so – in 23.5 chapters, what else?

The herons are building their nests in the heronry 200 yards away.

I

Astronomical spring

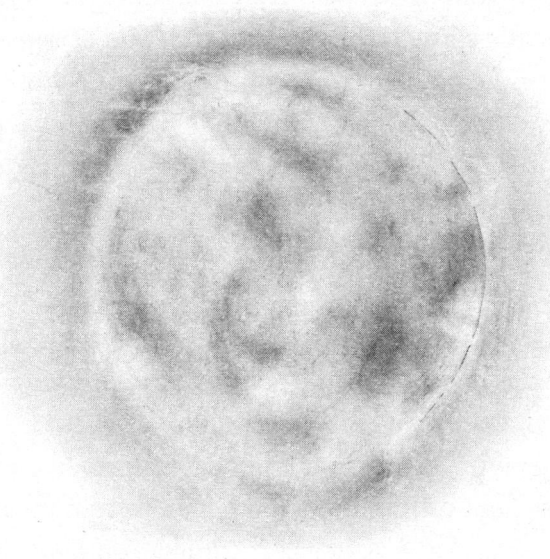

Let's begin at the beginning: with the formation of the earth 4.6 billion years ago. I suppose we could start with the beginning of the universe 9.2 billion years before that, but let's be parochial. Spring as it exists, if indeed it does exist on other planets, discovered or undiscovered, is beyond my scope. My prejudices, at least for the duration of this book, must be made clear: I'm an earthist. I make this claim with a certain gravity: indeed, I have no other option.

The earth began, as it continues, by way of gravity. Gravity is what brings us back down to earth again when we leap, preventing us from flying off into space, so we think of it – in our intuitive earthist way – as something the earth does. It's a little disconcerting to realise that you, the leaper, exert the same gravitational forces on the earth as the earth does on you; it's just that that earth, being rather bigger, doesn't pay your personal gravity much heed. Gravity is the force that pulls objects towards each other: everything that has mass has gravity, and you, dear reader, have mass.

So when there was a swirling cloud of dust and gas in the vastness of interstellar space, the small particles that made up that cloud acted on each other: for having mass just as you do, such gravity-powered interaction was inevitable. The cloud eventually collapsed under its own gravity. Some of it eddied and formed planets, and these kept on spinning and began to spin faster, in the same way that a skater performing a spin-sequence speeds up. The result of all this spinning was the solar system: the sun and the planets that continue to circle it were all formed at the same time, as part of the same event. The third rock from the sun was and is the earth: and having been formed it continues to revolve around the sun, prevented from whizzing off into space by the same force that formed it in the first place: gravity. The earth's sideways movement stops it crashing into the sun, the sun's gravity stops it flying off into the space that lies beyond the solar system. It is at once both captive and free: balanced to perfection in a knife-edge of gravity.

The swirling forces that created the earth also gave it a spin, and the earth continues spinning to this day because there's nothing to stop it. If you spin a coin on a table top, no matter how good a start you give it, it will eventually stop rotating. That's because gravity, air resistance and friction are all working against the spin: but in space the circumstances that stopped the spinning coin don't exist. So the earth spins round the sun and as it does so it spins around itself. It spins 365¼ times before it gets back to the same point and starts again, and each one of those rotations takes 24 hours: so let me state, in the unlikely event that you have missed the point, that the dual spinning motions define the way we understand time: days and years.

And if it had been left in that state earth would continue steadily, spinning and circling calmly. There would be no seasons and every part of the globe would have a roughly similar experience every single day: exactly as we do now on two days every year: days when everywhere on earth has 12 hours of daylight and 12 hours of night. But that's not how it works. Our experience from one part of the world to another – or to put the same thing another way, our experience from one part of the year to another – varies widely, wildly, almost incredibly. Because we have seasons.

We have seasons because the earth not only spins: it wobbles. This wobble directs the way we think and the way we live and the way we understand life. Everything that lives in the seasonal lands has no option but to lead a life shaped by wobble of the earth. This wobble was imparted by a collision very early in the earth's history. I attempted to achieve an intuitive grasp of this wobble by upgrading from the spinning coin to a desk toy: a spinning top designed to perform for a slightly uncanny length of time. It cost me £4.68 and it was a good investment. Staring at it as it spun on and on helped me to move on from our natural, intuitive and inevitable conviction – our *idée fixe* – that the earth itself is fixed. It is, of course, dynamic – far more dynamic than the top spinning away between my Spring Notebook and the fossil ammonite that serves as a paperweight.

I touched a pen to the spinning top to simulate the great collision of the early years of the earth's history, and was pleased to see that the top continued to spin, but now with a pronounced wobble. The parallel is far from exact, as the top is not spinning in the vastness of space but, like the spinning coin, is subject to friction from the wood of my desk, air resistance in the hut that I work in and the gravity of the earth on which desk, spinning top and spin-imparting human have their being. But there it was: it spun, and as it spun it wobbled, and that helped me to make sense of the wobbling earth beneath me.

The earth, however, is not on my desk, so once it started spinning it stayed spinning, and once it started wobbling it stayed wobbling. It wobbles on at an angle of 23.5 degrees. A wobble is not unique to the earth: all planets wobble: Mercury at an almost imperceptible 0.03 degrees and Uranus at a dramatic 98 degrees. Deep astronomical study has revealed that the earth's wobble varies very slightly: it shifts between 22.1 degrees and 24.5 degrees over a cycle of 41,000 years. That figure of 23.5 – more correctly 23.44 – is where we are right now and it'll be there or thereabouts for the next few millennia, after which I may have to update this text.

And it's this wobble that brings the seasons – but it only brings them to the seasonal lands. These lands lie north of the Tropic of Cancer, which encircles the earth 23.5 degrees north of the Equator, and south of the Tropic of Capricorn, 23.5 degrees south of the Equator. The areas in between, which we tend to refer to, a shade misleadingly, as the Tropics, have, inevitably, a tropical climate, characterised by alternations of wet and dry, or wetter and drier. These systems of alternation inevitably have their own effects on everything that lives there, including human culture. But the changes that come to the seasonal lands are far greater, far more dramatic, and they demand a complex and profound response from every living thing north of Cancer or south of Capricorn.

We mark the wobble in our calendar and in our lives by the solstice: the point at which the tilt is at its most extreme. It is also the point at which the earth begins to tilt back the other way. The solstices take place each year – roughly, it varies very slightly from year to year – on 21 December and 21 June; astronomers routinely calculate the precise time down to the second. The halfway points between the two solstices are the equinoxes, which means equal night. On these days every place on earth has roughly the same length of day and the same length of night, hence the name – though some prefer equilux, equal light, to reflect our dependence, not just for morale but for life itself, on light.

We are warmer at the summer solstice – June in the northern hemisphere, December in the southern – than we are at the opposite time of year, and the reason for that seems obvious enough: we naturally assume that the tilt brings us nearer to the sun: when our own half of the earth is tilted towards the sun in summer, we are closer to it than we were in winter and therefore warmer. But that's not the case: those of us in the northern hemisphere are actually closer to the sun during the winter. The earth's orbit is not a perfect circle; it's an ellipse, so at some parts of the year we are closer to the sun than at others.

It's not the distance that makes the difference of temperature in the seasons: it's the attitude. The tilt. In the northern hemisphere spring the northern part of the earth is pointing towards the sun so, although we are now further away from it, we are getting better value from it. You can demonstrate this with a simple experiment. Close this book and hold it up. Now take a torch. A smartphone with the flashlight app will do, though a hand torch with a tighter beam will give you a better result. All right? Shine the beam directly on the book. That will give you a neat circle of light. Now tilt the book backwards, so the top is pointing away from the light. Your circle of light is now an elongated egg. Each beam of light is spread out over a much greater area of the book's cover: so the light at every point is less intense than it was when the light struck the book head-on, as a circle.

And that also affects the earth in terms of warmth, for the sun's rays bring heat as well as light. These rays are more concentrated on the northern hemisphere between the equinoxes of March and September than they are in the opposite months, and so these periods are (all things being equal) warmer than they are between September and March.

This warmth is more than pleasant relief for humans and greater relief for all the wild creatures that have somehow survived the winter. The warmth means that plants can grow. Grass needs a soil temperature of 8 degrees Celsius to grow, but it takes 9 degrees for a grass seed to germinate. Other germination temperatures: spinach 2 degrees, broad bean, pea, cabbage at 8, tomato 10, aubergine, pepper and cucumber at 16.

The wobble of the earth doesn't just mean more warmth. It also means more hours of daylight. When the northern part of the earth is tilted towards the sun the revolution of the earth – which gives us the alternation between day and night – presents us towards the sun for more hours in 24 than it does when we are tilted the other way. The further north you live, the more extreme the contrast between the daylight available in winter and in summer.

SPRING IS THE ONLY SEASON

In Cornwall, where you find Lizard Point, the most southerly spot on the British mainland, the time between sunrise and sunset on the winter solstice is around 8 hours 2 minutes; this compares with 5 hours and 49 minutes on the Shetland Isles north of the Scottish mainland. The summer solstice brings a slightly greater difference: 16 hours and 26 minutes in Cornwall, compared to 18 hours 55 minutes in the Shetlands.

This peak sunlight allowance, generous as it is, is drastically extended by the phenomenon of twilight. In the tropics you don't really get twilight: the sun goes down as if in an express lift and then it's dark. In some tropical countries there's a tradition of sundowners: a drink to celebrate the spectacular end to the day: a huge sun racing to the horizon. You have to be quick with your drink or you miss the magic moment. But the further you go towards the nearest pole, the greater the angle the sun makes with the horizon. That means that there is still light – spilling over the horizon from the unseen sun – for a substantial period after the sun has gone down, and again before it rises again. If you find yourself in the north of Scotland in the weeks either side of the June solstice you will hard pushed to see any darkness at all. This phenomenon – sometimes referred to as 'da simmer dim' – is extraordinarily uplifting. We know that light is good for us, not as an intellectual fact, but in the marrow of our bones.

The payback for such joys is obvious enough. In the winter the cruel pangs of darkness affect the human spirits, and, of course, the sustained deprivation of light affects everything else that lives. Humans in the northern latitudes have tended to compensate by establishing rich traditions of distillation: whisky, whiskey, vodka, applejack, poteen, akavit, bennivín and on and on: spirits to lighten the darkness. The word 'whiskey' comes from the Gaelic *uisce beatha*, meaning the water of life. The dark times are associated with depression and seasonally affected disorder, or SAD. At its worst they bring despair and suicide.

Our need for the heat and light of the sun is made more acute by the months of deprivation. Our efforts to make the most of the grudging light of winter led to the convention of daylight saving: manipulating the clock so that we can get more daylight when we need it most. The day that 'the clocks go back' in late October in the UK is one of long-anticipated lowering of the spirits: suddenly, at a stroke, it's dark in late afternoon rather than early evening. It's as if our rulers had seized control of the sun, tormenting us with deprivation of light and hope. But the world comes right again on the weekend at the end of March when, though we may lose an hour in bed, we are suddenly given the priceless gift of sunlit evenings.

In the winter of 1977–8 the British government decided to scrap this hour business and carry on straight through. It was even more depressing. I remember getting up in the dark, going to work in the dark, catching the train in the dark, working all day in the office of the *Stratford Express* and then going home in the dark. My daily commute involved a walk over London

Bridge: every morning, looking east, towards Tower Bridge, I would see the sun make its reluctant way above the horizon as if freshly painted by Monet, and I would mutter T. S. Eliot's words: 'A crowd flowed over London Bridge, so many. I had not thought death had undone so many.'[1]

The sun is the centre of this book as well as the centre of the solar system, so it's worth taking a look at it from a non-earthist point of view, if only for a moment. It looks small and manageable up in the sky, especially in the seasonal lands where its heat is usually comfortable. It looks much smaller than, say, London. But it is – and I mean this literally – unimaginably colossal. To any non-earthist observer – or non-Venusist or non-Jovist – the sun *is* the solar system: so huge and so dominant that nothing else at all could possibly be of the slightest importance. It has a radius of 695,000km, or 109 times that of the earth, which is impressive. But when it comes to mass the difference is so enormous that the earth can be forgotten, along with all the other planets. The mass of the sun is 333,000 times that of the earth: more than 99 per cent of all the mass in the solar system is the sun.

It was formed from that molecular cloud we talked about earlier, most of the cloud turning in on itself while the rest orbited it in the form of a flattened disc. This disc was to become the rest of the solar system, most notably the planets, and most significantly for us, the

---

[1] From *The Waste Land*; more on this poem in Chapter 22.

earth. The earth can be understood as an afterthought of the sun.

The centre of the cloud that was to become the sun got so hot and so dense that nuclear fusion took place in its core: that's how a star is born. The sun now contains 73 per cent hydrogen and 25 per cent helium: the one is transformed into the other by the process of fusion. (The rest of the sun is oxygen, carbon, neon and iron.) The process of fusion creates tremendous energy: every second the sun converts four million tonnes of matter into energy. This can take between 10,000 and 170,000 years to escape from the core: it eventually does so in the form of light and heat.

The sun is not as small a star as we sometimes like to pretend, either out of uncharacteristic modesty or because the idea of living so close to this unimaginably powerful generator of energy is really rather alarming: for it is way beyond human control, and its power is way beyond any realistic human ambition. It is classified as a yellow dwarf, but it gives out, as we know by simply looking out of the window, white light.

The sun has no definite boundary, as the solid earth does; the calculations mentioned earlier are based on the apparent visible surface, the photosphere. The sun has an atmosphere, some of which – the corona – becomes visible at times of total eclipse. The sun is not solid – only gases can exist at the sun's temperatures – and the sun revolves more quickly at its equator than it does at its poles. Unlike the earth – an oblate spheroid, that is to say, a ball that is flattened slightly at the poles – it is an almost perfect sphere.

The sun will eventually collapse in on itself, but it's not in any itchin' hurry to do so. In the film *Annie Hall* the schoolboy Woody Allen character refuses to do his homework because the universe is expanding, so there's no point. ('You're here in Brooklyn! Brooklyn is not expanding!') The sun's impending collapse is unlikely to affect modern education: though in about five billion years the sun's core will increase dramatically in density and temperature. Its outer layers will expand beyond the orbits of Mercury and Venus and that will make the earth uninhabitable; while the sun itself acquires the status of red giant. It will then cool, shed its outer layers and become a white dwarf.

The second nearest star to earth (the nearest after the sun) is Proxima Centauri, and it's 250,000 times further away than the sun. What matters right now, to every living thing on the planet, is that the sun continues as a constant and stable source of energy. We have all of those five billion years in which to create something worthwhile. And while the forces of evolution have created otters and kingfishers and swifts as well as humans, and humans have created the Goldberg Variations and *Ulysses*, it strikes me that in some areas there is room for improvement. (There is a story that Isaac Asimov criticised the idea of sending Bach's music into space as part of a message to other civilisations that may exist in the vastness of space. He said it was showing off.)

The sun dominates our lives and has been an object of veneration in perhaps every civilisation that existed before modern times. It has been an explicit object of worship in many of these. The sun is said by some to be at the heart of all the religions that worship a single god: the phrase 'solar monotheism' is used here. There are shifting and complex sun myths in many civilisations; these include the Germanic Sól, the Vedic Surya, the Aztec Huitzilopochtli and Tezcatlipoca, both agog for human sacrifice, and Ra of Egypt. Mesopotamian royalty was addressed as 'my sun'. According to a Chinese story there were once ten suns, all brothers, and they loved to play. One day they all came out together to enjoy themselves and as a result the earth was in danger of frazzling up. But the heroic Hou Yi got his bow and shot down nine of them and the earth was saved.

The equation of the sun with danger is perhaps most vividly to be found in the story of Phaeton, son of the Greek god Helios; it is Helios who drives the sun across the sky every day in a chariot drawn by the most tremendous horses. The story is best told in Ovid's *Metamorphoses*: Phaeton, granted a favour by his unwise father, asks if he can pilot the sun for a day. Reluctantly his father agrees, and Phaeton sets off on his journey and inevitably loses control of the horses. As a result, he takes the sun far too close to the earth:

> The earth now burst into flames and all of the hills and the mountains,

split into huge wide cracks, and dried as it lost its
    moisture.
The corn turned white and the trees were charred
    into leafless skeletons;
parched grain offered the perfect fuel for
    self-ruination.[2]

Further disaster is prevented when Zeus slays Phaeton with a thunderbolt.

The story of a power too great for its wielders to control is part of ancient myth and modern fact. That of Phaeton has been interpreted as a parable about nuclear warfare, and, though that remains a potential threat, the story can now be understood for an actual threat that is being realised now, even as you read these words: for we live in a world that is getting more dangerously hot with every passing minute. The sun represents life: but it also brings death. More of that later.

The idea that the sun directs our lives sounds a bit rum to us twenty-first-century humans. After all, we have taken over the planet and had our will over a very great deal of it. When we want light we flick a switch, when we want warmth we flick another switch, and yet another should we want cool. In cities the limited times we spend outside in winter are generally passed in hurrying from one well-heated, well-lit place to the next,

---

[2] Also Penguin Classics translation by David Raeburn, published in 2004.

often travelling between them in well-heated, well-lit forms of transport. It might seem – at least to hypothetical naturalists from Mars, especially if they're inclined to skimp on their research – that our civilisation has been designed with the aim of escaping the tyranny of the seasons, and that we have succeeded triumphantly in that aim.

And though these Martians might seem to have a point, this is not yet fact. Light and warmth come pouring from the sun, bringing not just relief from cold and dark but also acting as a great life-possibilising generator of energy. The rhythm of the sun, as appreciated by those of us on earth who live in the lands most subject to the planet's tilting, dictates the rhythm of our own lives and, with it, the working of our own hearts and minds.

The sun is life, nothing less. And if it goes away in the winter – or at least is pretty stingy with its daily allocation of light and heat – it comes back in the spring. The spinning top collides briefly with the mouse mat and this creates a tilt as it turns back towards the ammonite. The tilt that gives us inequalities of sunlight is nothing less than the way we understand life. That's because the tilt brings winter.

And then it brings spring.

Signs of spring
December 2023

All observations from our place in the Broads, South Norfolk, unless stated.

22	Solstice 0327
	Floods. Buds on ash and hazel
24	Hazel catkins, Huntingfield, Suffolk
28	Alder catkins
	Daisies (maybe left over from last year but never mind)
29	Stock dove calling
	Half a wren song
	Great tit song
30	Exotic plants in flower, an umbellifer and a periwinkle species, Yoxford, Suffolk
31	More great tit song in garden

2

Botanical spring

In 2022 Sir David Attenborough presented a five-part TV blockbuster. This one was about plants and was called *The Green Planet*. It took us back to the Attenborough of old: throughout the series he kept cropping up in front of the cameras, in cities and forests and deserts: there he was rowing a boat across a lake full of water plants, or showing us the oldest tree in the world, or demonstrating the seed dispersal of bulrushes or, on one memorable occasion, manhandling a cactus in stout leather gauntlets, the better to show off the plant's spiny defences. It was a sequence that made it clear that the stout leather gauntlets weren't nearly stout enough: he finished this bravura piece of television in eye-watering discomfort. Anyone else would have stopped dead and gone for another take, but not Attenborough – and that made it vivid and unforgettable television. It was all great stuff and I was asked to write the book of the series. It was a fascinating experience – and by the end of it I was filled with an urgent need to write this book.

The *Green Planet* book followed the pattern of the television series and came in five chapters. The first was set in rainforest: and I delighted in this mighty opening challenge. I have walked in rainforests and slept in rainforests and every second I was there I was filled with a sense of awe that enriched life forever after. I once planted a dipterocarp seedling in an area of cleared forest in Borneo: I have played a tiny part in the fightback of the forests. Rainforests are supported by columns more mighty than those of any cathedral ever built and they bring the thrill of biodiversity in every step you take.

The second chapter was about deserts, and here the delight was not in the diversity and luxuriance of life but in the extraordinary fact that life can continue at all. I have less experience of desert than of rainforest, but enough to be transported back to some inspirational spots, especially the long clefts in the Namib Desert: rainfall from many miles away occasionally reaches them and allows them – in their subtle desert way – to flourish. Here were sunken groves of tamarisk, making an impossible contrast with the miles and miles of cat litter we had travelled through to get there. These are the favourite places of desert rhinos.

Chapter three was about home. And it was at this point that I felt aware – as a sensation in my essential guts rather than as an intellectual concept – that home is every bit as miraculous as the sky-reaching buttress-rooted trees of Borneo or the impossible blooming of the Namibian desert. That's because chapter three was about the lands of the seasons.

To those of us who live in these places, every vista is comfortable, homely and understood: the stuff of reassurance rather than awe. But if we could see in four dimensions rather than the usual three, and bring time into our visual understanding, we would never be in any doubt that the stuff outside our own front doors is a miracle on a par with every teeming acre of rainforest and every scant scrap of life in the desert. Right now, as I sit here typing away or groping for the right word, I can turn my head left through 90 degrees and look out over Norfolk marshland. Last winter brought a ten-day killing frost: the place was brown picked out with startling highlights of white: a tenacious hoarfrost that gave a lethal beauty to everything it touched. The trees were black skeletons, and not a flower in sight.

Six months earlier the place had been a luscious green, the nearest tree, an ash, radiant with fronded leaves. Two alder carrs on either side showed a different shade of green, while the willows that line the river half a mile away were covered in the sharp-pointed leaves that gave William Morris such delight. Yellow flags of iris stood out dramatically from the green of the young reeds and in the wetter places you could see spikes of purple loosestrife and the raspberries-and-cream colour of hemp agrimony.

In winter you can hear the distant gabble of geese, the quacking of mallards and gadwall, the chack-chack-chacking of fieldfares and the soft song of robins, the only birds that sing a proper tune in the British winter. A few months later the place is echoing with song: blackcap, reed warbler, sedge warbler, Cetti's warbler, whitethroat and blackbird, along with grunts and roars from the heronry half a mile off. It even smells different: in winter on those frosty days a rather thrilling nothingness, a cleanness, a clearing of the decks for the action of the spring, on wet days a tough peatiness, and as the spring advances the indefinable scent of growth is set off by more forthright odours of meadowsweet and water mint.

The marsh in summer, the marsh in winter: they're either two different places or a single miracle. The same is true of every other place that hasn't been concreted over: a London plane tree growing from the pavement in the heart of town is in one season bare and stark, in another rich with lush-green palmate leaves; Japanese flowering cherries in suburban streets turn the place shockingly pink before winter is truly over. If we could gaze across time – say, from one solstice to the next – we would think of our own seasonal lands with the awe we routinely give to rainforest and desert.

The seasonal lands are about change, about movement: this is a system that keeps its balance because it is never still. It's the same principle as the spinning top on my desk: or better, as a bicycle. Stand a bicycle up on its two wheels and it falls over. But the same bike is wonderfully stable when it's in motion: miraculously balanced for as long as you keep pedalling. In the seasonal lands the flowers bloom because they fade: they flourish every year because every year they also die.

And it starts with plants. Of course it does: everything starts with plants. If you're not a plant yourself you are either an eater of plants or you eat the eaters of plants. Or both, of course. Plants themselves start with the sun – yes, we're back to that again: because we can never escape it.

So here's an equation: sun plus water equals life. You get both ingredients pretty well all the time in the rainforest, which is why they are so lush. It's also why they are able to keep their steady state, for they are the most stable ecosystems on earth. In the hot deserts – what we think of as deserts, rather than cold deserts like the Gobi or those in Patagonia – there is plenty of sun but hardly any water, which is why the existence of any life at all strikes wonder. This wonder comes at least partly from the fact that in the seasonal lands we are mostly

OK for water: at any rate what we call a drought is a period without rain for a few weeks, rather than a few years. But, as the earth wobbles onward on the course of its annual journey, the sun comes and goes. This means that some periods are highly suitable for making and sustaining life, while at other times simply not dying is a serious challenge.

As the earth tilts back towards the sun and spring advances from winter solstice onward, so each day there is more light available. Every tiny advance in day length increases the possibilities of life: and that's because, alone among living things, plants eat light. (Again for completion I should point out that cyanobacteria – blue-green algae – are also capable of photosynthesis. But unlike plants they are not at the base of almost all ecosystems on earth.) To be more accurate, plants use the energy of light to power the making of their own food. No animal, and, for that matter, no fungus can do that: we must all get our food from something outside our selves. All of us – insects and humans, whales and herrings, mushrooms and toadstools – are plant parasites. We can't exist on our own: we need plants, plants need light to make their food, and so we humans are as dependent on light as any plant that ever lived.

The earth was about a billion years old when some species of bacteria acquired the trick of feeding on light. This is photosynthesis: using light, using the sun's energy to make food. These proto-plants took hydrogen from the atmosphere as an essential part of the process, using the element as a source for electrons in the complex process of food manufacture. Over the next billion years, they found another source for hydrogen: they started to take it from water. It's the one chemical formula almost everyone knows: water is H_2O, two molecules of hydrogen to one of oxygen. They began to take hydrogen from water and to excrete the waste product: oxygen.

It was a disaster. At least at first. Very few forms of life could cope with this newfangled oxygen-rich atmosphere, and a great extinction followed. It's known as the Great Oxidation Event, or sometimes, by less oxygenist observers, as the Great Oxidation Catastrophe. It changed the nature of life on earth and opened opportunities for any form of life that could exploit this new wealth of oxygen.

This was when earth became the green planet. Green is essential to the processes of life as we know it: it's the colour of chlorophyll, the essential stuff that makes possible the process of photosynthesis, and it comes from the chloroplasts that exist inside plant cells. These allow the cell to use the energy of light to convert carbon dioxide and water into glucose. It was a breakthrough: life was now able to proceed with an efficiency never seen before on this planet. They made their own food by using light: they were photoautotrophs. As a result of the success of this stratagem, green algae were able to outperform the red and the brown, and 750 million years ago plants were colonising the land and the earth got greener and greener. At least until very recently.

SPRING IS THE ONLY SEASON

Every year in the seasonal lands there is a recapitulation of history: a re-greening of the earth. Different plants respond in different ways to the return of the light. Trees, if I may state the obvious, are not entirely green: their structural parts, trunks and branches and twigs, are (mostly) unable to perform photosynthesis. They delegate this task to specialist organs, and these, if they are to function, have to be green. We mostly call them leaves, but we prefer needles for conifers, the cone-bearing trees, including the three native to the UK, Scots pine, yew and juniper.

Conifers keep their leaves all the year. These leaves – needles – are very tough. Very few animal species can feed on them. They resist freezing and water loss through their waxy coating. A pine tree covered in needles doesn't put up much more wind resistance than it would if its branches and twigs were bare, so it can usually stand its ground in winter gales. Conifers are good at cold; they are also good at dry, so they tend to dominate challenging environments. What's more they can perform photosynthesis throughout the year, taking advantage of even the shortest winter days to make food and keep going.

The broadleaf trees that grow in the seasonal lands operate a far more extravagant strategy. They lose their leaves in the autumn, having made enough food from their copious leafage during the warmer and better-lit months. They then enter a period of shutdown: a kind of hibernation, a time in which they are not so much growing as existing. The cold of the winter is an important part of the rhythm of their year. The trees then respond to the warming of the soil and the increasing hours of daylight: they wake up and start to make buds, sometimes startlingly early in the year.

We talk about the sap rising in spring. We use the expression as a metaphor for many aspects of the annual miracle, but so far as a tree is concerned it's the literal truth. The sap contains moisture and sugars, energy it has stored during the previous growing season. The plant needs to transfer this substance from the roots to the growing tips, for only once the new leaves have been produced can the tree start to make its own food again. The sap rises through tubes of improbable narrowness, drawn up by negative air pressure: once it has done so the tree can create new leaves. The buds burst, the leaves spread out before the sun and the tree can start again on the process of photosynthesis. This production of extraordinary quantities of photosynthesising devices – a great acreage of sunward-facing surfaces – allows them to make food in quantities no conifer could manage. The payback is that this extravagance gives them a great deal of wind resistance and makes them vulnerable to gales. Gales are more common in winter, but by then the seasonal broadleaf trees have shed their leaves and gone back to sleep. It's a winning strategy for the deciduous broadleaf trees until you get to a point – of latitude or of altitude – at which it no longer works with the same efficiency. And that's the point where conifers start to outcompete the rest.

Even in January, when the daylight hours are only slightly longer than they are at their very shortest, you can find a new growth of stinging nettles: young, tender, thrillingly green and already capable of delivering a painful sting. They rise not from seeds but from the hidden parts of the plant, the underground parts that we refer to casually as roots. Nettles are perennials: that is to say the same plant rises up every year. They can do this because of the remarkable efficiency of their underground storage system. This is a network not of roots, which exist to anchor the plants and to bring in water and nutrients, but of rhizomes and stolons. These are different types of underground stems: a way of storing food for future use while keeping out of sight, unavailable to animals that might want to appropriate the food store for themselves.

New stems rise from old parts. They produce their serrated leaves, they flower with little droopy green catkins and then they set seed, which, if all goes well, will land elsewhere and later germinate to become new plants. But the old plant, though it dies back in the autumn, is still living, and when the time comes round again it will be ready to produce new shoots, often very early in the year. In past centuries the return of nettles was a thing of joy to the human population: it meant that at last, after months of living only on what could be stored and salted and pickled and preserved, a fresh green vegetable could be consumed. Apparently the stings vanish with the cooking,

Cow parsley, almost as common as nettles along country roads, operates the same policy: flourish in the warmer months, die back to the ground when it gets colder and darker, leaving no tender and delicate parts to be damaged by tough conditions and hungry animals. But the show goes on underground, and when conditions change, up come the new shoots, not new plants but new expressions of the old.

Many plants operate this policy of starting again from the ground up, often becoming strong and dominant features of a landscape before shrinking back again. The marshland before me puts up many green shoots of reeds long before the March equinox, springing up from the stolons, the horizontal stems that grow beneath the surface. The yellow flag irises seem far too solid to be the product of just a few months' growth, and in a sense they're not: for they rise annually from rhizomes that are packed with the nutrients they need for growth.

We are most of us familiar with the strategy of the bulb. Plant a bulb and it's a near certainty that flowers will rise from it when spring comes around. Bulbs are another form of modified stem, another food store. They will flower every year, so long as you allow them to carry on living after they have flowered, so that the green leaves that remain can continue the job of photosynthesis and store some of the food they make in the bulbs. The green parts will then die back of their own accord, but the bulb remains, ready to spring into life when the year turns. We associate bulbs most obviously with daffodils. They come in 56 species; the pale, single-coloured one that is sometimes known as Lent lily is (probably) native to the British Isles.

The ploy of keeping such a useful food store means that a flower can rise from a bulb early in the year and reach an impressive size; the drawback is that other living things find a bulb good eating. Daffodils defend themselves by producing a poison, lycorine. Other bulbs are comfortably edible, onions being the most obvious example, but wild boars, great rootlers in the forest floor, have a taste for such bulbs as are palatable. It's possible that the great bluebell woods of Britain are relatively recent things: only able to thrive in such devastating beauty since the eradication of wild boars 400 years ago. Their accidental reintroduction in recent years – there are now more than 2,000 in several different breeding populations – will change the ecology of the places they live in, bringing new opportunities for some and unexpected problems for others.

Trying to live forever may look like the best possible strategy to us, but not all plants agree. Many of them, especially those in the gentler parts of the seasonal lands, work on a two-year plan. These are biennials, plants that have a quiet first year, consolidating, making and storing food and building up for the big year that follows. In its first year the new plants establish themselves, usually as something pretty inconspicuous, like a flat rosette of leaves that's reasonably safe from grazing animals, allowing them to build up a supply of nutrients. Many of them die right back above the ground when the cold weather comes again, like some of the perennials we have just discussed. That might look as if the effort put into the first year has been wasted, but not so: it's all there in the food store below ground, which, when the second spring comes around, will fuel the growth of the plant. That will bring us some glorious things like foxgloves, standing almost head-high with a great spike of striking flowers. In this second year the plant will flower, fruit and set seeds. Once that's done, it will die: if all has gone well at least some seeds will have landed in helpful places, where they will grow and set seeds in their turn, and so the original plant becomes an ancestor: its genes living on in its progeny.

The carrot is a perennial, storing its nutrients after the first year in a taproot. If it was allowed to survive the winter, it would then put up a flowering stalk, a rather gorgeous umbellifer, but when humans grow domesticated varieties of carrots we dig them up after the first year in order to consume that taproot, its nutrients fuelling us rather than the future growth of the plant.

Other plants operate a strategy based on an even shorter life: they grow from seeds, come to flower, scatter their own seeds and then die, never to bloom again, save in their progeny. Some will go through their entire life cycle in a matter of weeks, putting up soft, fragile stems, flowering and dying at express pace. Chickweed is a classic example of these plants in a hurry: gardeners are always in a hurry themselves, trying to root them out before they set seeds, for the new plants will come up in great profusion. This policy of a short life and a merry one is, in its own way, every bit as effective as that of the centuries-old oak: if both become ancestors then both have operated successful strategies. Probably the most spectacular UK annual is the field poppy, the bright red flowers that love disturbed ground, often seen on the edge of cornfields, though in these days of powerful herbicides very seldom within it.

I have written a fair amount about food stores and nutrients in this chapter: various devices that plants use so that they can grow without immediate reference to the sun: they can survive the winter and then start growing with food they already have. Once the plant is established and its green parts are photosynthesising, it can make its own food. But this ability to store the energy of the sun and use it when the moment is right is what allows so many forms of life to survive in the cold times and flourish again when the warmth returns.

This need for a store of food, this need for something to kick-start the processes of living until the plant is capable of photosynthesising again, is also found in seeds. A seed is not just a plant embryo; it is also a starter pack of nutrients.[1] These allow the plant, once germinated, to produce a shoot and get it above the surface, so its small green first leaves can start functioning. Seeds are full of nutrients and that's why seeds supply so much of our own food needs: bread is made from the seeds of wheat, sometimes from other kinds of corn. You can get an understanding of the nutritious nature of the seed itself in a dish of baked beans on toast or a packet of peanuts: seeds packed with what it takes to

---

[1] Unless it's an orchid. This is why humans found them impossible to cultivate until 1922.

fuel the growth of future plants, food that we steal for ourselves.

The way that many plants shut down for the winter is a kind of miracle in itself: but the greater miracle, at least to our eyes, is that it all starts all over again. The trigger mechanisms for this change from dormancy to vibrancy are various and complex. Many plants require a sharp taste of cold not just to sleep but to wake up again: cold is an essential part of their rhythm of their lives. Desert plants can be dormant for years, often as seeds, until a rare burst of rain awakens them and the desert is briefly in flower. In temperate places there is usually enough rain, and most of it falls in the winter, so water is no use as a trigger. Instead, day length and soil temperatures are factors in the waking process: as the prince kissed Sleeping Beauty, so the sun wakes the plants. This fairy tale is one of thousands of rebirth tales we use, partly to understand the spring better and partly to glorify it still more; more on that in Chapter 4.

Once plants have put out their working parts – the green bits of themselves – they are self-sufficient for as long as the sun lasts. That means they can move onto the next stage. For the angiosperms, that means making flowers.

Charles Darwin called the origin of flowering plants 'an abominable mystery': the fossil record appears to show a quite sudden leap into this new way of being. The earliest fossils date back to 145 million years, though finds of pollen indicate that they've been around rather longer. Whatever the origin, it's been a wild success: 80 per cent of all green plants are angiosperms, which are also referred to as flowering plants. This includes many more plants than those we refer to casually just as flowers. All broadleaf trees are angiosperms, and so are all grasses. A flower is a device for reproduction: it is about producing pollen (male) and moving it to the stigma (female) of another plant of the same species. Most flowers contain both male and female parts, though a good few separate the sexes.

The flowers of grasses seldom attract the attention – of human or any other kind of eye. They have no need to do so. Their pollen is distributed by the wind. This sounds a random method, and indeed it is, insofar as it is driven by chance. But grasses of the same species are often very close together, so it's not a big stretch to get the pollen to the right species.

But many flowers are very noticeable. They are not only noticeable: they are attractive, in the way that their roots are not. That's not a merely subjective judgement, nor is it a generalisation about human aesthetics. It's also a statement of hard evolutionary fact: many flowers are there to attract. That's their job. They are there to attract animals, and these animals will take the pollen from one flower to another: picking up male parts and taking them to female parts. They bring these animals in by means of an attractive scent and an attractive appearance.

This strategy of employing animals as go-betweens changed the earth. The pollinators are mostly flying insects. Some insects – most obviously moths – are active at night, so many plants put up their best odours at night. Gardeners sometimes exploit this trait by making a night garden, a place to sit in the late twilight of late spring to savour the odours. Though insects do most of the pollinating, plenty of other groups will happily take it on in the right circumstances. Worldwide, these include bats, birds, monkeys, lemurs, kinkajous, rodents and lizards.

All these animals take on the job of pollination because there is something in it for them: a fair payment, if you like. The payment is usually in nectar, a sweet energy drink put out by flowers for the specific purpose of luring pollinators. But for some — notably many bee species — the payment is also the pollen itself. The bees take this rich and nutritious substance back to the hive to feed the rising generation of grubs. It's more expensive for the plants, but it still works for any plant that can overproduce pollen. Pollen-laden bees move from plant to plant and, as they do so, at least some of the pollen reaches the female parts of a different flower of the same species.

The distribution of pollen by dedicated animal couriers is extremely effective. A good deal of pollen will almost certainly end up in a different flower, as the courier makes its next stop, and there's a decent chance that this will be a flower of the same species. This system is much more purposeful and accurate than wind pollination: and it has allowed the flowering plants to come up with many different forms: about 300,000 of them alive to today, an extraordinary adaptive radiation of species.

Let me add here, should it need saying, that the pollinators don't do the job on purpose. It's an inadvertent result of their progress from flower to flower in pursuit of their own needs: the collection and consumption of nectar and pollen. It's a contract of self-interest on both parts, but it mostly works out well and both get what they want. But not always. The famous bee orchid resembles a bee, and dupes a certain species of bee to try and copulate with it. If all goes well – for the plant rather than the bee – it will then fly off and get fooled all over again by another plant of the same species. The cuckoo pint, sometimes called arum lily, is a plant common in Britain, and it also works by deception. It puts out a foul smell – it quite literally smells like shit – and this attracts various species of fly. The plant then traps them, and while trapped they become covered in pollen. After a while, they are released – and off they go, and if all goes well for the plant at least one of them will be fooled again, and in their quest for more shit will inadvertently pollinate another flower of the same species.

The first flower of spring is always a moment of joy: at the same time surprising and utterly predictable. It's usually a snowdrop, springing up early with the strength of its stored food in the hidden bulb. They are so early they are mostly ahead of the pollinating insects, and so very seldom able to make their own seeds. They propagate from division of the bulb. They are usually reckoned to be native to the south and west of England, but they've been widely introduced elsewhere.

Other plants time their flowering for the moment when the very earliest insects are out and flying. The classic example is the primrose: the *prima rosa*, the first rose of the spring. This may seem a reckless thing to do: the weather can change for the worse and there aren't all that many insects about: mostly the furry queen bumblebees, waking from their winter-long diapause, in a hurry to establish a new colony. There aren't so many insects – but there isn't much competition from other flowers. The early flowerers are taking a punt: that they will catch a period of decent weather when the insects are up and about. If that works out well, they will have these insects all to themselves.

It's with this in mind that some tree species come into blossom before they come into leaf, and do so startlingly early. That strategy makes the flowers available to these early insects without any distraction from leaves: the advertisement is loud and clear, and any insect on the wing will make a beeline for them. Wild plum is generally the first in Britain, often seen on roadsides with a sudden improbable confection of white blossom. Blackthorn, much planted in hedges, follows shortly afterwards: and to human observers it's all that can be hoped for: indisputable confirmation of the fact that winter is coming to an end, that spring is coming and that hard times come again no more.

Signs of spring
January 2024

1. Great tit singing in top field
2. Three marsh harriers, two prob. males (a long way off) in a brief grapple
3. New growth of nettles under the ash tree
4. Song thrush sub-song, perhaps half-strength
   Wood pigeon singing
5. Song thrush louder than yesterday
6. Two little egrets, wondering about pairing up
   Blue tit singing a few phrases

3

Spring comes to Streatham

On the eve of the Sunday that followed the first full moon after the March equinox – the spring equinox, as we call it in the northern hemisphere – a community of like-minded people would meet up in Streatham in south London, all of us gathering together a little before midnight. It was part of my boyhood. I would join them with my parents and my two sisters: it was the natural and inevitable thing to do, and in many ways it was the high point of the year. At the beginning one of the celebrants would ritually make new fire, striking it from a flint. From this fire, a single huge candle would be lit. The youngest of the celebrants, always male, would then carry it into a darkened building where the rest of us had been waiting, and then, in a high, chanting, musical voice, he would announce the arrival of the new light. We would chant back an appropriate response, welcoming the light and giving thanks for it.

As the candle advanced through the building, we would each light our own small candle from the flame of the one great candle: candle by candle the once dark space became ablaze with light: the darkness destroyed by a light of 200 candlepower. The celebrant would then set his candle – the one great candle – on a high place where its flame was visible to us all, and then he would sing a song of exultation: praising the light that had returned to us, thanking even the bees from whose wax the candle had been made. 'Rejoice O earth in shining splendour ... darkness vanishes forever ... accept this candle, a solemn offering, the work of bees ... a fire into many flames divided, but never dimmed by sharing of its light.' I find myself chanting the words as I write them down and feel the faintest prickle of a tear for the wonder of the moment, for the glory of the light, for the memories of family and for the abandoned beliefs of childhood.

The place where this strange cult met was St Peter's Church in Leigham Court Road. It belonged – and still does – to the Church of England and stands in the diocese of Southwark. This was the Easter Vigil: the most holy night of the year. God had died and left us forever; God had been reborn and would be with us always ... and so we celebrated by means of light. As light returned to the world in spring, so we brought new light into the church and chanted our thanks. The long and complex chant that follows is called the *Exultet* or *Exsultet* (they revised the Latin in 1955) and makes an inseparable link between the resurrection of Christ and the returning of the light.

All this is further linked with the Jewish Passover, the flight from Egypt, the pillar of fire and the freedom from sin made possible by Christ's death. 'Oh happy fault! Oh necessary sin of Adam, which gained for us so great a redeemer!' But these historical and theological connections increasingly seemed to me, as I stood there with my candle and the glorious words of the *Exultet* filled the squat Victorian church, that what mattered above all else was the light. The deep emotions I felt were about the returning of the light: everything else was secondary to the fact that the year, once dark almost beyond bearing, was now not only light, but would get brighter every day.

The same rites are performed in Roman Catholic churches across the world, and very similar ones in the Orthodox churches. They are preceded by the 40 days of Lent, a season of austerity that mimics winter and mostly takes place before the equinox, which is technically still winter: a time in which the hours of daylight are shorter than the hours of darkness. In Lent the music is muted, religious objects in the church, even the crucifixes, are shrouded in purple cloth and the Gloria is not sung: God cannot be glorified in Lent, for this is not a time of joy. It is a time to reflect on our shortcomings, live more simply and do a lot of praying. No one says alleluia: the word, Hallelujah, from the Hebrew meaning praise to Yahweh or God, becomes a prohibited word: inappropriate to the time of sorrow, austerity and repentance.

The last week of Lent is Holy Week, which ends in the triduum or three days of intense churchgoing. Thursday – Maundy Thursday – marks the Last Supper and Christ's betrayal. Good Friday is, of course, the death of Christ: the one day in the year in which mass is not said and the sacrament, in the form of consecrated wafers, is removed from the altar; the church is desolate and – almost – without God. Everything is irredeemably bleak, as it must be. Even the sweet tinkle of the silver hand bell is replaced by wooden clappers: nothing could explain more eloquently the desperate nature of the day.

And then on Holy Saturday, the eve of Easter, the resurrection of Christ is all the more vivid for the weeks of hardship that preceded it. After the candle is in place and the *Exultet* has been sung we have the first Hallelujah of Easter: the forbidden word is once again permitted. The Gloria is sung again and mass is said after the 48 hours of holding off – and at the last, just before we all get up to leave, the sacrament is brought in procession back to the altar again. At St Peter's the organist always played the Hallelujah Chorus from *Messiah*.

And he shall reign forever and ever
Forever
And ever ...

After that, in the early hours of Easter morning we would spill down the steps onto the pavement of Leigham Court Road, saluting friends and acquaintances, and greeting each other in the manner we had picked up from a television adaptation of Tolstoy's *Resurrection*. I would say to my father: 'Christ is risen, Edward Hubertovich!', to which he would reply, 'He is risen indeed!', ending it there, not having enough grasp of Russian nomenclature to greet me as Simon Edwardovich. After that we would all go home and when we were considered old enough, we would drink the drink known as Troublesome Whisky: hot toddies made from brown sugar, lemon juice, a fat tot of whisky and boiling water, poured into a glass that had a spoon in it to prevent cracking.

This was our rite of spring, and it marked me for life. Though I set the religion aside long ago, I still rejoice – I still exult – in the rituals of shared joy, the combination of beauty and duty, the need for family, the music, the sequence of austerity followed by celebration, the taste for whisky – *uisce beatha* – and above all in the celebration of the return of life and light to the land after the cold, darkness and deprivation of winter.

I tell this as a personal memoir, but I am not unique. For two millennia the church has been celebrating the arrival of spring by way of Easter. Every year, the season of death, the time when nothing grows and scarcely a bird will sing, is followed by the season of life, when the land turns green again and the air is clamouring with the voices of birds. Every year has its time of death: every year life returns.

In the Christian tradition Easter is the great festival of spring, and the church has no monopoly on the way we celebrate it. The seasons came first and we have naturally and inevitably celebrated them since the dawn of humanity. The Christian church and other religions developed festivals that fit in with the seasonal round: we celebrate the northern hemisphere winter solstice with Christmas and the spring equinox with Easter. There are spring festivals in most of the cultures and religions that arose in the seasonal lands, and we will take a proper look at them in Chapter 8. For the moment, we will consider Easter, which has always been as much a secular and a vernacular feast as a religious experience. It is marked not only by intense churchgoing among the religious, but with customs that go back many centuries, some with only a tangential relationship with organised religion, and in many cases probably – impossible to be certain about anything to do with folklore – predating it. They tend to centre around four great symbols of springtime: eggs, chicks, lambs and bunnies.

We take eggs for granted these days. It may be the day of the winter solstice, the darkest day of the year, but you can still go down to the supermarket for a dozen eggs and make yourself a beautiful fat omelette for supper, perhaps with a vegetable from the high summer like green peas, or even fresh asparagus. But if you have ever kept chickens at home, as I have, you soon discover — well, it's a discovery if you approach the problem as a recently lapsed townie, as I did — that chickens don't lay eggs in the winter. The darkness causes them to shut down. That makes it a great day when the hens start laying again: when you feed them in the morning and discover a warm egg in the straw, or when you hear a hen's startled celebration of what she has just brought into the world. If you want your hens to lay eggs in the winter, you must supply them with artificial light, so the day seems longer to them and fools them into 12-month productivity. The 12-month fresh egg is a relatively recent thing.

There is a weight of Christian symbolism attached to the egg. Perhaps this has been spatchcocked onto more ancient traditions, or perhaps there is just an inextricable commonality between all symbols of new life. Certainly nothing represents new life more vividly than the hatching of an egg: the first tentative tapping, the miraculous emergence of a viable if somewhat bedraggled living being, the transformation from unliving to living, from non-existence to existence. In some Christian traditions the broken egg represents the newly empty tomb; there are traditional rites of egg-rolling said to represent the rolling away of the stone that closed the entrance to the tomb.

The link between eggs and Easter can be traced back nearly 2,000 years to Mesopotamia, where there was a tradition of staining eggs red, to show that the new birth is related to death and the blood of Christ. Decorated ostrich eggs 60,000 years old have been found in Africa, so the idea of the ornamented egg comfortably predates Christianity. There are many traditions of colouring eggs by boiling them with flowers that possess staining petals. It's all about making something special: doing something special to mark a special time. It's great to have eggs again, let's make it even more special by making the new eggs look even more glorious.

Eggs were especially welcome at Easter because they were forbidden during Lent: that's why you use up all your spare eggs the day before Lent begins, on Shrove Tuesday or Pancake Day. Such eggs as were laid during this period of self-denial had to be preserved: salted or pickled. There's a further Christian gloss on the egg: it represents the trinity, three parts of one whole: the yolk, the white or albumen, and the shell. But whether you deny yourself eggs during Lent or not, fresh eggs were, until very recently, a seasonal treat that returned when the world got warmer and lighter. Every spring reminded you just how good it is to eat an egg.

It was natural that the egg tradition should be taken a step further by the elite. The first chocolate eggs were eaten at the court of Louis XIV of France. In 1725, the widow Giambone of Turin was filling eggshells with melted chocolate as an Easter delicacy. In 1873 J. S. Fry and Co. were selling the first chocolate eggs in Britain;

Cadbury's later came up with a form of chocolate that could be moulded, and from then on Easter eggs were straightforward to make and available to all. Around 80 million Easter eggs are sold every year in the UK.

Lambs are all tied up with Easter, not just as obvious and gambolling signs of new life, but also for the complex idea of sacrifice. Lambs are born in the spring. There's nothing coincidental about this: even in these days when domesticated animals live in highly controlled conditions, the annual rhythm of ewes brings them into oestrus in the autumn, when the tup – the ram or male sheep given the job of covering the females – is introduced to the flock. Thus the lambs are born in spring, to coincide with the times when the resources are renewed: when the grazing gets more lush every day, giving the ewe the best possible food to stimulate her production of milk to feed her new offspring. As we move on into the summer the weaning lambs can feed on the best grass of all. The sheep population is at its maximum just at the time when there is most food for them all. That timing and the reasons for this are inherited from wild ancestors, but they are still relevant to sheep farming today. You need fresh grass, you need warmth in the soil – as said earlier, grass won't grow below 8 degrees C – and for that you need spring.

So lambs tend to be born around the March equinox, as daylight hours get longer and the opportunities for photosynthesis are consequently greater. The days get warmer and the leaping lamb is once again an irresistible emblem of spring: ungainly gambols performed by creatures with legs twice as long they apparently need to be, the animals themselves apparently unsure how many of them they possess and very little idea of the best way to use them.

But these woolly charmers exist for their edibility, for all that many meat-eating people prefer to compartmentalise their delight in the leaping and their delight in the eating ... though some joker will always enjoy puncturing overmuch delight in such a sight by saying 'mint sauce'. It's just one more jocular response to the delights of spring, reminding us once again how deeply they affect the world and those who live in the seasonal lands, human and non-human alike.

Our joy in life's renewal cannot be savoured without awareness of death: in this case, the death of the lamb who must provide the feast. Lamb is the traditional meal of the Jewish Passover as well as of Christian Easter. The meals that commemorate them both are inextricable from the idea of sacrifice: the lamb isn't just a celebration of the spring but, in a way, a guarantee that spring will come again. Animal sacrifices have been found in almost every ancient culture across the world. They exist to thank the gods for their favours and to ask them for more. Sacrifice is both an act of joyous worship and an act of fearful propitiation. If we sacrifice something we want for ourselves the gods will surely take note, ease up on their hostility, and things will turn out all right, the harvest will come in safe in its season and spring will return the following year when the time is right.

The sacrifice is less painful when the sacrificial victim is then consumed by the participants in the ritual: this perhaps slightly cheating kind of sacrifice seems to imply a gentle and formal ritual rather than an act of desperation; it's all gone a long way from the notion of human sacrifice that holds such a fascination for us. We still use the phrase sacrificial lamb as a semi-jocular reference to people knowingly placed in an impossible position: the Conservative candidate who fights an election in an ultra-safe Labour seat (and vice versa) is traditionally referred to as a sacrificial lamb: those with political intelligence seek to get some profit from this, sometimes by setting up a maverick candidate who will try some new ideas and garner some merry publicity without there being too much at stake.

The sacrificial lamb ties in with the notion of Jesus as the sacrificial victim: Jesus is referred to again and again as the Lamb of God. These words are repeated every time mass is said: *Agnus dei, qui tollis peccata mundi, miserere nobis*: Lamb of God who taketh away the sins of the world, have mercy upon us, in the words used in the Anglican church during my boyhood. The Latin words are sung to some of the noblest music ever written. The theological idea is that God sacrificed his own son so that humans should be free from original sin: that is to say, our innate sinfulness. The idea is gloriously spoofed by the great American humourist Tom Lehrer in 'The Vatican Rag', in which, inspired by the Roman Catholic Church's desire to be more modern, he puts a few Catholic notions to ragtime music and sings:

> Get in line in that processional
> Step into that small confessional
> There the guy who's got religion'll
> Tell you if your sin's original ...

The notion of Jesus as the sacrificial victim is represented by the Lamb of God image, traditionally shown with the lamb delicately holding a cross behind its off-fore fetlock: so once again the visceral, life-giving nature of spring is inextricably tangled up with the theology and iconography of the Christian Easter. The turning of the year is right at the heart of the Christian experience – and that makes it an inescapable part of the way people from the related culture think and see the world. We may live in a largely secular society and we may live in a world that is less obviously dependent than it was before on the rise and fall of the seasons, but our ancestors have bequeathed us their thought patterns and their understanding of the nature of existence.

We may spend an awful lot of our time looking at different screens, but when spring comes, when the sun bursts free and sends us some real warmth at last, lying across our shoulders like a warm shawl, and the daffodils leap up on roadsides and traffic roundabouts, when the buds burst and the birds sing and when we pass a field full of leaping lambs – we cannot help but rejoice and feel that, for all life's difficulties, things are going to be all right from now on – or even if not entirely all right, certainly a fair bit better. Then Easter comes and we give each other chocolate eggs, exchange cards decorated with fluffy chicks, and many people eat a festive meal of lamb, life moves into the lighter, brighter, warmer and richer part of the year – and as we do so we exchange jests about Easter bunny.

Easter bunny is not a rabbit, though often enough depicted as one: an anthropomorphic rabbit, often wearing clothes, distributing eggs, either real or chocolate. He dates back to at least the seventeenth century in Germany, and once had the Santa-like property of judging children before the egg distribution began: eggs were only for the good.

But the fact – if that can ever be the correct word when dealing with folklore – is that Easter bunny is a hare. A moment of thought puts this into the realm of the bleeding obvious. Rabbits are not especially interesting to humans during the months of early spring – around Eastertime – but hares most emphatically are. Rabbits give birth to blind, naked kits in a hole in the ground, and all rabbits dive underground at the threat of danger. Hares live wholly above the ground, and they give birth to young that are good to go: ready to gallop within the hour. And in March the adult hares go mad.

They are easy to see at this time of year, when the crops are still low. Those used to looking out for them in hare country – East Anglia most obviously – can pick them out at a distance, subtly humped, often sky-lined in this flat countryside. And in March – even in February – they get excited about sex and chase each other in mad circles, and often stand up and spar: not males seeking to establish dominance over each other but females attacking pursuing males, either because they are not ready to mate or because they want to put their potential mate to a test that examines both his speed and his strength. Hares, then, go in for flamboyantly sexy behaviour good and early in the year, before most other creatures are in the mood.

The hare is said to be the special animal of Eostre or Ostara, a spring goddess who has her origins in Germany: the wild sex-mad behaviour of hares makes them an obvious choice. Rabbits have a well-deserved reputation for speedy reproduction, but most of these activities take place underground, out of sight of humans. Hares perform spectacularly and in public. The monk known as the Venerable Bede wrote about Eostre in 731, referring to the month-long celebration of Eosturmonath. He wrote (translated from his original Latin): 'Now they designate that paschal season by her name, calling the joys of the new rite by the time-honoured name of the old observances.'

Most cultures celebrate Easter as Pasqua, Pascuas, Pasen, Páscoa, and Pâques, ultimately from the Hebrew Pesah or Passover. English has Easter and German, from the same root, Ostern. When we use the term Easter, according to Bede, we are referring to a pagan tradition that has been incorporated into Christian practices, both formal and informal. This takes us to one of the classic disputes among folklorists: there is not much hard evidence for the cult of Eostre and her hare, and it's even been suggested that Bede made the whole thing up, though it's not clear why he would have done so.

Never mind: hares, whether or not they accompany a goddess, have long been an inescapable part of early spring in open country. They were associated with witchcraft, like all largely nocturnal beasts, including cats, bats, owls and toads. It's a link with the powers of darkness. Hares are a little bit sinister – but because of their attractive nature they also give great delight. They have an ambiguity that bats and toads can never hope for. It was believed that witches sometimes took the form of hares to carry out mischief under the cover of darkness. Witches, of course, are at their most powerful in the winter months, when there is more darkness to operate in. So there grew up a tradition of eating hares at Easter: the time when the witches were banished. It was a moment of profound liberation from fear as well as from darkness and cold – and dark and fear go together.

We humans love contradictions and paradoxes, and the hare embodies that as well as any other symbolic beast. Pliny the Elder, the great Roman encyclopaedist, reported that Archelaus, a pre-Socratic philosopher, 'says that some individual possesses the characteristics of the two sexes and that it becomes pregnant just as well without the aid of a male'. This intriguing (and zoologically incorrect) idea means that the hare stands for both outrageous sexiness and virginity: for virgin birth, no less. Hares sometimes turn up in paintings of the Virgin Mary. They can also be found in church windows: the famous image of three hares, forming a circle, all of which, in a neat illusion, have just three ears between them but appear to have the usual two each. They are at the same time a hint of our pagan past, an example of the virtues of virginity and a symbol of the Holy Trinity.

But why eggs? The idea that rabbits (and/or hares) lay eggs is ancient and not entirely extinct: after all, Easter Bunny is in charge of the distribution of eggs and he must get them from somewhere. An example of this turns up in Rudyard Kipling's school stories, collected as *Stalky & Co.*, from the late nineteenth century. There is a minor but important character called Rabbits-Eggs in the first of these stories to be written; he is a local carter (the school is in Devon and a carter was in charge of local transport of people and goods). 'Rabbits-Eggs was the local carrier – an outcrop of early Devonian formation. It was Stalky who had invented his unlovely name.'

This is explained by J. C. Dunsterville, the model for the brilliant but anarchic Stalky, in a later memoir.[1] 'His nickname of "Rabbits-Eggs" was due to his having offered for sale six partridge eggs which he stoutly maintained were "rabbut's aigs". He genuinely believed them to be so. He was passing a clump of bushes when a rabbit ran out of them, and for some reason or another

---

[1] Quoted in the notes of the 1987 Oxford University Press edition of *Stalky & Co.*

he peered into the bushes, and there, sure enough, were the six eggs, obviously the produce of the rabbit.'

It's an ancient confusion. Hares are visible from a long way off in early spring – you traditionally acknowledge the early growth of crops by pointing out that it had reached the stage when 'it would hide a hare'. At the same time, in earlier days when agriculture was a good deal less intensive, there were many ground-nesting birds, like grey partridges and especially lapwings, who would nest in fields. (Lapwing eggs, usually described as plovers' eggs, were considered a delicacy; Sebastian Flyte offers them to his guests in *Brideshead Revisited*. It's now illegal to take eggs from the nests of wild birds.) These eggs, found in the open where the hares had so recently been sighted, often chasing and boxing, seemed to be just what Rabbits-Eggs believed them to be. And when spring comes and the countryside is full of both eggs and hares, it is natural to create a benevolent (to good children at least) figure distributing eggs: a figure who told us that spring was back and the world was kind again. The air and the soil were warm, the days were full of light: rejoice oh earth in shining splendour ... darkness vanishes forever.

Signs of spring
January 2024

9	Great tit singing well in garden
10	A few lapwings – just a hint of display flight as one comes in to land
11	Great spotted woodpecker drumming
13	More wood pigeon song
	Two egrets together on next-door field
14	Hazel catkins on the marsh
	Singing stock dove
15	Two egrets flying over the river, clearly very taken up with each other
16	Cindy reports boxing hares on nearby Raveningham estate
	Muntjac pair grazing very close to each other
	Hint of marsh tit song

4
Mythological spring

Tim Finnegan, an Irish hod carrier, is still pissed the next morning. As a result he falls from his ladder and dies. So it goes. Naturally they hold a wake for him, and equally naturally it gets out of hand. As a result a good deal of whiskey is spilt on the corpse – who instantly revives:

> Whirl your whiskey round like blazes
> Thundering Jesus do you think I'm dead?

And that is *The Ballad of Finnegan's Wake*, a song that celebrates both life and *uisce beatha*, and it was borrowed by James Joyce for his mad masterpiece of eternal recurrences, rising and falling only to rise once again, the gloriously unapostrophied *Finnegans Wake*. From which you will gather that stories of death and rebirth are not exclusive to mainstream Christianity and St Peter's, Streatham. The idea of apparent death turning into incontrovertible life is found again and again. It seems to be a constant of Mediterranean, West Asian and European civilisation – all lands governed by the rhythm of the seasons.

This theme is spelled out in the English folk song 'John Barleycorn', in which three mysterious men come from the west – from where the sun sets – swearing that John Barleycorn must die.

> Well they've ploughed,
> They've sown, they've harrowed him in,
> Threw clods upon his head,
> Till these three men were satisfied
> John Barleycorn was dead.

But then Sir John springs up again, much in the manner of Tim Finnegan, and amazes them all. He springs up in the spring, when else? For that is the time when seeds germinate and life returns to the land. The three men go to all sorts of bother to kill him again with scything and threshing, only to find that Sir John thrives on such treatment.

> But little Sir John with his nut brown bowl
> Proved the strongest man at last.

We'll note in passing that both these songs are about drinking, for both beer and whisky are (usually) made from barley, and are traditionally the preferred drinks in places where grapes can't be grown – the more northerly places, where the difference between the seasons is most marked. As we have already seen, whisky (whiskey if you are Irish or American) is the water of life, and the places with the darkest winters tend to be best at distillation. Must find some way or another of coping with all that darkness.

The theme of death and rebirth carries on into our most powerful and enduring mythologies and beliefs, most obviously in the form of Christianity. C. S. Lewis, the great Christian apologist and author of *The Chronicles of Narnia*, suggested that the earlier myths of death and rebirth were a pagan anticipation of the Christian story: a groping towards a truth that would later become clear. He also wrote one of the greatest evocations of spring in all literature, and we'll turn to that shortly. Meanwhile, I leave Lewis's thoughts with you in the interests of impartiality.

Lewis loved the tales of King Arthur, in all their various contradictory forms. The stories are, of course, all entwined with the legend of the Holy Grail, which plays a central role in the unfolding story of knights and truth and love and adventure and the quest to save the world. The grail is sometimes a cup, sometimes a plate and sometimes a stone: all that's clear is that it's the difference between life and death. The stories have been interpreted, most famously in Jesse Weston's *From Ritual to Romance*,[1] as tales that can trace their origin to oriental fertility rites; they subsequently went through complex cultural transitions until they became relatively polite medieval romances. As they developed, they became increasingly Christianised, showcasing virtues like purity and virginity, while the Grail became the vessel that Jesus drank from at the Last Supper when he established the ritual of the Eucharist, the symbolic shared meal of bread and wine. Celtic legends and Christian beliefs fuse as the knights seek the Holy Grail. It's all about the human love of a good story, and our undying fascination with the idea of the conquest of death. That is to say, the annual arrival of spring.

Because beneath all the 'of your courtesy' and 'I pray you' of Sir Thomas Malory's *Le Morte d'Arthur* there is something atavistic going on, something that gets down to the bones of mythology. That is to say, matters of life and death. In all its forms, the Grail is important because it is the bringer of life and the conqueror of death. Naturally, this being mythology, there are many

---

[1] The book was a major inspiration for T. S. Eliot's poem *The Waste Land*; more on this in Chapter 22.

different versions of what its powers are – healing, eternal youth, infinite abundance – but it's essentially the difference between deprivation and plenty, sickness and health, death and life. The quest for the Holy Grail is tied to the health of the land: the ailing, wounded figure of the Fisher King ruling over a dying land. If the king can be restored to life by the finding of the Grail, the land itself will become fecund again ... and that is the terrible situation that happens to us every year: winter is upon us once again and only spring can save us. So the knights set off to seek the Grail: Lancelot had every talent but wasn't pure enough, compromised forever by his adulterous love for Arthur's Queen Guinevere. Perceval (or Parsifal) set eyes on the Grail but failed to understand what he saw. Eventually the virginal Sir Galahad, Lancelot's son and a better – or at least a less flawed – person than his father, sets eyes on it and was so enraptured that he died on the spot.

The essentials of the story are constant: a person and a place are both ailing and dying, and both must be brought back to life and health. Only a miracle can save us: and somehow, every year, the miracle takes place. Spring arrives in the nick of time to rescue us as a knight-errant rescues a damsel in distress: death is avoided, we are saved by the skin of our teeth and life can continue, more gloriously than ever before.

These stories of death and rebirth – winter and spring – were collected by Sir James Frazer in his famous book of 1890, *The Golden Bough*. It is a pioneering work of social anthropology and folklore, one that explores the continuity between our ancestors and our modern selves. Frazer claimed that death and rebirth is a universal theme, common to all cultures. This is disputed by his modern successors in this rich and complex field, one that is always spectacularly short of certainties. But it's usually accepted that Frazer's conclusions are chiefly applicable to West Asian, Mediterranean and European cultures: all places strongly affected by seasonal change. They add up to what Jung called archetypal processes and 'trans-personal symbolism': all part of his central notion of the collective unconscious. These themes, then, are not just known to us all: they are part of us all.

The Nile Valley might seem – at least in Britain – to be rather too far south to feel the rhythms of the seasons in the intense manner that we do in the British Isles, but Cairo is also well north of the tropic of Cancer, at 30 degrees. And Egypt is – or, rather, was before the construction of the Aswan Dam between 1960 and 1970 – subject to annual life-giving floods. This is the result of the annual monsoon rainfall on the Ethiopian highlands, which sends prodigious quantities of water into the Nile Valley.

The Nile Valley is part of the Fertile Crescent, which extends north and east into Mesopotamia, the land between the Tigris and the Euphrates. In these places agriculture was invented 12,000 years ago. (It was invented at the same time in other places across the world as well; the Fertile Crescent development is especially relevant to the history of surrounding lands, including Europe.) By turning to agriculture, humans swapped the uncertainties of nomadic hunter-gathering and pastoralism for a fixed abode. This was made possible by a life of back-breaking labour, now essential for all but the elite. The annual flooding of the Nile brought rich silt which annually revitalised the flood plain and made it possible to grow rich and nourishing crops with relative ease. And it was associated with the ancient Egyptian god Osiris.

Osiris is normally depicted with a green skin, a pharaoh's beard, legs swathed in a mummy's bandages and a feathered crown, the *atef*. He holds a crook and flail, demonstrating his responsibilities for both livestock and arable farming. I should stress here that versions differ over place and time, and that there are different emphases and downright contradictions in the many versions of every story. Folklore is not something you can ever be dogmatic about. But certainly at times Osiris has been celebrated as the son of the earth god Geb and the sky goddess Nut. He is both brother and husband to Isis, who has vast magical powers, protects the kingdom from its enemies, governs the skies, along with all nature, and even has power over fate.

Osiris was a judge, the ruler of the dead and the underworld, and was called the Lord of Silence. He is in charge of the sprouting of vegetation and the annual flooding of the Nile; he is invariably benign and permanently youthful. These immense virtues perhaps made it inevitable that his brother Set should turn against him; Set killed him and cut him up into pieces. But Set had reckoned without the power of Isis, who gathered the pieces and wrapped them up. That allowed Osiris to come back to life. He was worshipped in annual rites as the land itself was brought back to life with the annual life-bringing floods.

Osiris and Isis had a son, Horus, the falcon-headed god who is perhaps the best-known of the Egyptian pantheon; the pharaohs claimed direct descent from him. Thus we have a tradition of a god who dies and who comes back to life. He is associated with a land that is annually depleted and annually restored. The god has green skin with feathers in his crown; perhaps there's even a faint echo of this in Robin Hood, dressed in Lincoln green and a hat with a feather in it. I once had such a hat myself and it gave me deep joy.

There are also hints of the Green Man: an image familiar to most of us. There are roof bosses in Norwich Cathedral that show a human face growing out of leaves – or are the leaves growing out of him? These images, in the cloisters on the southern side, are 600 years old and the idea behind them is incalculably ancient. An unapologetically pagan figure is an integral part of one of the loveliest cathedrals ever built. I have listened to both the great Bach Passions in the cathedral and afterwards walked the cloisters and gazed up at the Green Man images: reminding myself once again that though Christianity is ancient, humanity itself is a good deal older, and that rising up after death is something that nature does as a matter of routine.

The Green Man myths are not specifically about death and rebirth, though perhaps that is implied. Certainly they are about fertility: representing an almost insolent fecundity and telling us that nature happens everywhere: we owe it everything and we are also subject to it. The knowing leafy face looking down from the roof hints at secrets and understandings far older than Christianity. Since the invention of agriculture human history has become a story of a combat with nature: combat, if you like, with the Green Man. And though humanity appears to be winning the war — in some places achieving something close to a rout — nature is incapable of giving up. More of that in due course.

And while anthropologists and folklorists can argue the degree of relatedness of these reborn gods and discuss forever which tales influence which traditions and how direct this influence was, we observers can marvel at the commonality, take pleasure in the stories and rejoice in the fact that, once again, death itself is working backwards. There is, for example, the story of the Mesopotamian god Tammuz and his consort Inanna (Ishtar in some traditions).

Tammuz is the herdsman god, Inanna goddess of fertility and erotic love. Inanna goes down to the underworld, the world of the dead, for motives that are unclear and sinister. She passes through seven gates; at each one she must leave behind a garment or ornament: finally, naked as the day she was born, she enters. There she is turned into a corpse and hung on a nail. As a result there is no more fertility on earth and no more sex either. Her tale is told in *The Descent of Inanna*, which still survives, an older work even than the more famous *Epic of Gilgamesh*.

That corpsification is by no means the end of Inanna. She is angered by the failure of Tammuz to mourn her as she thinks fit, and so, to pay him back, she has demons drag him down to the underworld as well. Now the whole earth is in ruins.

> As for me, Inanna
> Who will plough my vulva?
> Who will plough my high field?
> Who will plough my wet land?

Eventually she relents, and Tammuz is permitted to return to the upper world for six months every year: to set death aside for half a year and bring life back to the ailing land. The other half of the year he must spend with Inanna. Life departs, life returns, and another year is done, and so another begins.

It's generally agreed that Adonis is a reasonably direct descendant of Tammuz. These days Adonis is mostly celebrated as an epitome of youthful male beauty, but there is more to his story than good looks. As a beautiful child he was admired by both Aphrodite (in Roman times Venus), the goddess of love, and by Persephone (Proserpina to Romans), queen of the underworld, so there's tension in the story from the very beginning. When he grows up he becomes the lover of both. But

Adonis loves – perhaps more than both goddesses put together – to go hunting, and on one expedition he is mortally wounded by a wild boar and dies in Aphrodite's arms. Anemones spring from the blood that reaches the ground. He must now, of course, go down to the underworld with the rest of the dead but (in some versions of the story) Zeus intervenes and Adonis spends half the year on earth with the goddess of love, and the other half beneath it in the arms of the queen of the underworld. Adonis is the lover of life and beauty; he is also the lover of darkness and death. A cult of Adonis developed, celebrated by women, who ritually tore their garments and beat their breasts in grief at his annual death.

Shakespeare took up the idea of Adonis as reluctant lover with immense enthusiasm. In his lifetime, *Venus and Adonis* was his most popular published work. Venus tells Adonis:

> Graze on my lips, if these hills be dry,
> Stray lower, where the pleasant fountains lie.

James Joyce had fun with this, equating Shakespeare's Venus with his wife Anne Hathaway: 'The greyeyed goddess who bends over him, stooping to conquer, as prologue to the swelling act, is a boldfaced Stratford wench who tumbles a lover younger than herself.'

Erotic love and fertility, the swelling actions not just of human lovers but of the earth itself, are closely interlinked in all these tales of rebirth. Attis is a figure who crops up (note the *mot juste*) in Phrygian (a people from

Anatolia in what is now Turkey) and Greek mythology, and he's another vegetation god, consort of the Cybele, mother of the gods. He castrates himself and dies as a result, but he is resurrected.

Baldr is a god from Norse and Germanic mythologies, son of Odin and Frigg, brother to Thor and several others. He is beautiful, just and immune to all harm; this gift amuses the other gods and they throw all kinds of stuff at him for the pleasure of seeing it bounce off. But the evil Loki discovers that mistletoe is the one thing that can harm Baldr; he persuades another god to use mistletoe as a missile and that kills Baldr. At his funeral another god – though it's probably Loki in disguise – refuses to weep for him, and so prevents Baldr from coming back to life.

There are rebirth stories from cultures remote from the interlocking cultures of Europe. Quetzalcoatl of Mesoamerica, associated with both the morning and the evening star – with both the arrival and the departure of darkness – goes to hell and comes back bearing the bones of the dead, and gives them life with his own blood; they become the people of the world.

Izanami is a Japanese goddess with duties over both creation and death, familiar companions, a contradiction that we instinctively understand. She and her consort Izanagi were able to produce many islands from their union, but Izanami has a terrible accident with fire and is forced to retreat to the underworld. Izanagi pursues her there with a view to bringing her back, but when he finds her rotting and maggot-eaten, he runs away and barricades her in.

The cult of Dionysus – Bacchus for the Romans – takes us back in the European tradition and reunites life and rebirth with drunkenness in the Finnegan or Barleycorn way. Dionysus is the god of the grape harvest and wine-making, presiding over the great celebration of fruit and vegetation. He is a god of insanity, ritual madness, religious ecstasy and theatre. Wine and ecstatic dance freed his followers from self-consciousness, fear and care, and wine was at the centre of religious experience. The annual celebration of the Bacchanalia mixed the classes and genders in an ecstatic free-for-all and was later banned; taking part became a capital offence.

The story of Dionysus begins, as so many stories do, with Zeus's infidelity, this time with the mortal Semele, daughter of the king of Thebes, who becomes pregnant as a result. Hera, Zeus's long-suffering and intemperate wife, persuades Semele to ask Zeus to appear before them. He does so because he must, but it's all too much: Semele is killed by a stray thunderbolt. But Zeus saves Dionysus, sewing him up in his thigh and letting him out when he reaches maturity – so he was twice born.

In time these stories shifted and were understood in different ways. Some of these characters turn up in Milton's *Paradise Lost*, no longer heroes of their own myths but as 'bestial gods':

> Thammuz came next behind,
> Whose annual wound in Lebanon allured
> The Syrian damsels to lament his fate
> In amorous ditties all a summer's day,
> While smooth Adonis from his native rock
> Ran purple to the sea ...

These rebirth stories, apparently killed off and consigned to the archives of the myth collectors as Christianity became the only orthodoxy, acquired a strange habit of coming back to life again in different forms. They are found in many fairy tales, often shockingly violent when read in their more ancient forms. The Brothers Grimm have a story, 'The Two Brothers', in which a huntsman kills a dragon, a fine deed; he is then beheaded by someone jealous of his feat. But a magic root is found and the head is returned to the body – but, alas, it's put on back to front, so the huntsman must be killed all over again so that his head can be put back the right way. As the story continues, the huntsman then beheads his own innocent brother, but all is well: having plenty of magic root left, he restores the head and they all live on in the way that people always live on at the end of a fairy tale.

We are more familiar with the story of Snow White, first published by the brothers in 1812, with a final revised version in 1857. The essentials are familiar to us all, though a fair amount of the Grimms' violence has been allowed to fall into disuse: the wicked queen, Snow White's stepmother, plans to eat Snow White's heart so that she can become immortal. But the huntsman, the queen's hired assassin, fails to go through with the job and brings her a boar's heart instead.

The rest of the tale is more familiar: the queen herself then seeks out Snow White and attempts to kill her. In the Grimms' version this involves the traditional three attempts: first with a bodice that constricts her until the dwarfs bring her round; second with a comb which poisons her, until again the dwarfs revive her. But they can do nothing about the poisonous apple: Snow White is clearly dead. But she is beautiful even in death and a passing prince, observing her in a glass coffin, is entranced. The coffin continues towards the grave but one of the bearers stumbles, and this dislodges the apple from Snow White's throat. She comes alive again, marries the prince and it all ends happily for everyone apart from the wicked queen, who must dance to her death in red-hot shoes. There is an intriguing confusion about snow, winter, spring, death and life: and ultimately all shall be well.

The tale of Sleeping Beauty is another story of apparent death and glorious revival. There are many versions; the earliest can be traced to the fourteenth century. Naturally, the Grimms have a version. In its essentials, the story is about a beautiful princess who is doomed to die, usually when she pricks her finger. But this sentence is commuted into a 100-year sleep; the good fairy makes sure that all the birds and animals in the castle and the surrounding forest also sleep – so all nature, as well as the princess herself, is awakened with the prince's kiss.

The fairy-tale tradition of death and revival is adapted by C. S. Lewis in a tale that consciously links fairy tales, Christian salvation, sacrifice, death, rebirth and spring. In the first of *The Chronicles of Narnia*, *The Lion, the Witch and the Wardrobe*, the four human children find their way to a new world – Narnia – which has been enchanted by the White Witch so that it's always winter and never Christmas. The only hope lies in the possibility of the return of Aslan, the great Lion.

> Wrong will be right when Aslan comes in sight,
> At the sound of his roar, sorrows will be no more,
> When he bares his teeth, winter meets its death,
> And when he shakes his mane, we shall have spring again.

The enchantment begins to break, Father Christmas arrives, bringing solemn, martial gifts, and then, in an entrancing passage, the children walk to meet Aslan as the country moves in the course of a morning from early January to mid-May. 'This is no thaw,' says the dwarf, henchman of the wicked queen. 'This is *Spring*. What are we to do? Your winter had been destroyed, I tell you! This is Aslan's doing.'

The superhero stories, first as comics and then as films, are generally thought of as essentially modern, certainly as a twentieth-century art form. But, of course, they are in their essentials far older than that: the warrior with exceptional powers, setting all to right, is as ancient as any story on earth: he can be found in *The*

Iliad, *The Epic of Gilgamesh* and *Beowulf*. These superhero tales often involve a rebirth: Peter Parker, awkward and geeky, is bitten by a radioactive spider and finds that he has miraculous powers: he is effectively reborn. The discovery of these is the best part of the two films that concern Spiderman's beginnings.

Achilles, star of *The Iliad*, became – almost – invulnerable after his mother Thetis dipped him into the River Styx, holding him by his heel – which turns out to be his one point of weakness. To move from a morbid, sickly state to one of fabulous power: here is a theme that recurs with Iron Man, close to death, revived by a suit of scintillating technology. Superman is always being trapped by green kryptonite, the one substance that can harm him – but he always revives and is soon back to his best again. The Fantastic Four, apparently disastrously affected by exposure to cosmic rays during a space flight, find they have acquired miraculous powers and so become a team of unbeatable superheroes.

The hugely successful Avengers films, which also feature a team of superheroes, was apparently concluded in 2018 when they all died ... but they all came back to life the following year in *Avengers: Endgame*, which became the highest grossing film ever made. One more example: the Captain America films are based on the premise that the eponymous Second World War hero was frozen and brought back to life to take on the troubles of the twenty-first century. Whether as a shameless plot device or as a central part of the entire concept, the idea of rebirth is constantly coming back to life again.

Just as it seems things could get no worse, they get better — better even than they were before. It's a thought that haunts us, and always has. Osiris and Adonis, Iron Man and Captain America, the handsome prince and Aslan himself will return to set things aright. We know that winter will come and bring untold hardships, for even today winter is reliably lethal, and in early times it was always an annual time of dying. But we also know that winter will end, and that what follows will be so much better than the mere ending of hardship. It's not just that winter ends. It's also that spring begins. Aslan has shaken his mane: surely only good can follow. The long history and the convoluted mythologies of death and rebirth: of the dead land coming back to life again, were all summed up by James Joyce in *Finnegans Wake* in a single word: single word that is also a masterpiece.

Cropse.

Signs of spring
January 2024

17 Three muntjac on the marsh, a male and a female very close together
18 Pair of stonechat on the Common
    Drumming great spotted woodpecker
19 Two red kites flying together, very close – they can't keep their wings off each other
20 Four Chinese water deer – two very close to each other
22 Two swans in dykes on the Common, apparently paired up
23 Singing dunnock
24 Two squirrels playing chase
    Two egrets in a newly dug-out dyke. They get up and make a circuit of the marsh before heading off, still together
    Two buzzards flying together

5

The song of spring

You're no kind of nature writer until a publisher has taken you to lunch and invited you to write the new *Silent Spring*. The only problem with this thrilling idea is that it can't be done. You can't repeat the shock of the original revelation in Rachel Carson's book of 1962. She spelled out the truth we should have seen for ourselves years earlier: that humans are destroying nature.

The easy assumptions of humanity — assumptions a million years in the making — had to be revised. It was an apocalyptic vision, not of the future but of what is happening right now. Carson's conclusions demanded a radical new understanding of the way humans interact with nature: and, behind it, a realisation that operating outside nature is not within the range of long-term options open to humanity. More on this in Chapter 21. Right now we're talking about birdsong.

It's highly possible that Carson's book wouldn't have had the effect it did without its brilliant, chilling, attention-seizing title. It is a reference to John Keats's poem 'La Belle Dame Sans Merci':

> O what can ail thee, knight at arms
> Alone and palely loitering!
> The sedge has wither'd from the lake
> And no birds sing.

The idea of spring without the sound of birds gives a sense of horror and desolation, and when the book was published it concentrated the mind most wonderfully. Before Carson we had been working on the idea that certain species were coming under threat and that we needed to save them: but it was accepted that we would be doing this from the goodness of our hearts. Carson made it clear that by destroying nature we are destroying ourselves. It was widely and rightly agreed that nature conservation is a noble cause: Carson showed us that it is also dictated by self-interest and common sense.

Spring is not silent, not yet. It is still the time of birdsong. We understand this as a joyous inevitability: as much a basic human as a basic avian right. In the winter most of the sounds we hear from birds are sharp, monosyllabic, informative and functional: calls that express alarm or the need to be in touch with other birds. The second of these – contact calls – have an approximate meaning: I'm here, where are you? They are especially important for birds operating in flocks, and in winter many species switch from being half a pair to being one of many, and naturally they need to keep in touch with each other. And, like the roots of flowering plants, these contact calls and alarm calls are not intended to please anyone: they just have to work. But in spring many birds make sounds that are complex, musical and give pleasure far beyond the target audience of their own species. Like flowers they are *supposed* to be attractive, and that's because the function of both is attraction. And, of course, with both, it's all about sex.

Well, let's not be narrow-minded. We are twenty-first-century humans and inclined to think of sex as an end in itself. The song of birds is about establishing a territory. This is not to be confused with property: to a bird a territory is a place in which a pair can create a nest in a good, sheltered and safe spot, and all around it find the food they need to raise a number of young birds until they can fend for themselves.

A song must attract a mate. It's mostly the males that sing, but there have been new discoveries in this area that we'll look at a little later. A good song also suggests that rival males keep away – keep clear of the male, the female and the resources of the territory. The process takes place in spring because spring is the time of increasing resources, especially those of invertebrates, which are mostly feeding on the newly emerged botanical richness we looked at in Chapter 2. We have singing birds because we have active insects because we have growing plants; most of the birds that sing will be feeding themselves and their new families on invertebrates. Every bird aims to have a territory and a nest full of gaping chicks at precisely the time when the resources are at their peak. It's about surfing the wave of spring: catching it at just the right moment to get the longest and most rewarding ride. A late freeze, like the 'Beast from the East' in 2018, is a killer: those that survive have no option but to try again as soon as conditions change.

There's no point in setting up a nesting territory in the autumn. True, you wouldn't have much competition, but by the time the young hatched there wouldn't be enough easily found food for a nestful of chicks. There's hardly enough for you. For birds in the seasonal lands, as for most non-human living things, procreation is a strictly seasonal business.

It's not easy to grasp this. We humans are, for much of our lives, capable of reproducing at any time of the year and we consequently think of ourselves as sexual beings on a year-round basis, and assume that's what it must be like for everything that lives. In us humans the sexual urge is not something that comes and goes from one month to the next: in men it reaches a sustained peak before falling away, in terms of performance if not always in terms of desire. The years of male lust are, it has often been said, like being shackled to a lunatic; a much-quoted line originally found in Plato's *Republic*, in which he quotes Sophocles, who says, in one translation: '[I] feel as if I had escaped from a frantic and savage master.'

All male birds have a pair of testes inside the body. At the start of the breeding season – in spring for the species we're discussing here – these become 200 times larger. He becomes, more or less, overnight, something not far short of a completely different bird, with different behaviour, different motivations, different ambitions and in some cases a radically different appearance. More or less overnight, he finds himself shackled to a greater lunatic than any human ever knew; a few months later sanity will return and the lunatic will let him alone as if he had never existed ... until the following spring. In female birds the ovary and the oviduct swell.

Both genders are filled with unaccustomed and life-changing hormones, notably androgen for the males and oestrogen for females. And for the next few weeks or months they live in a completely different way, with completely different reasons for existence. Instead of hanging around in flocks and getting on with their neighbours, they will pair up and – in some cases literally – fight off any birds of the same species. Instead of holding on and seeking only to survive, they will risk everything as they give themselves over to the immense task of making more birds: their new priority is to secure the future of their immortal genes, rather than the survival of their mortal selves.

And for very many of these utterly changed birds, music becomes the centre of their lives, whether they are making it or listening to it and judging it. The males lift up their voices and sing: and even in cities, even in the heart of the open-air food factories of the intensively farmed countryside, we humans rejoice in the fact that spring is not yet silent: that the song of birds can be heard above the roar of machinery.

Most of the birds that sing are passerines, or perching birds: birds that usually have three toes facing forward and another one facing back, which makes perching easier. And there are thousands of them. If you have ever tried to identify a bird with the help of a field guide, you'll know that at the start it all seems relatively simple, with ducks and herons and waders that are, mostly, quite obviously different from each other, at least when reasonably close. But before you get halfway a certain dismaying sameness creeps in. A smallish size and a roughly similar sort of shape start to dominate, and many of the birds share a similarly discreet range of colours in mottled browns and olive greens. These are passerines, and even in the least ambitious field guide there is species after species after species: enough to make a timid beginner give up on the spot. The very many small drab passerines are often referred to as LBJs, Little Brown Jobs.

There are about 6,500 extant species of passerines in the world, or about 60 per cent of all bird species. Of these, two are New Zealand wrens, or *Acanthasitti*, and about 1,000 are *Tyranni*, which are almost all found in South America, and are deeply perplexing to any Old-World birder trying to get a grasp of the New. All the rest are songbirds: classified as Passeri or as Oscines (pronounced oss-signs). This sub-order is noted for the development of the syrinx, as you would expect: the syrinx is the bird's voice box. We humans are able to speak because we possess a larynx at the top of our windpipes; birds possess a syrinx at the bottom of theirs.

It is named for Syrinx, a beautiful nymph who took a vow of perpetual virginity; good luck with that, as to all beautiful females in classical mythology. She was pursued by the lustful Pan and, rather than submit, she flung herself into the river and was transformed into a reedbed. The wind passed over the hollow stems of these reeds and created a series of sweet sounds; Pan gathered them together and made a musical instrument: Pan pipes.

The syrinx is a (comparatively) large and bony organ lined with a membrane. Syrinxes vary in size and complexity from one species to another, though it's usually reckoned that the length of the windpipe is more significant when it comes to the complexity of the song produced. All birds possess a syrinx and most use it to produce sounds of different kinds. Unless you're an Oscine, these are relatively simple. Cuckoos are not Oscines, though reasonably closely related; all

150 species of cuckoo are capable of rich, far-carrying sounds, but not songs of complexity or variety.

But most songbirds really do *sing*, and their songs are often complex and musical. In many species they are also wonderfully various, differing not just from one species to another, but also from one individual to another. Many have an extensive personal repertoire. Every song imparts a great deal of important information, and it's aimed at every member of the same species within earshot. The first and most obvious information is the location of the singer. The second is the species the singer belongs to. This is so clearly — almost pedantically — spelled out by the songs themselves that even humans, with a much coarser sense of hearing, are capable of distinguishing one species from another without need for special equipment.[1]

And if you would care to try and do so yourself, start in November. At that time of year in Britain there is only one song of complexity and beauty that you are likely to hear and that's robin. Both male and female robins sing through the winter, and their sweet, thin, pretty song is one that many people — not me — find mournful. They sing because, unlike every other species of British songbird or Oscine, they maintain a personal feeding territory which they defend from others of the same species. Males and females both sing, and both defend

---

[1] Birds hear more detail than we do, and can distinguish much shorter sounds. When a wren's song is slowed down, we can hear many more notes than we did at full speed.

their separate territories, not as if but because their lives depend on it. They do so by means of a three-stage system that mostly allows territorial disputes to be settled without violence; violence, usually costly to both parties, is to be avoided whenever possible.

Territorial defence begins with song: in winter a robin's song is not intended to be attractive at all, its intention is entirely repulsive, and it's perhaps the most beautiful way of saying 'piss off' that you will ever hear. If a rival, driven by ambition or desperation, chooses to defy that unequivocal message the two birds will hold a pose-off, reminiscent of those occasions when one body-builder mimics the pose of another, to show that he or she can do it better. With robins it's about showing off not pecs and lats but that defining red breast. Such a performance should make the identity of the dominant bird obvious to both, and the subordinate one backs down – but if they seem to be well matched a punch-up will follow, sometimes with fatal results.

As winter turns to spring other birds join the chorus, one by one. The meaning remains the same, so far as male-on-male interactions are concerned, and so does the hierarchy of confrontation: sing, display, fight. For all that we like to think of nature as being red in tooth and claw (and beak), fighting is always the last resort, never the first. The first resort of a songbird is song. This has an important biological function for the birds, but it also brings deep delight to humans. I suspect that it also gives deep delight to female birds, for that is the second and more important aspect of its biological function. If the song doesn't please a female, the male singer is wasting his time.

As said, the performance of a song gives important information about the location and the species of the singer. It also gives information about the singer himself as an individual. (At this point we will concentrate on the singing male.) The first information about the male bird concerns his health and vigour. A male establishes his territory by singing loud and long. His ability to do so depends on how good a bird he is. He must be healthy and strong: if he isn't he won't be able to give as good a performance as the bird in the next tree. In other words, song is an honest indicator of the bird's value, as a potential opponent, if you're male, and as a potential mate, if you're female.

These messages come from the volume of the song, and also from the hours spent singing. A bird who gets knackered after ten minutes is obviously inferior to a bird who can keep going for an hour. The longer and louder singer is both sexier and more fearsome than his neighbour.

A further message comes from the content. Broadly speaking, there are two types of singers: those that sing the same song again and again, and those that have a wide vocabulary of song: stereotypical singers and repertory singers. Among the repertory singers variation is what admiring females love and rivals males fear: variation shows that the bird is experienced, knowledgeable and capable: all in all, a bird to be reckoned with. But who decides which variations are good? Who decides which song is the right sort of song? The answer is staring you in the face, though it was anathema to the Victorians: it's about female choice, and it's called sexual selection. Darwin explained natural selection, which is about the struggle between species.[2] He also explained sexual selection, which is a form of competition that can take place only within a species. The first kind is about which individual gets to survive, the second is about which individual gets to breed. Darwin nailed this one as well, of course.

Birdsong is a response to changing conditions: the arrival of warmer weather and increasing hours of daylight. It doesn't happen overnight, though sometimes it seems that way, when a day of startling loveliness pierces the January chill. And it's never a perfectly smooth transition: it comprises a series of advances and retreats: a day of singing is followed by a foul day full of avian silences. There are obvious advantages in being the first bird to set up a territory, start singing and start wooing; but there are equally obvious disadvantages: a sudden cold spell could be fatal not just to the singer's chances but to the singer himself. It's a high-wire act: do you get ahead of your rivals or play the waiting game? In the words of the song by the glam-rock band Sparks

> Choose your partners everyone
> If you hesitate
> The good ones are gone!

---

[2] This comes down to individual survival, but it's not a struggle *between* individuals.

SPRING IS THE ONLY SEASON

Gardens in the east of England (including mine) are often full of male blackbirds in winter, sleek, black and glossy with sunshine-yellow bills. Why so few females? These cocks are mostly Scandinavian birds, coming south to enjoy our gentler winters – so where are the hens? They fly even farther south, into southern Europe where the weather and the food supply are more reliable and the chances of survival are greater. The cocks take the risk of a more northerly winter so they can get back to Scandinavia as soon as the weather changes. They race each other back so they can commandeer the best territories by means of their incomparable flute solos. By the time the females arrive the most effective male birds are ready to receive them. It's not just about what you sing, it's also when.

Robins, as said, sing through the winter. On nice days – days that seem like a promise of spring – other birds join in, anticipating spring rather than taking a premature part in it. In British cities, suburbs and countryside the song of the robin is interrupted on a sunny January day by the cheery jumble of notes from a dunnock, or the startlingly loud trill of wren. Such outbreaks can take place even before the winter solstice: a few years back I heard singing woodlark in Suffolk on 20 December.

The birds don't start singing all at once: there is instead an annual succession, one that marks the advance of spring and the retreat of wintery woes. Learn a little birdsong and it becomes gloriously clear that the winter months are actually about the gradual advance of spring: on a short bright day in January, spirits already lifted by the sun are lifted farther by a repeated two-note song. It's not the most complex piece of music you've ever heard in your life, but context is all: this is the full-hearted spring song of the great tit, often written as 'teacher-teacher-teacher'; or compared to the sound of a squeaky pump.

On the same day you might hear a sharp rattle from above your head. This is a great spotted woodpecker, no songbird but a very decent percussionist. This drum solo has the same function as song: it's an honest indicator of the bird's fitness by means of a sound that carries a fair old distance.

This succession of melody and percussion, this series of additions to the orchestra, is a little like Mike Oldfield's *Tubular Bells*; perhaps it should be accompanied by Viv Stanshall's lavishly voiced announcements: 'Two slightly distorted guitars ... mandolin ... Spanish guitar and introducing acoustic guitar ... dunnock ... great tit ... mistle thrush and introducing song thrush ...'

For the next big moment is often the song thrush, a repertoire singer with a much richer range than most of his predecessors of the spring, repeating each phrase two or three times before moving on to another. The song is inventive and imaginative, often taking sounds from the locality – nuthatches, ring tones, car alarms – and reinterpreting them. After that, British blackbirds express their hope to breed by means of a sweet, relaxed whistling song that comes tumbling down from the chimney pots. In open country you hear skylark, singing not from a chimney or a perch in a high tree, but from the sky itself, singing on and on while flying at the same time, pouring and pelting music in a fashion that has the least scientific person wondering how it can do so for so long without taking a breath.

They can do it because birds don't breathe like us mammals. They don't go in for in-out diaphragmatic breathing. For a bird, breathing is a continuous process: a constant fresh intake is made possible by a body filled with air sacs and air even passing through hollow bones. Perpetual access to the freshest of fresh air is a huge help when it comes to flight, the most energy-expensive form of locomotion; anyone who has ever broken into a run can only envy the birds the fresh air they have always at their disposal. This wonderful adaptation also powers the singing: the length and volume of a bird's vocal performance depends on it. For the skylark it's both at the same time: virtuosity and endurance in both flight and song as he delivers his rash-fresh, re-winded new-skeinèd score.[3]

The spring continues with the arrival of the migrant singers: those that have wintered elsewhere but come to our shores to breed. And before they breed they must sing. The first of these is the chiffchaff, who sings a steady two-note song, different from the great tit and simple enough, but always particularly pleasing as it marks a shift in the year: in two notes we move from

---

[3] From 'The Sea and the Skylark' by Gerard Manley Hopkins.

early spring into middle spring. These days many chiffchaffs over-winter in Britain, but it's still the case that a new phase begins when they start singing.

The chiffchaffs are followed by other species of warbler. The blackcap is not as famous a singer as the nightingale, but the rich and melodious song is reckoned by many people to be just as good. It's certainly far more widespread, penetrating cities and suburbs and reaching deeper into Britain – the bird is sometimes called 'the northern nightingale'. They usually begin with a few plain, even scratchy notes before breaking into the melody: recitative and aria, as the writer Nick Acheson has it. Warblers are hard to see, and even when seen plain they're hard to tell apart: they're all of them pretty much LBJs. To appreciate warblers you need your ears. The sedge warbler's song is so complex and various that it's said never to sing the same song twice.

It always seemed to me that the last period of spring – high spring – arrives with the song of the willow warbler. When I was first able to pull this song from the background it was as if a door had opened: I felt as if I understood not just a single species but all birds, and it seemed, all nature. I was an initiate ... though the true meaning of this initiation was that a world of new questions and new discoveries was now available. It was at the same time an arrival and a point of departure. The song of the willow warbler is marvellously sweet, shifting sibilantly down the scale. It was once ubiquitous: when I was a Londoner I picked it out on Barnes Common and Hadley Wood railway station. But in recent years it is heard far less often in such places: and we'll look at the reasons for that later.

The undisputed champion singer of the British Isles is the nightingale. Its lofty reputation is not in the slightest way exaggerated. Certainly it sings in the night; it also sings throughout the day, when the surrounding chorus offers not distraction – still less competition – but a humble and modest accompaniment. It's been calculated that whereas a blackbird can produce 108 different syllables and a skylark 341, a nightingale can manage 1,160; and this, it is claimed, correlates to a larger and more complex brain.

What is certain to the human listener is that it's a song of extraordinary power, volume, expression, variation and unstoppability. The nightingale is a bird of paradise: the demented extravagance that you find in the plumage of these extraordinary birds can be found in the nightingale's voice. It's perhaps the ultimate expression of the British spring.

And, yes, female birds do sing. The issue is clouded with all kinds of confusing stuff to do with human sexual politics, and issues about which gender more often leads scientific investigations. There is also a fair amount of wishful thinking ladled on top of the established facts. But it's a fact that if you've done any serious birding in the tropics, you won't be shocked by the idea of singing females. In more stable ecosystems than our own, those less affected by the radical seasonal changes we know so well, many species hold a territory throughout the year by means of song duets. Both male and female sing and their songs have the dual function of maintaining both their territory and the bond between the pair. But in the seasonal lands, birdsong mostly comes and goes with the spring, and any female participation is less obvious – not least because in many of our commonest singing species, male and female are near as damn it identical: you can't sex a dunnock, wren and robin at a glance, as you can mallards and kestrels. Blackbirds, as we have seen, are unusual here. Most warblers, apart from blackcaps, are impossible to separate.

You can study the behaviour of birds of known gender when this has been established by previous examination in the hand and then made obvious by the fitting of coloured rings. Observation of such birds has shown that females also sing, though they do so less often than males, often with shorter and less elaborate songs. An American study of 2020, one that got a fair amount of publicity, showed that female swallows sing.

Birds sing. The fact is celebrated in a million poems and songs that humans sing. Birds gave us music: we took the melody they bring us every spring and added it to the rhythm of our own heartbeats – the rhythm we spent the first nine months of our existence dancing to – and we've been lifting our own voices in song ever since. To recap:

Hey ding a ding a ding
Sweet lovers love the spring.

Signs of spring
January 2024

25	Great tit singing by the water butts
27	Two red kites flying very close
29	Two, maybe three song thrush singing
	Two great tits singing
	Snowdrops under weeping willow
	Single gnat
30	Very good song thrush very close to my hut
	One buzzard chasing another over alder carr, both calling hard
	Great tit with classic teacher-teacher-teacher song
31	Dunnocks in full song
	Aconites in flower
	Green woodpeckers yaffling

6

Poetic spring

Poetry and spring are inextricable. At least they are in the British imagination: the poet of national archetype is a young fellow with long hair and a garment that billows as he walks in his wild way around the springtime countryside, working himself up into a frenzy until he has no option but to yield to the inspiration that has overcome him and write his poem. The poem he writes is, of course, about springtime, taking in the consequent daffodils, and begins: 'I wandered lonely as a cloud ...'

The poem is a real one by William Wordsworth, and it became a staple of anthologies and school lessons. It established for all time our romantic view of Romanticism and of all poetry: poetry as something only a poet can do, driven by a kind of mad inspiration. You write your poem because you simply can't help it – after all, it's spring. Every reader empathises with those thrilling moments of joyous excess that come with the turning of the seasons and the sudden revelation that once again we are in the most marvellous time of year – and it's better than we remembered, even better than we could ever have hoped. This is an emotion experienced annually by every one of us: turning a street corner and seeing a tree in blossom when last time it was just bare boughs; hearing a blackbird burst into song just after they've announced that the train is delayed; coming across a sunken hollow suddenly filled with primroses. Or, for that matter, turning your head to see a host of golden daffodils.

We might want to shout hooray or yippee, we might want to throw the hat from our head or deliver a series of violent punches to the air; we might, if there are people about, content ourselves with a secret but jaw-busting smile – but certainly these great moments demand some kind of response. And as we rejoice we might find words welling up from deep in the memory where we thought they had been lost:

> Ten thousand saw I at a glance
> Tossing their heads in sprightly dance.

And in this way we confuse our own moment of joyous emotion with the creation of a poem: as if both were equally instant and instinctive; after all, that's how spring works. Daffodils spring from the earth; blossoms spring from the bare branches of a tree; birdsong springs from the top of another tree and a poem springs unstoppably and spontaneously from the pen of the inspired figure who witnesses it all, almost as a physiological process. Poetry should be like that.

There are a million poems about spring, because poems tend to be about stuff that goes really deep. Spring and love are perhaps the favourite subjects in all poetry and, often enough, we find them in the same poem. We associate both spring and poetry with a kind of madness: spring fever is an overflowing of optimism mixed with eagerness for love.

We relish the idea that only a poet can write poetry; unless you're Wordsworth don't bother reaching for your pen. Which is like saying that there's no point in playing football unless you're Pelé. I knew someone years back whose passport – he made a point of showing it to people – described his occupation as 'poet'. It was a bold claim, one that set him apart from everybody else, most of whom, in those distant days, wrote poems ... but while we wrote the damn things we wouldn't dare describe ourselves as poets. It's far too lofty a claim for almost everyone. That's because poetry, in our shared national fantasy, is instantaneous, utterly authentic and a pure gift. You've either got it or you haven't, and most of us haven't. We must let the few rare others find the words to express the spring we all share.

Real poetry, as lived and written, isn't quite like that. The fact is that Wordsworth wasn't lonely as a cloud when he took that walk in 1802. He was with his sister Dorothy, who recorded the incident at Glencoyne Bay in Ullswater in the Lake District in her diary, noting that the daffodils 'tossed and reeled and danced and seemed as if they verily laughed with the wind that blew upon them'. Her brother's poem was published five years later and it combines his thrill at the first vision of the daffodils with his hard-won technical mastery. The poem is the result of a very great deal of hard work, along with a little adept fictionalisation: 'I wandered lonely as a cloud' reads better than 'me and my sister went for a walk'. We prefer to think that all *real* poetry is, in Wordsworth's own words, the spontaneous overflow of powerful emotions. We forget that he didn't stop there: he continued his description of the poetic process by saying that poetry 'takes its origin from emotion recollected in tranquillity'. It may start in giddy inspiration and a few scribbled words: it generally moves into a long stage of thinking things through, along with a very great deal of conscious craftsmanship.

So as we look at the poetry of spring, let us also spare a thought for the poet as a person of craft, as someone who works long and hard to get it right, taking a first impulse, in this case one of wild joy, and spends hours of labour making sure that the finished poem is absolutely right. A good poem has as much good craftsmanship (non-sexist term, obviously) as a chair, and chairs are no good if they collapse when you sit on them. Just as Pelé's great goals came from a lifetime of practice, so the great poems of spring tend to spring from a base of solid, hard-won craft.

There's no ducking the craft in the opening lines of *The Canterbury Tales*. I remember being faced with them in my first week as a sixth-former: the first dizzying vision of apparently indecipherable spelling and, with it, an equally dizzying realisation that the code could be cracked. And, sure enough, within the hour I knew that these strange words were telling me about spring, and doing so in a way that is as lovely as anything else ever written about spring. At the same time I realised that our annual delight in spring is far older than I thought. As I read Chaucer's bouncy Middle English I seemed to be going back to the dawn of humankind, rather than the closing years of the fourteenth century, a few years after the Peasants' Revolt with Richard II still on the throne.

> Whan that Aprill with hise shoures soote
> The droghte of March hath perced to the roote ...

These words provoked the same disbelief in my mind as they have just done in my spelling corrector. They can be roughly updated to read: 'When April, with his sweet showers, has pierced the drought of March to the root ...' And on it goes, in a single sentence lasting 14 lines, telling us that when spring comes and smale foweles maken melodye, everybody is full of restless ambition and it's time to set off on a journey, a pilgrimage to Canterbury no less: so let's go: 29 sondry folk, all of them about to be described one by one, with vivid personal detail and a good few jokes. And it's all marvellous stuff, especially once you've got your eye in for the spelling, but even though *The Miller's Tale* of thunderclap farts and *The Clerk's Tale* of the improbably patient and cruelly abused Griselda have their compelling side, it's that opening evocation of spring that has stayed with me across the intervening half-century, and how April's longed-for rain has

> Bathed every veine in swich licour
> Of which vertu engendred is the flour ...

The time of growth and flowering is here again, so let's set out on a marvellous jaunt; we'll have a lovely time and we'll all tell our best tales as we go.

The idea of spring as a time of welcome rain is a little unexpected, for all its vividness. Perhaps the same notion of the life-giving rain that brings the spring is behind the greatest quatrain of longing ever written. It's said to have been the favourite verse of Henry VIII, and sometimes suggested that he actually wrote it. Let's have it twice, first with original spelling:

> Westron wynde when wyll thou blow
> The smalle rayne down can Rayne

> Cryst yf my love were in my Armys
> And I yn my bed Again.

And modernised:

> O Western Wind, when wilt thou blow
> The small rain down can rain?
> Christ! My love were in my arms
> And I in my bed again.

That exclamation mark makes its point like a sledgehammer, though that's no bad thing. It's a song rather than a poem, insofar as these things can be separated, and it was set to music around 1350; you can find a few versions, often beautifully sung, on YouTube ... and it makes me wonder if there aren't just two seasons that exist in the seasonal lands: spring, and the time of longing for spring.

Shakespeare was good at spring, as we saw at the end of the previous chapter. Perhaps all great writers are, for they are naturally at home with great themes. We'll take in a little more Shakespearian spring a bit later, but while we're looking at poems we can't miss Sonnet 98, which begins:

From you I have been absent in the spring ...

This is followed by a jaw-droppingly effortless catalogue of springtime loveliness before the poem makes the neatest possible about-turn and says that all these wonderful things were:

> But figures of delight
> Drawn after you.

Spring is nothing without his beloved. In fact, he adds, spring without you feels more like winter. As with all those brief and brilliant verses – all 154 sonnets – you can only hope that the beloved was suitably moved by the words and responded as the poet desired, for surely the poet deserved it.

Round about this time poets were beginning to admire a more polite version of nature, and, therefore, a more well-mannered version of spring. Their favourite open spaces were not wholly wild. They were gardens: places where human hands had nature under control: nature had been successfully fought in order to create places that pleased human senses. The right sort of garden was seen as a perfect cooperation between humans and nature: perhaps even between humanity and God.

The sort of nature that these poets praised was not purely natural beauty, but a beauty that was, like a great poem, the result of conscious human craft: craft that could be concealed to a greater or lesser extent, according to taste and changing fashion. This is at variance with orthodox modern taste, and to make sense of this we must contemplate a time when wild nature was not a treat. It was everywhere, impossible to escape. Gardens were special places, forests were ten a penny. The population of the UK in the seventeenth century was about 6.5 million, and of London

600,000. London didn't reach the million mark till the beginning of the nineteenth century. So there was an awful lot of space without people, and therefore an awful lot of nature. Nature wasn't rare or threatened or cherished or valued: it was just there, and more likely to be seen as an enemy that needed to be subdued than a place of beauty. Nature was only beautiful when tamed: when organised. Only in such circumstances could spring be truly understood, enjoyed and celebrated.

Andrew Marvell's poem 'The Garden' revels in this kind of nature, and it contains the famous lines about:

> Annihilating all that's made
> To a green thought in a green shade

which makes more sense than ever in the twenty-first century. The poem points out:

> How well the skilful gard'ner drew
> Of flow'rs and herbs this dial new ...

Who is this gardener? A skilful human? God? Two in one? This is poetry, so relish the ambiguity and savour everything that's green.

A century later Alexander Pope was speaking up for managed nature – but not over-managed. He praised above all 'artful wildness' and in *An Epistle to the Right Honourable Richard Earl of Burlington* he suggested that Nature was a damn good thing:

> But treat the goddess like a modest fair,
> Nor overdress her, nor leave her wholly bare

In another poem, also called 'The Garden', he writes about 'the humble glories of the youthful spring' and revels in what nature can do when consigned to skilful hands: we've got spring just where we want it. But perhaps his most important lines about spring were in another context altogether, one in which he wasn't writing specifically about the season or of nature or of natural beauty. Rather, this was his poem about life, the universe and everything and is entitled *An Essay on Man*. It's a rum piece in many ways, and its resounding conclusion, 'One truth is clear, Whatever is, is right', can be understood as an acceptance of the laws of nature, as established under the pioneer scientists of the Enlightenment, and/or as an uncritical acceptance of the stratified society we live in. But that's not the line that has stayed with us across the centuries; that's not the line that has entered the English vernacular and is quoted widely by people who don't even know it's a quotation, still less where it comes from:

> Hope springs eternal in the human breast.

The words have retained their power, and perhaps they've gained more along the way, by brilliantly and artfully conflating hope and spring. Hope and spring: spring and hope: two great inseparables, two great eternals, the two things that keep us going in troubled times: the belief – the certainty – that however shitty things are, better times will come.

The most painful form of love is triggered by loss. The revolutionary nature of Wordsworth's daffodil poem was not that he took delight in flowers, but that he wrote with love about a wholly wild landscape. This was wilderness, pure wilderness unmodified by human hands, and yet it was portrayed as a place of profoundly meaningful beauty: a beauty you could reach and understand best in spring:

> Then my heart with pleasure fills
> And dances with the daffodils.

Even as he wrote – and laboured over – these words, the wild places of Britain were already becoming fewer and less wild. We were losing wild nature, and doing so at pace. The Industrial Revolution was beginning: powered by new technologies that required unprecedented mining and burning of fuels: wood from trees and fossil fuels, or coal, from trees long dead. Up till then nature had invariably been seen as an infinite resource as well as a place of perpetual hostility to humans.

The conquest of nature began 12,000 years ago with the simultaneous invention of agriculture in several places around the world; it gathered pace with unprecedented force as the Industrial Revolution began and the human population began to increase with a new and devastating rapidity. People needed more room, more fuel, and more resources: and it was all there to be taken from nature. As the Industrial Revolution advanced, it became clear for the first time that we were losing wild places and that we were losing touch with nature. And while all that seemed to many a glorious advance, other people, including poets, were already looking at its cost. The idea that nature, that wilderness, actually mattered: this was a shattering new concept. And it's there in the poem about daffodils, it's there in the awakening of wilderness in spring.

The Romantic movement was in a great part a response to the Industrial Revolution. It was also a response to the Age of Enlightenment, in which hitherto unquestioned religious orthodoxies came up against newfangled scientific exploration. The Romantics placed a high value on emotion, individuality and nature: and also on artists, who were seen as the true interpreters of the world.

The movement took place across Europe and spread to the Americas. The dates are a matter of argument and interpretation, but the first half of the nineteenth century saw most of the high points, with anticipatory Romantics going back a good 30 years earlier, and later Romantics still hard at it in the mid-twentieth century. Many of the pioneers came from Germany and Britain; in Britain the Romantic poets were in the vanguard. And again and again, they made their points by writing about spring. The joy we take in the new season, the joy that nature brings us every year, the consequent belief that things will get better – this was the natural subject of the Romantic poets, whether they were writing

POETIC SPRING

about flowers or the French Revolution. The heart of the Romantic movement was in the coming of spring: a new start: a belief that we have it within us to make all things better.

William Blake, the primordial Romantic, wrote tersely about spring in his *Songs of Innocence and of Experience*, and, more memorably, in words that are perhaps even more deeply embedded in the English language than Pope's hope, that we shall strive on and on:

'til we have built Jerusalem
In England's green and pleasant land.

A song of verdant – and vernal – hope if ever there was one. Perhaps the most famous spring poem and the most famous Romantic poem (after Wordsworth's daffs) is Keats's 'Ode to a Nightingale'. This addresses not spring itself but the great voice of spring, a voice that is only heard in spring. Keats writes about an ecstasy brought about by listening to the song – he heard it on Hampstead Heath in 1819 – and it's the poet's own elevated state that concerns him rather than the bird itself. We aren't invited to listen to the bird, but instead rejoice in Keats's resolution to fly 'on the viewless wings of poesy'.

If Wordsworth's poem captures the spirit of romantic wandering, Keats captures that of romantic contemplation. Between them they create a diptych of what the Romantic poet should be: either striding vigorously about the wilds in search of nature in the spring or sitting alone and still as nature comes to him in the spring, each in his different way not only reaching new levels of understanding but sharing them with the rest of us.

A year later Shelley wrote his own hymn to spring, to birdsong and to nature in 'To a Skylark', the one that begins 'Hail to thee, blithe spirit'. Noël Coward stole the last two words as the title for a play, one about a disembodied spirit; there's a beach hut in Southwold, near the mouth of the River Blyth, called Blyth Spirit.

This poem can be seen as the third leg of the great tripod of English Romantic poetry and its celebration of nature by way of spring. The skylark sings only in spring, and, for that matter, is a ground bird for most of the year. The skylark likes open places with no convenient song-post, and so the male sings on the wing. And Shelley, while travelling with his wife Mary (author of *Frankenstein*) in Livorno in Italy, was thrilled by the sustained, never-ending song of the skylark and responded in 21 stanzas in which he seeks to understand all of nature and with it the meaning of life. Naturally – again the *mot juste* – he falls short in everything save rejoicing:

> Teach us half the gladness
> That thy brain must know ...

The trouble with being any kind of naturalist is that you cannot help but be aware that an awful lot of nature poetry is patchily observed, imprecise, sometimes plain wrong and anyway more inclined to be about the poet's perception than the nature perceived. As a result the Romantic poet favoured by naturalists is John Clare, son of a farm labourer, and much re-evaluated and revived in the twentieth century. He's not quite in the same league as a poet when compared to the big three just discussed, certainly not in terms of widely remembered greatest hits, but he's a much better observer than them all. When he wrote about nature, he wrote about nature: what he actually saw rather than what he fancied he experienced. Here's an example, from 'On A Lane in Spring':

> And there a fly
> Rests on the Arum leaf in bottle green
> And all the spring in this sweet lane is seen.

The fly will likely be trapped by the lily and be held there, as we saw in Chapter 2, later to emerge covered in pollen, ready, if all goes well for the plant, to fertilise another arum with the precious dust.

But perhaps my favourite poet of the spring – there's something about poetry that excites an almost frenzied partisanship, as if an anthology of verse was a kind of Premier League competition – is Gerard Manley Hopkins, devout Catholic and perhaps even more devout observer of nature. His sonnet 'Spring' is a highly complicated poem that begins with welcoming simplicity:

> Nothing is so beautiful as spring.

In certain moods I will claim this as the best spring poem of all, if only for the line 'thrush's eggs look little low heavens', a line that has four Ls in three words and is a brilliant description of the mottled sky-blue of a thrush's eggs. Hopkins takes the optimism of spring a step farther:

> What is all this juice and all this joy?
> A strain of the earth's sweet being in the beginning
> Of Eden garden.

Spring is not just the nicest time of the year, it's the closest we get to paradise, which lies both in the past, in the story of Eden, and perhaps in the future, when we die. The implication to the non-religious is also clear enough: revel in spring, and in the now, for nothing else is certain.

I shouldn't be too snobbish about the naturalist credentials of Romantic poets: Robert Browning's famous 'Home-Thoughts, from Abroad' is very well observed. It begins, of course,

> Oh, to be in England
> Now that April's there

and describes the song of the song thrush who repeats each phrase:

> Lest you should think he never could recapture
> That first fine careless rapture!

POETIC SPRING

The last two words have gone into the English language in the manner of Pope's line about hope springing eternal, and it's been borrowed for all kinds of other purposes. But as we saw in Chapter 5, it's as accurate a description of the song thrush's song as you could wish for.

The custom of writing about spring didn't die out with the end of the Romantic movement, though the understanding of spring and what it means shifted and changed, and we shall look at that in Chapter 22. But the last century is still full of poems that celebrate spring without ambiguity. D. H. Lawrence gave us 'The Enkindled Spring', one of his early efforts, first published in a collection of 1916:

> This spring as it comes bursts up in bonfires green ...

But we'll let Ted Hughes have the last word in spring celebrations. His poems about nature were often ferocious, visceral and violent, sometimes with only tenuous relationship to the actual creatures described, but his poem 'Swifts' is clearly about the birds themselves, and thrillingly observed at that:

> Controlled scream of skid
> Round the house-end and away under the cherries.
> Gone.

But that's not the line that has stayed with me. In every poem that you carry in your mind – at the same time half-remembered and never forgotten – there's always a single line or half a phrase that sticks like a bur. Every time I see and hear the first swifts of the year, the words come to me:

> They've made it again,
> Which means the globe's still working ...

The clear implication is that there is some uncertainty – some annual uncertainty – about the working of the globe and, with it, the operation of spring. One year we might find evidence that shows that the globe really isn't working any more. So the return of the swifts is no longer a pure enkindled joy: it's also shot through with relief. And that, too, we'll examine further.

Signs of spring
February 2024

1. Two loud dunnocks
   Single daffodil in flower on the lane
2. New growth of ground ivy, nettles, cuckoo pint leaves and ground elder along lane
3. Wren singing in garden with full trill
   Half-arsed display from a pair of great crested grebes on River Yare
   Pussy willow on sallows on banks of the Yare
4. Raveningham estate: snowdrop walk
   One primrose
   Active honeybees
   Back home, bat glimpsed at twilight
5. Two green woodpeckers yaffling on marsh
7. Four mad hares on the marsh, much chasing
8. Two egrets together on Common again

7
Spring on the wing

The first butterfly is one of the year's fanfare moments: like the song of the chiffchaff or the first blackthorn in blossom it seems to signal a transition from promise to achievement. True, spring can and should be seen as a continuing process that lasts (roughly, in everything bar astronomy) between the December and the June solstices, but there are moments of glory when we can pause for a moment and savour the thought: the longing is over and we've got there at last. I thought it would never happen, but now it has. Huzzah!

It happened to me a few weeks earlier, as I write these words on a sweet afternoon in late May. I was looking from kitchen to garden and there was a glimpse of movement – bright yellow movement, as if a sunbeam had got loose and was blazing against the cotoneaster. If that's a touch too fanciful I apologise: butterflies, especially the earliest butterflies of the year, tend to inspire thoughts that are extravagant, would-be poetic and often unabashedly sentimental.

This butterfly was, of course, a male brimstone, named for his sulphurous colour. It is one of four or five species of butterfly likely to turn up in gardens and parks early in the year, where they move jerkily but concentratedly about their business, seeking both flowers and each other and leaving a trail of huzzahs in their wake.

I expect we all have a pretty clear idea of what a butterfly is: this little flutterer is obviously a butterfly because it's obviously not a moth. Moths are drab and nocturnal, butterflies are colourful and dance in the sunlight. Alas, that simple, vernacular distinction doesn't stand up to examination: there are plenty of day-flying moths, including the gorgeous six-spot burnet and equally lovely cinnabar moth, also the less extravagant but often numerous silver Y moth. What's more there are a good few extravagantly coloured nocturnal moths, like the elephant hawk moth and garden tiger, both of which could challenge most butterflies in a gaudiness competition.

The scientific differences have to be hedged about with words like 'mostly' and 'mainly' and 'though there are exceptions' – but – in the main – the antennae of butterfly are bullous or clubbed at the tips, while those of moths are tapered or feathery. A butterfly at rest – when its wings are not spread right out in a full bask to absorb the heat of the sun – generally holds its wings high and together, like praying hands, while a moth is more likely to fold them in a neat triangle. But when it comes down to it, the principal and most obvious differences between butterflies and moths are cultural rather than scientific. We know and like butterflies and they send us good messages about the turning of the year; we don't know much about moths and we distrust them, seeing them as irritating light-bulb orbiters, or (blaming all species for the crimes of one) devourers of clothes.

Butterflies and moths are insects in the order of Lepidoptera, which means scaly wing; should you do a good deed and escort a house-trapped moth or butterfly back into the open, you might find a light dust on your hands; fallen scales from the wings. Taxonomists argue about their degree of relatedness: which separate groups share the most recent common ancestor. Moths are usually divided into two groups, macromoths and micromoths; it seems obvious that the larger ones, the macros, have more in common with butterflies than the little guys, but recent research suggests that this is wrong, and they're probably more closely related to the micros: tiny moths that even experts find hard to tell one from another.

One fact is indisputable: moths are more successful than butterflies, if we judge success by the number of species. There are about 165,000 species of Lepidoptera worldwide, of which only 18,000 are butterflies. That difference is even more exaggerated in British populations: there are around 2,500 species of moths, of which 1,600 are micros and 59 species of breeding butterfly. We'll look at moths in more detail in Chapter 13: in this chapter we'll concentrate on butterflies, because everybody knows that butterflies appear in the spring.

But where do they appear *from*? Where were they before? Or to put that another way, *what* were they before? Belize, in Central America, is about one-tenth the size of the UK. It has 700 species of butterfly: almost 12 times more than the UK. Why this dramatic discrepancy? The UK has something that Belize lacks: winter.

In the heavily seasonal lands winter is an annual catastrophe. Dealing with it requires a complex and sometimes desperate strategy. Winter makes problems for everything that lives, including the dominant and planet-changing species, but it has a special meaning for every animal species that is neither a mammal nor a bird. That's because they all require an external source of heat. We often call them cold-blooded, but that's misleading: they often have an internal temperature greater than that of the surrounding world. Butterflies reach such heights by basking in the sun, spreading their wings to absorb its energy, energy they will use to power their flight in search of flowers and other butterflies. They can also increase temperature by agitating their flight muscles: a sort of shivering process, energy-expensive but effective.

All the same, butterflies, like most invertebrates, can't be active without a reliable external source of heat. If they are to survive in Britain and the other seasonal lands, they must find a way of getting through winter – even though winter is insupportable to them. They manage this by means of any one of four obvious potential strategies – and one other rather unexpected ploy, which I'll save for last.

When that brimstone appeared in my garden it was as if it had appeared from nowhere: a rabbit from the great green hat of spring (apologies, another fanciful phrase). That sense of magic is an ineluctable aspect of spring: but magic won't do as an explanation in the twenty-first century – and besides, what actually happens always turns out to be more extraordinary than anything we could make up.

Butterflies are not just butterflies – and that's *not* a fanciful phrase, it's an undisputed fact. Like most other insects, they go through life in four radically different phases: egg, larva (for butterflies and moths that's caterpillar), pupa and adult. In order to get through or over or round the apparently unpassable barrier of winter, a butterfly must deal with it in one of those four forms. Which is the best option? Which one do butterflies choose? You'd think that one strategy would be optimal and they'd all follow it, but not so: all four are viable and different British species go for different ones. (One species, the speckled wood, operates on a choice-of-two basis, caterpillar or pupa.) Some species over-winter as eggs, others as caterpillars, others as pupae – and a few as adults.

The brimstone is one of the last kind: they wake as the year turns and, being fully-formed adults, they are already good to go. They've got all that tiresome, time-consuming business of hatching, eating – the caterpillar is basically an eating machine – and changing out of the way and so they head out into the spring as functional flying creatures, ready to mate, and after that, if female, to lay eggs. All of this brief and colourful life is fuelled by the nectar produced by the earliest plants to flower and by the weak but still welcome rays of the spring sun, still a long way from their most effective angle of impact. Spring in earnest has just begun, but the brimstones are at the climax of their lives, surviving for a scant week or two in which they take the final step towards becoming ancestors or die in the attempt.

Butterflies get through the winter by entering a phase of diapause. It's a near-total shutdown and it can operate in all four phases of a butterfly's life. Diapause is not unique to butterflies either; many other arthropods (the phylum to which insects belong) also use this state. It is far more drastic a state than hibernation:[1] if you like, a fair bit closer to death. You may have come across

---

[1] More on hibernation in Chapter 15.

over-wintering adult peacock butterflies: they turn up in sheds and other outbuildings and sometimes inside houses. In these circumstances they look dead and they act dead and can be handled and moved about just as if they were dead: but they are attached to life by a slim but mighty thread, and a great awakening will be triggered by changes in day length and/or temperature. Sometimes a peacock is woken from diapause by a hike in the central heating: if you have a good heart you will place it in a cardboard box until it has stopped fluttering and then transfer it to a suitable location outside: cool, sheltered and yet easy enough to escape from.

Small tortoiseshells and commas – both of these are species of butterfly – also over-winter as adults. Like the brimstone they are easily seen garden butterflies, familiar to all who take the trouble to notice them. The advantage of the strategy of over-wintering in adult form is that once they've emerged from diapause they have the new world of spring more or less to themselves: there is much less competition than they would find in high summer. The disadvantage, of course, is that there are fewer flowers – fewer sources of nectar, which they need to power their flight in their few days of active adult life. However, as we've seen, some plants also operate the early-is-good strategy and for the same reason: their pioneering flowers face far less competition for the services of flying insects than those that flower later. The insects that are up and about early in the spring have no option but to seek out the limited choice of early flowers.

The butterflies' most popular strategy for facing the winter is as a caterpillar: more than 30 of the UK's 59 butterflies go for it. Again there are different strategies available. Some go straight into diapause from hatching, some do so when part-grown, some when fully grown and almost ready to pupate; some of these are intermittently active in winter and feed on mild days. Other species get through winter as an egg or a pupa. Every strategy for over-wintering has its problems: in every phase of its life an immobile insect is at the same time tasty, nutritious and defenceless. The insect in winter must place its bet on concealment, and then on waking at the right time. The right time is not just when it's warm enough to be active: the moment of waking must coincide with the availability of nectar-rich plants (if you're an adult or imago) or the required food plants (if you're a caterpillar or larva).

Butterflies aren't fussy about which flowers they take nectar from: any accessible source will do. But caterpillars are very particular. If they aren't on the right plant they die. Some can manage a small range of plants, but the choice is still crucial. There's no point in a caterpillar coming out of diapause until there is something to eat: an adult female can bask in the sun and feed and mate but unless she can lay her eggs on the right plant, in season, growing well and unwillingly receptive to future caterpillars, she has wasted her life.

The first orange-tip is one of those critical spring moments. The male is small and white with, unsurprisingly, orange tips to his wings: he is, in a quiet way, spectacular. He is always, it seems, in the most terrible hurry, charging across the newly green world in search of nectar and a female; the females being rather more subtle, the tips to their wings a mottled charcoal. The caterpillars feed on lady's smock, a lovely and discreet little plant, and garlic mustard, rather more robust and obvious. Common blues like bird's-foot trefoil, holly blues – another unsurprising fact – like holly, and brimstone caterpillars feed on alder buckthorn and purging buckthorn, two small native trees.

But let us rejoice in nettles, and not just for the people who relished them as the first fresh green food of the year. Nettles are life itself to the caterpillars of those gorgeous garden butterflies mentioned earlier: peacock, small tortoiseshell and comma; also red admiral and painted lady; more on these species in a moment.

The one caterpillar food plant most people are clear about is cabbages: small and large whites both feed on brassicas, that is to say, cabbages and related plants, many of which grow wild as well as in allotments. These plants, when damaged by, for example, a very hungry caterpillar, defend themselves by putting out toxic oils. This is not the advantage to the plant that it seems, at least not so far as these caterpillars are concerned, though other potential predators are deterred. The large white caterpillar takes on these toxins without harm and uses them for its own purposes, by becoming toxic itself. It is brightly coloured, black and yellow, traditional warning colours: the caterpillar is easily found because it is informing all potential diners that consumption is contraindicated. The small white is less effective as a sequesterer of toxins and relies on green camouflage rather than warning colours. As adults both species look pretty similar, but only the large white is seriously toxic. Looking like a toxic butterfly does the small white no harm at all.

But here's a strange thing. Though we might refer colloquially to any white butterfly – at least four British species – as cabbage whites, there are very few other butterflies that non-naturalists can put any kind of name at all to. Most people can name a few birds – robins and swans, for example – and probably the odd flower, like daffs and roses. But butterflies are just butterflies. One name fits all. No non-naturalist would say: 'There's a brimstone.' What's more, there's an almost total lack of folk names for butterflies: no enjoyably colourful rustic nicknames for these bright and obvious creatures.

This is in sharp contrast to other easily seen things. Alternative and historic names for the kestrel go deep into double figures and include stannel hawk, hoverhawk, red hawk, keelie, field hawk, windhover and, less poetically, windfucker. The arum lily named by John Clare is also cuckoo pint, lords and ladies, Jack-in-the-pulpit, devils and angels, red-hot poker and, more recently, willy lily. But there are no dirty jokes inspired by butterfly species. The only folksy name for a butterfly is, well, butterfly: the most likely explanation for this unlikely term is that it's about the male brimstone, arriving early in the year and glowing in the colour of the best butter. For all the others, it seems that one generic term satisfies everybody: it's a butterfly and there's an end to the matter. The common names used casually by the people who do notice them were mostly given by the primordial naturalists who collected them and painted them, hence the painterly names like clouded yellow and Camberwell beauty. (Let me add in passing that the easiest possible way of getting more pleasure from nature is learning the names of a dozen garden butterflies: such knowledge makes you look more and look harder and brings a disproportionate degree of pleasure.)

Wordsworth wrote a couple of poems about butterflies without giving any clues as to which species delighted him:

> Come often to us, fear no wrong;
> Sit near us in the bough!

Capturing the feeling that most of us have experienced: the desire to tell the fleeing deer or alarm-calling bird: we mean no harm!

Emily Dickinson, the nineteenth-century American poet, almost unpublished in her lifetime, was keen on butterflies and wrote a wonderfully sardonic poem 'The butterfly obtains'. It's about the bad press the butterflies, for all their obvious beauty, tend to get:

> The circumspect are certain
> That he is dissolute ...

Butterflies are supposed to have butterfly minds. They are seen as inconsequent seekers of pleasure, drifting randomly from flower to flower in colours too gaudy for sobriety and good sense. But that erratic flight, in which the butterfly often seems to trip over his own feet in mid-air, is in fact a masterpiece of predator avoidance: try, as an exercise, to keep up with a moving butterfly. And don't believe that butterflies are feeble: and that brings us to the fifth way a butterfly can survive the British winter. By not being there when it happens.

A red admiral is the one butterfly a non-naturalist might name. Certainly it was the only I could name for many years. It's a big one, a black background strongly marked with red, black wing tips picked out with white punctuation. Observe it in flight and you will find nothing dilatory: this is a strong and purposeful insect, a butterfly that looks as if it could fly through a brick wall. They need to be strong: every year they fly to the British spring from southern Europe and even North Africa, reaching the most northerly Scottish islands and penetrating the altitudes of the Highlands. This astonishing migration brings red admirals here in spring: some as early as January (though a few individuals over-winter in adult form in diapause). Once in Britain they breed and die; subsequent generations undertake the return trip in the autumn. As the temperatures drop, the urge to migrate is triggered and off they go, picking a still, clear day to do so, setting off south without mating first, a flight of gaudy virgins heading towards the Mediterranean. Once there they encounter a fresh growth of nettles – parched and desiccated during the Mediterranean summer – and there they mate and the females lay eggs on the nettles, food plants that will sustain their caterpillars and allow the next generation to move on towards the great journeys of adulthood.

Red admirals are powerful and effective fliers, and the aerodynamics they exploit are complex and unconventional. One of the most pleasing tricks in their repertoire is known as the Weis-Fogh clap-and-fling: a movement named for a Danish zoologist, in which they clap their wings together and then fling them wide open. This allows them to rise effortlessly into the vortex created by the initial clap.

Two other migratory species of butterfly reach the UK. You never know how many clouded yellows you're going to get: a good year is something to celebrate. They arrive in July and August so they don't really count as spring arrivals. Painted ladies are more reliable, but they, too, have boom years, in which every buddleia seems to be drooping under their combined weight. They arrive early enough to count as spring butterflies: large and striking insects: the base colour of their wings is pale to deep orange, which is picked out with black marks; the wing tips are black with white spots.

The migration of the monarch butterflies of North America is justly famous, and vivid images of their roosts, with immense numbers gathered together, have established them as *the* migrating butterfly. But it's not mere chauvinism to claim that the painted lady is twice as remarkable, undertaking a journey of 12,000km, about twice that of the monarch. Painted ladies start in the African tropics and travel north as far as the Arctic Circle and, when their summer duties have been fulfilled, they travel back south again. This immense double journey is not performed by one single population of insects: rather, it's a narrative involving a series of generations, around six in all, an annual *Forsyte Saga* of butterflies. The butterflies arriving back in tropical Africa are likely to be the great-great-great grandchildren of those that set off. If humans ever travel beyond the solar system, we will travel in the same way as the painted lady: in a series of generations.

Butterflies are mostly extravagant and prominent. That makes them very good at finding each other, and that's the whole point of being a butterfly. They don't have to live long: merely long enough. That's long enough to mate and, if female, to lay eggs, and that can be and often is a matter of days. Butterflies are temporary: he that kisses a joy as it flies dwells in eternity's sunrise, said Blake; no doubt he was thinking of butterflies at the time. Neither butterflies nor spring last forever: that's why both are treasured.

Butterflies compartmentalise their lives. They do almost all the eating they need to do as caterpillars, so that when they are adults they can concentrate entirely on the task of making more butterflies. All they need are regular sips of energy-giving nectar. The males of some species engage in combat: hard to believe that something routinely associated in human minds with effete manners and an inability to concentrate should enter these aerial battles with such enthusiasm. Two bloodthirsty – or to be more accurate, haemolymph-thirsty – insects will rise as one, beating the crap out of each other as they do so. The males that win the battles – or find some other way of getting lucky – father the next generation: the females that accept the males must then lay eggs on the right food plant. (So if you have a garden it makes the best sense to allow a nettle patch to flourish; if all goes well you will be rewarded with the brightest butterflies when the spring comes.)

Butterflies, it sometimes seems, are there just to please humans. They are at the same time almost gratuitously beautiful and almost ostentatiously harmless. They seem to be telling us about a wholly benign world: and if that's an illusion it doesn't mean we can't enjoy it. A person who can't delight in a butterfly is leading a life of great deprivation.

Butterflies, being mostly highly visible, are relatively easy for humans to count (as opposed, say, to earthworms). Alas, most of the counting reveals decline. More of that later, but let's close this chapter by looking at one more species. Its British distribution map is a sad thing: there's England and Wales and Scotland and it's all empty apart from a tiny green blob on the right-hand side. This blob is the Norfolk Broads: the only place in the UK where you'll find swallowtails.

The Broads is a fine place in many ways (I live there) and it's worth paying a visit in late May and early June just for this butterfly. Swallowtails are immense, by butterfly standards, big as the palm of your hand, black and yellow, subtle blue spots on the rear band of black with red dots at the back of the rear wings and the two little streamers on the trailing edges that give the butterfly its name. Philip Howse, who writes brilliantly on animal perceptions, especially when butterflies are involved, suggests that when the swallowtail is in flight the little spikes, in combination with the red dot, give the impression of a bird with eyes and a hungry beak: enough to put off any potential predator for the half-second the butterfly needs to get away.

Swallowtails are insects of wet country, which explains why their population centre is the most watery landscape in Britain. They were once far more widespread, for the simple reason that there used to be much more wet country. They were common in the fen country of Cambridgeshire until the 1940s, and also found in the Thames Valley. But a great deal of wet country has been drained for agriculture and other purposes; much of the Fens were ploughed up for potatoes and carrots in the Second World War. Changes in management – otherwise known as neglect – affected the growth of milk parsley, the caterpillar's food plant.

Since then good conservation work has improved the quality of much of the swallowtail habitat in the Broads, and the population there is currently stable – so much so that every spring pilgrims come to places like Strumpshaw Fen and Hickling Broad to feast their eyes on this monstrously improbable beast. Swallowtails can appear in a sudden flash of yellow; they can remain in sight and in flight for a sustained period over reedbeds and open water, powering onwards with a wingbeat that looks as strong as a bird's, nothing remotely dissolute about it all; and occasionally they will alight within the pilgrims' view and spread their gorgeous wings for a prolonged bask, soaking up the sun and perhaps also the waves of silent applause that coming rolling towards them.

There's something miraculous about the swallowtail, but then there's something miraculous about all butterflies, particularly those that greet the spring at the earliest possible moment: and for a moment you can believe, with Pope, that everything that is, is right. And perhaps the swallowtails will spread from their fastness of the Broads, and perhaps we will find a way of reversing the decline in butterfly numbers. I feel a little foolish and naive at having allowed such a thought to come to the surface, and even more so to have written it down. But you know how it is. Hope does rather tend to spring eternal, especially where there are butterflies around.

Signs of spring
February 2024

9	Plum blossom on main road
10	Noisy activity in rookery
11	Greenfinch and chaffinch both singing
12	Wren signing with full trill
	Full wood pigeon song
13	Black-headed gull with black head
14	Rainbow, song thrush and chaffinch in song
	Greenfinch, dunnock singing
	Two hares together
15	Paired-up mute swans
	Herons calling from heronry

8

Feasting in spring

The year was 1979, the date 27 January, the time midnight, at which point it became 28 January. The Year of the Horse was over; the Year of the Goat had begun. And with it, the Third World War. Or so it seemed. The entire village before me was, in an instant of time, rocked by a series of mighty explosions. They came in tight clusters of a dozen or so, a pause, then more. Sometimes – often – these dozens overlapped. Within minutes the Bonfire Night stink of gunpowder filled the air: then came more bangs, more and more and more, for this was joy unleashed, this was happiness unbound, this was the great night of all great nights and the exultation could only be properly expressed by the most ferocious form of firecrackers. Spring was here at last and a new start could be made by all, last year's rotten luck had already been discarded and a new era of all the best luck in the world would surely follow, bringing with it a detonation of prosperity and joy. Certainly it worked that way for me, even if the prosperity was relative.

This was Chinese New Year, perhaps the greatest celebration of spring of them all, and certainly the noisiest. A few weeks earlier I had moved to Lamma Island, which lies due south of Hong Kong. That was because the rents were cheaper, the ambience better, the scenery more lovely and I had just been sacked by the *South China Morning Post*, a carefully timed dismissal that enabled them to avoid their contractual obligation to pay me a New Year bonus of a month's pay. So I settled in Yung Shue Wan, a village that specialised in market gardening and fishing, with a few commuters bringing in money from outside. It also attracted – there were 17 of them in total – a strange flotsam of Europeans, Americans and Antipodeans: artists, journos, transients, teachers of English as a foreign language, dodgy business people, losers, boozers and lost souls. Once there, and having no alternative, I set out on the bumpy road of the freelance writer and so found my vocation. The government of Hong Kong had long ago banned firecrackers for their obvious dangers, but no one bothered much about governments on Lamma – so when the magic moment came, a million firecrackers were lit and joy filled the air along with the smoke and the stench.

Hong Kong just about counts as tropical – its 22.3 degrees north – but it still has marked seasons: coolish dryish winters, steam-bath summers and, in a good year, a glorious spring. On Lamma this was marked by the roar of the bullfrogs in the irrigation tanks and the chanting of the Indian cuckoo, a sweet and endlessly repeated four-note call that expats understand as 'one more bottle', as if we needed encouraging. All of China north of Hong Kong is intensely seasonal and so, inevitably, the Chinese celebrate spring. The recognition and celebration of spring covers 360 degrees (longitude) of the globe: wherever there is a strongly seasonal climate people will be sad when winter comes and joyful when spring returns at last.

Like Easter, Chinese New Year doesn't have a set date every year but must take into account the phases of the moon. The lunisolar calendar[1] is perplexing for those not used to it – also I suspect for those who are – but it's roughly the case that the Chinese New Year begins on the second new moon after the December solstice. As this great day approaches, elaborate preparations must

---

[1] In the lunisolar year the months are lunar but the year is solar. A few extra days are squeezed in to make up the difference.

be made. One essential is a proper spring clean of the house, and not just for the sake of cleanliness: you're sweeping away all the bad luck from the preceding year and clearing a space for the good luck that will surely replace it.

Luck can be defined as the elements in your life that are beyond your control: the notion that you make your own luck is therefore a contradiction, and that's a truth that operates in all cultures. All cultures have traditions that attempt to propitiate whatever forces are in control of your luck, from touching wood and crossing fingers in the west to the elaborate celebrations of Chinese New Year.

The streets of Lamma were decorated with red papers that bore gold characters, often simply enough the character for *Fu*, or good fortune. An ancient story tells of a terrible monster called Nian who turned up every year to devour all the people and everything they possessed – but a wise old man discovered that Nian was terrified of the colour red and also of loud noises. With firecrackers and red papers evil and misfortune could be kept away for another year.

Chinese New Year's Eve is also a great family reunion, with lots of noise and feasting and togetherness. It's a time of new beginnings: the bad past has been swept away and for a while at least, new hopes seem like certainties. On New Year's Day you are likely to dress in a completely new set of clothes. Younger family members will be given gifts of money, always supplied in red packets. An odd sum of money is bad luck, and so is a sum that ends in four, because the word for four – *sei* in Cantonese, the language of Hong Kong – sounds a lot like the word for death.² Eight is the number that counts: the luckiest number of all,

And on New Year's Day everything changes. Now no one will touch a broom or do any cleaning at all, for fear of clearing out the good luck. You don't wash your hair – some prefer not to wash at all – and no one will use a knife or scissors, for fear of slicing away good luck. There are taboos against swearing and using words like 'death'. Bad news for authors: it's extremely unlucky to buy a book at this period, or to give one as a gift, because the word for book sounds like the word for lose. You must choose another time of the year to make a gift of the Chinese edition of *How to Be a Bad Birdwatcher*.³ In China everyone has seven consecutive days of holiday but the celebrations carry on until the fifteenth day, which is marked by the lovely Lantern Festival, and the Yung Shue Wan night was annually aglow with lanterns and no one could doubt that the world was a better place than it had been a fortnight ago.

---

² Also *sei* but spoken with a different tone. Chinese languages are rich with such puns and word associations. Eight is a lucky number because the Chinese word for eight – *ba* – sounds a bit like *fa*, which means make a fortune. That's why the Beijing Olympics began on 08-08-2008, even though August is the worst month for smog.

³ One of mine, first published in 2004.

I lived on Lamma for four years and remember how on every New Year's Day there would be lion dances in the street accompanied by drums, drummers and lions, combining to bring good fortune and drive out any possibility of bad luck. There was always a fizzing jollity and excitement all through the village, along with a faint scent of gunpowder, replaced as you neared the temple by the dizzying smoke of joss sticks. It was, every year, a time of celebration and joy and it was, above all, about hope.

Of course it was about hope. It was spring.

Now let's fast-forward to 15 March 2006. I was in Mumbai, covering a Test match between England and India; it was scheduled to begin after the festival of Holi, it being unthinkable to hold a cricket match while Holi was still going on. Naturally, as a good journo should, I went out into the streets to get some local colour. That, I should point out, is both a journo joke and a Holi joke: for Holi is the great festival of colour and as I walked around the open spaces around the Gateway of India and in the crowded, hooting streets inland, I passed through crowds high on holiday humour, all of them throwing powdered colours at each other. Many were already walking painter's palates, palates of an artist uninterested in muddied hues: red for love, fertility and marriage, blue for Krishna and, of course, green for renewal. For some reason they didn't throw any at me, perhaps unsure if I would take it in the right spirit and on this day of all days no one wants bad vibes. Holi is not just about colour: it's also about spring, love, reconciliation and the triumph of good over evil.

That, of course, is the crucial part of spring in every culture of the seasonal lands: every year, in a way that is both surprising and inevitable, light conquers darkness and life conquers death — so it's obvious that good is conquering evil at the same time, and while we're at it, love is conquering hate. Only the bottom half of India is tropical: the country lies between 8 and 38 degrees north, and covers a north–south distance of 3,300 km, so there's room for a lot of seasonal and climatic variation, and, naturally, there's more scope for the seasons as you move north. But winters here are not as barren as they are in the high north: there is traditionally a spring harvest of winter-sown crops, the *rabi* crops of wheat, barley, peas and gram (chickpeas).

Spring is welcomed in and Holi is annually celebrated at the full moon in the month of Falgun and this usually falls in the middle of March (we're back with the lunisolar calendar). The festival celebrates the divine love of Radha and Krishna and also the victory of Vishnu over the evil Hiranyakashipu, who is, it seems, invulnerable: he can't be killed by a human or by an animal; he can't be killed indoors or outdoors; he can't be killed in the day or in the night; he can't be killed by a missile or by a hand weapon; and he can't be killed on land or on water. Vishnu comes to him in the avatar of Narasimha, half-human and half-lion. He is neither human nor animal; he takes on his enemy at dusk, when it is neither night nor day; he does so on the threshold, which is neither indoors nor outdoors; he seats him on his lap, which is neither land nor water; and kills him with his lion's claws, which are neither projectile nor hand-held weapon.

This is a pleasing riddle-like story, the sort of thing deeply embedded in many cultures: Samson in the Bible, the sphinx in the encounter with Oedipus, and Shakespeare in *The Merchant of Venice*, to take three random examples. Holi begins the night before the day of colours, when bonfires are lit and an effigy of Holika can be burned: she is a fireproof female demon who entices Prahlad, son of Hiranyakashipu, to sit with her on a fire. Her plan is to punish him for his devotion to Vishnu but it all goes badly wrong: she is burned to death while Prahlad is saved.

The following day brings the playful throwing of colours; Krishna was concerned that his skin colour – blue (sometimes just dark) – was not pleasing to Radha, his beloved, but his mother told him to snap out of it and tell Radha she could paint him any colour she liked. This story has inspired the best-known part of the Holi festival, and, in the most vivid colours possible, it celebrates love, and love is both colourful and colour-blind.

Holi is more than a jolly-up. It is also a time to renew damaged relationships, and to forgive or to pay debts both fiscal and moral. It's also a time when – briefly – differences of status and caste can be set aside and for a while everyone is equal, or seems so. Ribald language and wild behaviour are generally tolerated on this occasion: there is something in common with the festivals of misrule that traditionally followed Christmas celebrations in England and elsewhere. After all the colour has been thrown, everybody calms down, goes home, washes and changes into clean or, better still, new clothes, white ones for choice, and then goes to visit friends and family and, of course, feast: especially on *gujiya*, dumplings filled with fruit, nuts and spices, especially cardamom.

Holi is frivolous and meaningful, playful and serious. It is largely unorganised and belongs to everyone. It is at the same time ancient and modern, traditional and every year new made, buried in time and annually relevant. Perhaps all enduring festivals are like that, or perhaps they just should be. Holi is essentially about love, joy and fun. I found that trip of 2006 very difficult, for I was swamped with a lingering post-viral lethargy that left me with low energy and lower spirits. A walk in the Holi streets of Mumbai kept despair at bay.

It's not really possible to hold a spring festival in Islam, even though the holy month of Ramadan has some aspects in common – notably piety and fasting – with the Christian Lent that precedes Easter and with the Jewish Passover, which we'll come to shortly. That's because the Islamic calendar is wholly lunar: the sun has no say in it at all. In the lunisolar calendars we looked at earlier, the lunar calendar is brought in sync with the solar calendar by a process called intercalation: basically, you stuff in a few extra days so you don't fall behind the sun. (The leap year is an example of intercalation and it's what makes the solar calendar work; without the extra day every four years the solar calendar itself would fall behind the sun at a rate of a quarter of a day every year.) The Islamic calendar doesn't do any intercalation at all, with the result that every Islamic year falls 10 or 11 days short of the solar calendar. That means that all festivals, tied as they are to the moon and not calibrated with the progress of the sun, migrate through the calendar year. They can't be tied to the annual rhythm of the seasons.

Ramadan involves prayer and a study of the Quran. It's also a time for reflection and for cherishing the community. It requires abstention from food, drink and tobacco between sunrise and sunset. I remember hearing the call from a mosque in Marrakesh during Ramadan, announcing that the sun was officially down and the time of fasting was over for the day: a white-haired man threw his mouth at a standpipe as if it were the lips of a lover: it had been a long hot day to go without liquids. Another, younger man dived hungrily for his cigarettes, lit up and inhaled life. A devout person is also expected to refrain from all sexual activity in the daylight hours of Ramadan, and all sinful behaviour.

Dispensations from strict fasting are accorded to the acutely and chronically ill, diabetics, breast-feeding mothers, the elderly, menstruating women and travellers. There are complications: when Ramadan falls in late June and you live in, say, the north of Norway, there are no hours of darkness in which to feast and replenish. There are various ways of coping with this devoutly: for example, you can align your day to the hours of sunrise and sunset in Mecca. Ramadan has the feel of a spring festival, since it involves an annual renewal: a fresh start by way of piety, devotion and self-discipline, and one that is followed by the joyous time of Eid, as the Christian Lent is followed by Easter. It's just that it doesn't march with the rise and fall of the seasons.

The Jewish Passover – in Hebrew Pesach – is a spring festival, based around the sacrifice and subsequent consumption of the Paschal Lamb. It was established long before the Christian Easter. The two feasts are closely linked and at the same time deeply estranged: quite a lot like family life, in short. There are theories that it has its roots – perhaps the right word in this context – with Canaanite[4] agriculture festivals celebrating the arrival of spring and of the spring harvest of winter-sown barley, so we are back once again to celebrations of fertility. Passover takes place on or around the first full moon after the March (in the northern hemisphere, the spring) equinox and, not exactly by coincidence, the Christian Easter takes place round about the same time: the Last Supper was a Passover feast.

Both festivals celebrate the spring, but both are also about complex religious ideas. Passover commemorates the departure of the Jewish people from their lives of

---

[4] The Canaanite civilisation flourished on land bordered on one side by the Eastern Mediterranean and on the other by the River Jordan during the second millennium BC.

slavery in Egypt. This departure – this exodus – was precipitated by the tenth plague of Egypt, brought down by God (Yahweh) on the Egyptians. The final plague was too dreadful to be borne: the killing of the firstborn son in every household. Only the Jews were exempt: they had been instructed by Moses to mark their doors with the blood of a lamb; that was so the angel of death could take note and pass over these households as he went about his terrible night's work. The Jews, unable to leave Egypt for so long, were now required to do so in a hurry and, so the story goes, they were unable to prepare their bread for the journey as they would have liked. There was no option but to make and eat unleavened bread, bread that hadn't been set aside to prove with yeast. And that is part of the Passover feast to this day, along, of course, with a sacrificed lamb. The feast also carries a requirement – in some interpretations an obligation – to drink wine with the meal, four cups for preference.

The Passover meal is the subject of one of the best-known paintings in the world, or at least in Western culture: for once the overused word 'iconic' is not inappropriate. That is Leonardo da Vinci's *The Last Supper*, which shows Jesus and 12 apostles around the table. The Last Supper was where, in Christian tradition, Jesus changed the meaning of the most important feast in Judaism by requesting that bread and wine should from henceforth be consumed in his memory: that was because he, and not the dish they were eating, was the paschal sacrifice.

So with Passover we have once again a feast of new beginnings. This meaning was taken still further in the

Christian tradition established subsequently, because, though Jesus will be sacrificed and killed, he will rise from the dead as spring does its annually impossible feat of rising from the death of winter.

There are spring festivals practised with different levels of intensity all over the world: wherever the shifting of the seasons makes a significant difference to daily life. These include Nowruz, in Iran and other parts of Central Asia, a festival of Zoroastrian extraction that lasts for a month and is associated with a feast that must include seven springtime items. In Thailand, Songkran is not entirely unlike Holi, but instead of colour they throw water. There is an annual spring gathering at the pyramid of Teotihuacán in Mexico. In Egypt, there is the charmingly named festival Sham el Nessim – Smelling the Breeze – which involves much giving and receiving of hard-boiled eggs.

One country has physically altered itself from top to bottom – from north to south, a difference of 3,000km, lying as it does between latitudes 20 degrees (just tropical) and 45 degrees – in order to celebrate the spring properly. This is Japan and the Japanese have planted cherry trees everywhere there is an open public space: in front of schools, in front of many public buildings, and of course in public parks.

For humans these trees have but one function: beauty. Their fruit is useless for humans. All – all! – they offer is a brief annual moment of loveliness: one that lasts a fortnight (if you're lucky). For the other 50 weeks of the year they're just another piece of street furniture.

The fleeting nature of this beauty is an important part of it, of course: beauty and, for that matter, life itself is fleeting, and that's all part of Buddhist and Shinto teaching. Which is all very fitting and pious and so forth: but the season of cherry blossom is also a time of celebration, for conviviality, for sharing and for loving, like all the other celebrations of spring that we have been looking at.

The great tradition of *hanami*, or blossom viewing, began in 812 under Emperor Saga, and it rapidly spread from the royal court to people everywhere. It is emphatically part of modern Japan: an aspect of being Japanese. The festival celebrates the continuity between the present day and the deep past: an ancient tradition of annual renewal that is itself annually renewed. The coming of spring is marked by the blossoming trees, but — because of the nature and the physical shape of the country — it doesn't happen everywhere at the same time. Rather, it marches from south to north and the blossom front is tracked avidly on television as it advances. The contemplation of the *sakura*, the cherry blossoms, is a fine and poetic thing, but it's just as good, or even better, when you're accompanied by a group of friends and a nice picnic, particularly if the picnic contains a decent bottle or two. In places like Ueno Park in Tokyo one picnic merges with another in a crowded country and an immensely crowded city, but as the haiku poet Issa wrote:

Under cherry trees
none are utter strangers.

FEASTING IN SPRING

The Japanese tradition of haiku has become a global one, though no one can write a haiku without thinking of Japan. In the strict Japanese tradition these poems should contain 17 syllables. A haiku is a response to a single thought, a moment of enlightenment, of enhanced understanding – and it should contain a *kigo*, a seasonal word, one that gives a clue – by no means always heavy-handed – to the season in question. In other words, no matter what subject the poet has chosen, every haiku has as its real subject the season itself, and, by extension, the procession of the seasons and the passing of time. Thus the bitterness of winter gives way to the relief and joy of spring. Let's have three examples from Bashō,[5] acknowledged as the greatest haiku master of them all. He can effortlessly shift gears from sublime thought to joyous wit to low comedy, sometimes all three at once, capturing human life in a double-handful of syllables:

The warbler sings
among new shoots of bamboo
of coming old age

For the white poppy
the butterfly breaks off its wing
As a keepsake

---

[5] Matsuo Bashō, 1644–94.

Mallow flowers
by the side of the road
devoured by my horse.

But we'll let Issa[6] have the last word:

Cherry blossom
made for haiku poets
to exploit.

[6] Kabayashi Issa, 1763–1828.

Signs of spring
February 2024

- 16   Cley in North Norfolk. Singing skylark
  Displaying Canada geese
  Alexanders in flower
  Toad in car park
- 17   Sky-dancing marsh harriers
  Paired-up Egyptian geese
  Two herons fly into the heronry together and start a racket
  Four oystercatchers, spring arrivals
- 18   Very loud dunnock
  Excellent wren song – two trills and a flourish at the end
  Rosemary in flower at Leiston
- 19   Oystercatchers calling
  Red dead nettles in good numbers
  Dark male marsh harrier, new arrival
- 20   Budburst on weeping willow
- 21   Heavy rain – chaffinch, song, thrush, great tit all singing
  Eight oystercatchers together
- 22   Seven herons in the air above the heronry, all in high excitement
  Two egrets fly out of the heronry in tight formation
  Ten oystercatchers
  A few gnats
- 23   Norwich: crocuses, jonquils, snowdrops
  Magnolia with buds ready to burst
  Lacewing in car

9

Springtime travellers

And then all at once they're here as if they'd never left and every year my heart rejoices a little more than it did the year before. Something about the way they fly, in circles and esses, with little jinks and darts and handbrake turns, seems not so much a search for food as an expression of joy: a promise of happy carefree days that will last for as long as the swallows stay with us. Of course, I know this is all folly – silly, sentimental, anthropomorphic – but I can no more stop my heart from rejoicing at their springtime arrival than I can stop the sun from rising earlier tomorrow than it did today. Swallows seem to be flying for the sole purpose of expressing their love of life: telling us with each steep-banking circle that we have done the year's hard yards and it's time to accept our reward.

This joy in the arrival of the swallows comes partly from delight in their aerial skills: in the sleek shape with swept-back wings and forked tails, their neat colouring, shining navy blue above, pale below, with that subtle hint of extravagance in their red faces. But it also comes from the fact that they weren't here yesterday. They haven't been here for the past seven months and more. All winter they've been somewhere else, but they crossed the world to be back with us, and as they fly into the outbuildings I will them to find a safe place inside where they can make more swallows.

A few years ago I was asked to come up with a suggestion for Britain's national bird; it was part of the debate in preparation for a nationwide vote on the subject. Swallow, I said. It has to be swallow. They bring us joy when they arrive, they sum up all the delights of the English summer, they make us sad when they go and they remind us that we in Britain are part of a global community: like everything else, we depend on everything else. The swallows we rejoice in can't live without safe migrations, safe wintering grounds and safe stopover points miles away from their nesting grounds in UK outbuildings. They are our swallows and they are the world's swallows. Wildlife is global, not local, and its conservation is all about community and connectivity. We are, I said, all in this together: and the swallows spell that out for us in the most beautiful fashion. (The vote was won by the robin.[1])

Never mind. Swallows still bring disproportionate joy when they arrive. One swallow doesn't make a summer, we are traditionally told, but the arrival of the first swallow certainly tells us important facts about spring. Swallows fascinated the great eighteenth-century naturalist Gilbert White, the archetypal chronicler of place: his *Natural History of Selborne* remains essential reading. Perhaps White was better on spring than he was on any other season, for, after all, it's the best subject. He was the first person to separate the three species of what we now know as the *Phylloscopus* warblers: they all look the same and, before he made his meticulous observations of the radically different songs they sing in spring, wood warbler, willow warbler and chiffchaff were regarded as a single species. He spent all his life in one place – Selborne, of course, in Hampshire – where he was a clergyman. And he spent a lot of time thinking about swallows. He longed to know what they did in the winter, why they suddenly disappeared and how, with equal suddenness, they came back.

---

[1] The event was organised in 2015 by the excellent David Lindo ('The Urban Birder'). Robins got 75,632 votes, or 34 per cent, beating barn owl in second and blackbird in third.

The idea of migration enthralled him without ever wholly convincing him: perhaps because he was a stay-at-home by nature. The last time he mentions swallows in *The Natural History* he says that he has 'great reason to suppose that they do not leave their wild haunts at all, but are secreted amidst the clefts & caves of the abrupt cliffs where they usually spend their summers'. After a lifetime of debate on the subject he eventually, it seems, plumped for hibernation rather than migration.

White[2] got so many things right that it seems mean to pick out one of the few things he got wrong, but his error shows us how extraordinary bird migration is, and how hard it is to get your mind round the idea of a very small bird making a physical slog across impossibly daunting distances. British swallows – well, African birders are more inclined to regard them as African swallows that happen to breed in Europe – take the most extreme long-haul option available and travel even further than those that breed on the European mainland. They spend their winters in South Africa and Namibia; if you see a swallow (a European swallow *Hirundo rustica*) in Cape Town, it probably hatched in the UK. When the moment is right – more on this in a moment – they leave their wintering grounds and set off on the 6,000-mile journey to the European spring.

Unlike many other migrants, they don't fatten up before they set off: they feed on aerial insects, so if all goes well they will feed as they travel. By the standards

---

[2] More Gilbert White in Chapter 21.

of many species, they move at a leisurely pace, say 300-plus km a day. They rest up at night in communal roosts, mostly in reedbeds. They fly from southern Africa to the Congo: ahead lies the Sahara. Some take the coastal option, a longer distance but a less fearsome prospect. Others go straight on across the world's widest desert. They then travel through Morocco, cross the Mediterranean, travel north by way of eastern Spain and western France, and then cross the Channel.

Many of them head back to the exact same place where they were hatched, or to the place they nested last year – and these might well be the same. One study reports that 44 per cent of swallows return to the nest they used the previous year, once there making all the repairs necessary with fresh mud. It's an unimaginably heroic journey, at least it seems that way to us, and it's as if they've done so specially to do us honour. As they make their belly-tickling runs across the insect-rich grass, gain 100 feet in a twist of the wings and then break into a sweet fragment of song, notes tossed towards the ground in careless handfuls, the ground-bound human below knows that spring has shifted from promise to achievement and politely gives thanks to the birds that have miraculously changed the world in a single sumptuous instant.

And it all comes down to another miracle: the extraordinary fact that birds can fly. Birds can fly and we can't – and that gives them a radically different way of understanding the world and its problems. More than any other creatures on earth, birds have the ability to avoid trouble by being somewhere else when it happens. Or to put the same thing another way, if there's something good happening almost anywhere in the world, birds have more chance than any other creatures on earth of making use of it.

The lightning brief Arctic spring and summer produce rich resources of food. There are comparatively few ground predators, because it's very hard for them to get through the long winter. What's more, there is almost continuous daylight for the critical weeks when food must be found for new-hatched young. So when the days in Britain and Ireland lengthen and the spring comes, the swans and geese that have spent their winters on and around the waters of these countries take to their wings and fly to the Arctic, where they can raise their young in the brief time of plenty. When the killing Arctic winter comes round again, they head back south to the balmy winters of the British Isles, where the days are short and cold, but not half so short and cold as they are in Iceland and Spitzbergen.

These winter visitors leave Britain with the spring, but many other species arrive as the British ecosystems wake up, the trees come to life, the flowers bloom, the insects reappear and a land that seemed half dead is teeming with life again: and the more it teems, the more life comes in to exploit the teeming. Life makes for more life: and that is what spring is all about. The swallows are here not for a sentimental attachment to old England, but because, as the weather warms up and the days get longer, the sky becomes filled with aerial plankton: small specks of life that exist in the air, mostly insects, but also tiny spiders, carried into the air on long streamers of web.

This largesse is only available for a few months of the year and resident British birds lack the specialist equipment to exploit it to the full. Black-headed gulls hawk for insects in the air: they're OK at it but not brilliant. They don't need to be: this is just one of a dozen or more feeding strategies they adopt: they are very effective generalists. But swallows, and their relatives, house martins and sand martins, and also swifts, which are not related but have a similar feeding strategy, are all specialists, and their speciality is aerial plankton. They come in and help themselves. They have no choice but to leave in the autumn as the supplies of aerial plankton diminish and they have no Plan B when it comes to feeding. And so they head back south to pursue their specialisation elsewhere, while the skies become empty of insects and spiderlings, and also of swallows, martins and swifts.

White found the idea of migration improbable, but it was perfectly acceptable to earlier writers. The prophet Jeremiah wrote: 'Yea, the stork in the heaven knoweth her appointed time; and the turtle and the crane and the swallow observe the time of their coming; but my people know not the judgment of the Lord.' The turtle is the turtle dove, so here is some good observation, all four species being migrants – and this fact must have been widely accepted or Jeremiah wouldn't have used it to contrast with people's ignorance of less delightful matters.

Aristotle is usually thought of as *the* philosopher: a man happy only when dealing with abstract ideas. Certainly he had a penchant for logic (never a popular subject with humanity), but he was also a pioneer in what was once termed 'natural philosophy': what today we call biology, ecology and ethology. And he had no problem with migration: 'Some of them find protection in their accustomed localities, others are migratory, and at the autumn equinox, escape at the approach of winter ... and in spring retreat gains before the approach of summer.'

Homer used migration in a famous example of the epic simile in *The Iliad*:

> As when the ringing cry of cranes goes up before the heaven
> When they flee the winter storms and monstrous rains ...

The ancients' meticulous attention to scientific detail can be exaggerated: Homer goes on to explain that the cranes set off on these journeys in order to wage war on the pygmies. But he was right about the basic fact of migration.

There was always resistance to the idea of migration, simply because it seems so unlikely. Travel was so difficult for humans that it was impossible to imagine the possibility of any non-human making continent-crossing journeys twice every year. Doubts about migration lingered into the nineteenth century. In continental

Europe storks were, and in places at least still are, the most obvious migrants of all: huge birds wholly absent for the winter, arriving in spring to form noisy colonies, nesting on chimney pots and church towers, clattering their bills and copulating enthusiastically in full view. Where had they been all these months? Did they hibernate at the bottom of the sea? In 1822 in the village of Klütz in Mecklenburg in what is now Germany, a stork arrived with an arrow in its neck. As if the poor thing hadn't had enough trouble, it was then shot down out of curiosity and the arrow was found to be from Sub-Saharan Africa. Several other examples have been found since then: such a specimen is a *Pfeilstorch* and there are around 20 of them in various museums.

Study of migration predates this: the *Pfeilstorch* merely ended the luxury of doubt. The pioneering work was done by Johann Andreas Naumann who was the first to identify the phenomenon of *Zugunruhe*, or pre-migration restlessness: he observed it in caged birds and concluded that they, too, felt the urge to migrate and that it was apparently triggered by changes in day length. You can observe *Zugunruhe* in wild swallows in September as they circle and perch in fidgety gangs, getting ready for the off.

Since Naumann's time migration has been widely studied in wild birds. The first efforts involved ringing (in American banding): catching birds, attaching a light ring to a leg and hoping for a recovery at some later date. This practice continues and has yielded much astonishing information. Birds are captured in nets set out for the purpose, often on known migration routes. They are handled with care, ringed (ringers prefer the strong verb 'rung') and released. With advancing technology more sophisticated equipment can now be attached to a bird without inconveniencing it: more of that in a moment.

The British spring begins, roughly speaking, with the December solstice, but the pace hots up with the arrival of the migrants around three months later. A trio of birds traditionally marks the moment when the great season changes gear: wheatear, sand martin and chiffchaff. Wheatears are mostly seen in England on the way through to breeding grounds in Scotland and Wales, especially when the distinctive white bum is revealed as they fly away; the name has nothing to do with wheat but is derived from white-arse. Sand martins are swallow-like and appear over open water with devastating suddenness as early as late March, making the idea of subaquatic hibernation briefly compelling. They fly with zip and energy, giving a let's-get-cracking vibe to the advancing season.

The moment the first chiffchaff lifts his voice in song is always a special one for people tuned in to birdsong: I will text 'Chiffchaff!' to birding friends when I hear the first of the year. It's the best kind of pleasure: a thrilling encounter with something wondrously new that tells you that everything is just as it always has been. The two-note call of the chiffchaff tells us that God is in his heaven, all's right with the world. The annual parade of migrant singers has already been touched on

SPRINGTIME TRAVELLERS

in Chapter 5: blackcaps and chiffchaffs sing throughout the daylight hours once they have established themselves, and as they do so they give the simultaneous feeling of adventure and comfort: of change and stability. These days both species are increasingly inclined to over-winter in Britain, which compromises the pleasure in their songs with more than a little worry. More on that in Chapter 23.

They are both species of warbler. Warblers are enigmatic to non-birders. They are all around us in season but seldom seen by a casual eye – and even if sighted, apparently impossible to tell apart, because one species looks alarmingly like every other. Birders train their ears (as Gilbert White did) so they can tune in to the growing springtime chorus and distinguish one warbler from another without needing to use their eyes.[3] Most warblers are migrants: of the dozen or so that are reasonably easy to find, only two species, Cetti's warbler and Dartford warbler, invariably stay at home for the winter. The others arrive, sometimes after a trans-Saharan journey, and change the soundscape when they do so. Reedbeds are suddenly filled with the song of reed warblers and sedge warbler; wood warblers light up the wet woods of the west.

But some migrants are worth using your eyes for. Ospreys, who migrate from Africa, are as fine a sight as you could hope for in Britain: birds of prey that plunge talons-first into the water after fish. Hobbies are slim,

---

[3] See my own *Birdwatching with Your Eyes Closed*, first published in 2011.

elegant falcons that hawk for dragonflies, and also hunt swallows and swifts in the air: clearly birds that like a challenge, because their chosen prey species are not the easiest of targets. If you're lucky you will see them plunging after hawking swallows in that wonderfully dramatic anchor shape. They, too, are African migrants. Birds of prey are, compared to warblers, massive. That means powered flight is even more expensive in energy for them. They couldn't make it if they had to flap all the way, so they do as much of their journey as possible at the glide, gaining height in thermals – rising columns of warmer air – by spiralling, often in large numbers. They get this free lift from the environment and then glide onwards, gradually losing height until they find another thermal. Thermals can only form over land, so they avoid the sea as much as possible, most of them crossing the intervening seas at Gibraltar or the Bosphorus.

These days the most obvious migrants are swifts, often seen in the sky above cities; ancestrally they were cave dwellers but modern swifts more often nest in roof spaces. These are the birds whose arrival was celebrated by Ted Hughes in Chapter 6. Swifts are with us for as little time as possible: they arrive in May and are gone by early August. Young swifts come from Africa to Europe with the grown-ups but aren't ready to breed yet, so they spend the whole time they are with us in flight. They fly up from Africa, feed on aerial plankton, and by late July form mad screaming parties in which they speed along streets in low-level runs, apparently using the houses as markers for a drag-racing track. A swift, once fledged from a nest in this country, can go as long as four years without leaving the sky, without perching even for a moment: for they can feed and rest and socialise on the wing, even while travelling to and from Africa, and, when the time comes, they will mate on the wing as well.

There are more migrants to be found if you turn your eyes seaward. Terns are like gulls made slim and elegant, sports cars rather than all-purpose runabouts. They often feed by plunge-diving after fish: slamming into the water head-first from a height of 10m and more. Common terns also use inland waters. Arctic terns look very similar but live very different lives, for they are one of the world's migration champions. The UK population breeds mostly in north Scotland and the Western Isles; there are other populations still further north. Almost unbelievably, all these birds arrive from the Antarctic: from the opposite end of the world, an annual round trip of 35,000 km. No living thing sees more light in the course of a year than an Arctic tern. One was rung in Wales and, with a fine sense of colonial and onomastic history, was recovered six months later in New South Wales, Australia, 20,000km away.

How do they do it? Bird migration remains one of the great mysteries of life, though many advances have been made. Daylight fliers use the sun as a compass, and that doesn't work unless you know the time – exactly – and are capable of perceiving the sun's passage through the sky even on cloudy days. Birds have also been shown to use the magnetic field of the earth to navigate. They can also find their way at night by using the stars. They sometimes also use visual landmarks, like rivers and coasts, and carry mental maps.

Some travel what seem to be impossible distances all in one go, doing so by massively increasing their fat reserves before they depart. The bar-tailed godwit, which is found in the UK among other places, makes the longest non-stop flight: flying from Alaska to New Zealand, 11,000km, in just five days. Bar-headed geese have the altitude record; they fly high for the excellent reason that the Himalaya is in the way. They have been tracked at 7,720m and there is anecdotal evidence of them overflying Mount Everest, so more than 8,000m. It's been speculated that their migration route was well established before the Himalaya was created, squeezed up by the collision of tectonic plates between 40 and 50 million years ago.

So let us burst into song once again and sing that great thirteenth-century welcome to the spring and the anticipation of the season that follows:

> Sumer is icumen in
> Lhude sing cuccu!

Or, summer is a-coming in, loudly sing cuckoo. Cuckoos sing from late April to mid-June, sometimes even a little later. I used to hear them on Streatham Common when I was a boy; alas, they're no longer found there but where I live now, in the Broads in

Norfolk, cuckoos still sing out with mad passion when the spring comes.

We manage a little bit of marshland for wildlife and it was there, on 17 May 2023, that the British Trust for Ornithology caught two cuckoos. They did so by setting up mist nets at dawn, alongside a dummy cuckoo, adding to its enchantment by playing the call of a female cuckoo. This brought not one but two males barrelling down out of the alder carrs in jig-time. Both were fitted with satellite tags and then released: they are now part of a BTO study of cuckoo decline. It's been going on since 2011 and more than 100 birds have been tagged. Our birds have been called George and Michael – not my choice – and their progress can be followed on the BTO website: a search for 'BTO cuckoo' should do the trick. I can walk their favourite springtime places when spring has long departed, lift my phone and check on their travels – Michael in northern Spain at the beginning of August and George already over the Sahara.

I say 'our cuckoos' with very little conviction. Data from the project has shown that cuckoos spend just 15 per cent of their year – or their lives – in the UK. They spend 47 per cent at their wintering grounds in the Congo rainforest and the rest – 38 per cent – on their travels. They travel south by two different routes: some go down through Spain and over Gibraltar and across Morocco, others prefer to go through Italy or the Balkans and across the middle of Africa. All of them have to cross the Sahara. Most birds return by a different route, making an annual circle, as the map on the BTO website shows. Important facts have been revealed about the relative safety of different routes, the importance of stopover points in West Africa and their relationship with the timing and the availability of the invertebrates they feed on. We now know a great deal more about cuckoos than we did before.

But I don't suppose these birds, making their heroic journeys with the best BTO bling on their backs, will be able to explain a still greater mystery. Cuckoos, famously, have no domestic life. The males sing 'cuckoo' in the hope that a female will hear them from a great distance: that's why the call is loud and clear and simple. Should that happen, the tryst is brief, generally followed by the glorious bubbling call of a female. After that she will lay her egg in the nest of some unfortunate bird – usually dunnock, meadow pipit, pied wagtail or reed warbler – and then her job is done. The chick will grow into a monster, or so it seems, bigger than its unwitting foster-parents. Once fledged, it will fly off and become part of the great migratory tradition of the species.

But who tells them to go? Who tells them when? Who tells them where? They have no parent to show the way, no siblings for moral support, and no flocks of their own kind to learn from. They just do it: and if all goes well, they end up in the Congo for half the year, until the urge to travel takes them over again. George and Michael set off merrily enough and I followed their journey south on my screen. But, alas, both tags stopped working and the rest of their stories is unknown. The following spring at least one cuckoo took up residence again. I was unable to ask him his name, but he was certainly giving it everything.

Wel singes þu cuccu!
Ne swik þu nauer nu![4]

Signs of spring
February 2024

24	Local river, kayak. Catkins on alders
25	Bumblebee
	Territorial tawny owls calling competitively at dusk
26	Cuckoo pint in leaf
	Pair of oystercatchers
27	Goldfinch song
	Five herons fly into heronry in 15 minutes
	Whisper of blackbird at dusk
28	Ladybird on outside wall of my hut
	Two Egyptian geese, paired up
	Bat in flight round stables
29	Goldcrest song
	Big noises in heronry
	Gnats by garden gate

---

[4] You sing well, cuckoo – never stop now!

10

Sporting spring

Who told us? How did we know? Why was any other step unthinkable? Questions I can't answer and nor can John, but it was the same every year. There came a time – in memory a single day, and after that, it was always impossible to go back – when we crossed the road to Streatham Common and instead of throwing jumpers to the ground to make a goal, we drove stumps into the earth – three together and then, after John had measured out 22 paces with his longer stride, we drove in one more. The first three were for the batter to defend, and the fourth to mark the place where the bowler bowled.

It wasn't just us. It was as if an irresistible divine voice had spoken to each individual's soul and pronounced: football is no more. From this day forth you will play cricket. And, in a transition as radical as the one when all of spring arrived on a single day in Narnia, the landscape of the Common was transformed. Instead of scattered groups of boys kicking a large ball, there were groups of boys bowling and smiting a small one. In a day the world was changed.

John Murtagh, who lived three doors down from me, can't remember what triggered the transition either. It was, he thinks, something to do with the Easter holidays, and perhaps with his own feeling that, as school cricket captain, it was time he got his eye in. I remember it as a feeling of inevitability: a shared conviction that no other course of action was possible. When he shakes his mane, we shall have cricket again. To play football would have been a kind of blasphemy against the power of spring.

The association of cricket with better and easier days has created a wagonload of sentimentality, with the breathless hush in the close tonight – ten to make and the match to win – and the ghostly batsman who plays to the bowling of a ghost: two quite different but equally sentimental poems, both still much treasured and much quoted, even if these days with a little irony.[1] And I must confess that I'm tempted to paint an even more sentimental picture of those days on Streatham Common, in the years around the fifties/sixties cusp, when boyhood was very different, distractions were harder to find and paedophiliaphobia had yet to become universal.

I long to recall the time when John, always much better than me, would smite the ball almost into the Rookery, the formal garden across the road, while my mightiest hits were never more than a stroll away for him: but that didn't matter because I was essential: without me he would have had no game: nothing to smite and for that matter no one to bowl at. These days existed all right, but our innocence should be set against the evening when John blagged us into Streatham Odeon to watch *Dr. No*, the first James Bond film with Ursula Andress emerging from the sea in her bikini – a primal image and a very reasonable application for the job as goddess of the spring.

In later life I played cricket for mighty Tewin Irregulars Cricket Club, though I wasn't much better at the game than I was on Streatham Common. I remember a game in mid-June: I was batting and I stopped a fast bowler in his delivery stride to point out a cuckoo flying over the pitch. It was fortunate that our opponents

---

[1] 'Vitaï Lampada' by Sir Henry Newbolt, and 'At Lord's' by Francis Thompson.

were the RSPB;[2] the bowler followed my pointing finger, remarked 'good spot' and went back to his mark.

We acknowledge the changing seasons by changing our behaviour as well as our garments, so naturally we change the sports we play and watch. Advancing technology has made great changes, of course: satellites bounce television coverage of major sporting events into our homes from all over the world, so in the depth of winter English people can watch cricket being played in the Australian summer. The science of ground maintenance has been revolutionised: many games can now be played in seasons when it was previously impossible: rugby, either code, requires a pitch soft enough to dive about on and was once impossible between May and August: these days, with sprinklers available at the touch of a button, rugby league has made a transition from a winter to a summer sport.

Sport is trivial – that's rather the point – but it is not only trivial. The idea of play lies deep in human nature: and goes even deeper. Play behaviour has been observed in many animals, including octopuses. I have often watched lion cubs play-hunting, mock-fighting and stalking the tip of their mother's tail; I have seen a mature lioness initiate play, grasping a cub in huge soft paws while lying on her back and tossing it up, so it landed on her chest, where it fought with playful ferocity. Play, for lions as for humans, is serious fun. With the

---

[2] Royal Society for the Protection of Birds.

cubs it's a way of learning; with humans it has become an end in itself: one that we take into grown-up life.

So we have formalised play and called it sport – and inevitably, reflecting the way that we have to live, we suited our sports to the seasons. You can't play cricket in winter: it just doesn't work. Even at the level of Tewin Irregulars, a match takes five or six hours, much of it spent standing still, in a reasonably intense sort of way. You need a certain level of warmth for that: and even if you could wrap up warm enough for a winter day and still move, catching a hard ball with cold hands is difficult and painful; in early spring serious players put hand-warmers in their pockets. To make things worse, you can't bowl properly on a muddy pitch: not only are you likely to slip, but the ball won't bounce, so the batter can't hit it. And it rains more in winter than summer, even though it doesn't always feel that way if you're a cricketer. Once or twice I have played on through the rain, in the belief that we've all gone to considerable trouble to get here, so we might as well do what we came for: and it's always been awful. You can't grip and throw the ball properly, you can't see it properly, you can't bowl it properly. Cricket doesn't work in the rain; it needs a nice spring day before it can start and a decent summer to bring it to a climax. In England cricket is always an act of hope in the face of experience.

But you can play football in the rain and for that matter, you can play it on a bog. Football as a vernacular game is played in streets and playgrounds, for falls are comparatively few and the ball is usually near the floor and less likely to break windows than in many games. Falling over and diving about are luxuries: you can't rugby-tackle in the street. For that you need a field, which is fine if you live a rural life or a privileged one in which space can be set aside for games. But that's not for everyone, which is why football has always been the game of the poor, and therefore of the world. It is also the best game for the British winter: short and with plenty of running about; the goalkeeper is kept warm by anxiety.

The transition from winter to summer games – one that naturally takes place in the spring – also affects spectators. If you're watching a football match you're out in the weather for a couple of hours: a period often bookended by visits to the pub or other places of refreshment. Half-time offers a break for a warming drink: Bovril[3] is traditional, along with a hand-held pie for nourishment, warmth and soaking up some of the pre-match booze.

The rhythm is roughly similar at rugby union matches, though there is a strong tradition of taking nips from a hip-flask to keep yourself going. But as the spring advances, the weather and the increased hours of daylight make it possible to pursue sport in a more leisurely way: a full day sitting at the cricket is pleasant enough in midsummer, punitive in winter. Tennis matches can last four hours: not a pleasant option in winter but when Wimbledon comes around people

---

[3] A potted meat extract, used for making what is sometimes called beef tea.

will queue for hours and, historically, even days, for the privilege. The tennis year has a tendency to follow the advancing spring, following the ripening strawberries with the clay court season within it starts in Spain before moving to Rome, on to Paris, and then switching to grass and to Wimbledon.

Sport has always produced seasonal festivals: rites of spring no less. These have got blurred over time, with changing technical possibilities and increasing financial incentives, but the basic idea remains. The FA Cup final was always a spring festival, a sporting maypole dance. It is still the last domestic match to be played in the football season, and traditionally takes place on the second Saturday in May. It is, then, an event of the high spring, one that celebrates the end of winter and the coming of summer: a sporting version of *Sumer is icumen in*.

The singular wasp-waisted shape of the FA Cup, the trophy itself, makes it a symbol not just of sporting glory but also of the passing year and the ultimate triumph of the spring. It was for years the only football match on live television: for many people it was the one chance in the year to watch football and see those names, much read in the papers, as real, moving people. I remember watching the 1961 final when Tottenham Hotspur beat Leicester City 2-0 to complete the double of FA Cup and league championship; I think it was the first proper football match I watched. The FA Cup final is remembered by some as the best day of the year after birthday and Christmas. It was perhaps on the Sunday after the FA Cup final that John and I got out the cricket stumps.

Rowing is traditionally a summer sport, but the Boat Race – the annual aquatic contest between the universities of Oxford and Cambridge[4] – is held around Easter and is another rite of spring. The competition is a private affair – hardly elite sport, though the standard is pretty high – and as ostentatious a celebration of privilege as exists in modern Britain. But it is also a great vernacular festival, and the towpath along the River Thames between Putney and Mortlake, the Boat Race course, is every year lined with people who have no connection with either university and little interest in the question of which of them can row faster. It's just a great day out: pubs open all day (and for many years that was a rare thing), spring in the air, and the passing pleasure of watching a bunch of toffs (imported and homegrown varieties) flogging themselves to death. These days there are also women's races along that often turbulent stretch of water.

Boat Race Day often coincides with another sporting rite of spring: the Grand National. This is a horse race, and one that routinely dismays foreign visitors used to a less robust form of equestrian sport. It is the longest race of the season,[5] over the highest and most

---

[4] Quotation from the P. G. Wodehouse story 'Without the Option', found in the 1925 collection *Carry On, Jeeves*.

[5] By a pleasing coincidence the Boat Race and the Grand National are roughly equal in length: the horses travel 4 miles 2½ furlongs and the rowers 4 miles 375 yards.

dangerous obstacles: falls are inevitable and the death of horses is frequent enough. Between 2000 and 2023, 16 horses have been killed during the race; a total of 90 since the race was first run in 1839. This has been a cause of increasing concern, illustrating changing times: in recent years the fences have been made safer and the number of runners has been reduced so there is less outright mayhem than before. But even in this modernised — some say sanitised — form, riders fall, injuries are frequent and horses still sometimes die. I could, I suppose, draw parallels between the annual sacrifice of horses and other sacrificial offerings that traditionally come with the turning of the year: sacrificial lambs and all that ... though it's a thought better hinted at than spelled out. Certainly spring is a traditional time of madness, as any hare will tell you: the madness of the Grand National has a certain macabre appropriateness to its season.

The race marks the great transition from jump racing, the sport of winter, to flat racing, the sport of summer. Again, the boundaries have blurred in recent times, and flat racing on all-weather tracks is available all through the year for those interested (it's more a medium for gambling than a pursuit of equine excellence). In Britain and Ireland racing, over the jumps or on the flat, has traditionally taken place on grass — the word turf is preferred — and mostly still does. Jumping a horse requires a softish landing and not just for falling jockeys: a horse must take all its weight on the leading leg as it lands, which puts a huge stress on the tendons between hoof and knee.[6] Hard ground adds to the shock and jarring, damaging to the horses, and also to riders who fall off. Jump races are mostly contested by geldings: mature horses that have been castrated.

Flat racing is different all the way through. Jump racing brings up old favourites from past seasons who keep going for year after year: flat racing is about the love of the new, the very latest thing. I remember standing on the gallops at Arundel Castle with the trainer John Dunlop, looking at this year's crop of unraced two-year-olds. It was a bright, biting spring morning, the sun lighting up the long uphill gallop without spreading much warmth, making me long to gallop a horse up the slope myself. And Dunlop said: 'I love this time of year above all. Look at these horses – any one of them – any single one of them – might turn out to be the greatest racehorse that ever set foot on a track. That's almost certainly not the case – but no one can say it's not possible.' And that is flat racing for you in a few phrases. It also sums up the beginning of spring pretty neatly: the best year ever might just be opening up before us.

Flat racing is essentially a test of young horses: two-year-olds in their first season and three-year-olds in their second. The five classic races of the season are all for three-year-olds: the best of these will go on and breed and if all goes well they will beget champions in their turn. It's a race for the right to become an ancestor: a paradigm of Darwinism. Flat racing can't take place in

---

[6] The knee joint on the foreleg is in fact equivalent to the human wrist joint.

winter (on grass) because wet and boggy ground damages the fragile legs of young horses: thoroughbred racehorses are bred for speed, and are delicate, vulnerable creatures, no more capable of surviving in the wild than a Persian cat. Gallop a two-year-old colt in the mud and he'll probably never race again,

Jump racing brings an earlier rite of spring than the Grand National. The Cheltenham Festival is held a little before the March equinox and it's the biggest week of the year for everyone involved in the sport: you can have a bad year, but a good Cheltenham will rescue it; you can have a good year, but a bad Cheltenham will spoil it. Soon afterwards flat racing – on grass as it should be – is in full swing.

And flat racing can be seen as a string of spring festivals. They start with the Lincoln, which is, confusingly, run at Doncaster, and it's a race that reassures the racing world that life continues as it should. Round about May Day we get the first two classics of the season, both run at Newmarket: the 1,000 Guineas for three-year-old fillies (females) and the 2,000 Guineas for three-year-old colts (males). But the greatest festival of them all is the Derby meeting, which is, of course, centred around the Derby, a race for the best three-year-old colts of the year. It takes place around Epsom racecourse, it's a great sporting event – and also another vernacular festival. For years it was always on the first Wednesday in June, but it shifted to Saturday in 1995 for financial reasons, seeking a larger television audience and because the live audience was falling.

The race was first held in 1780 and is celebrated in the famous picture of 1856–8 by William Powell Frith – and although it's called *Derby Day* there isn't a single horse in the painting. Either he couldn't draw horses or he wanted to make the point that the Derby is a people-fest and the horses are peripheral. The picture shows no species but humans, hundreds and hundreds of them, with the racecourse and main stand in the background. The focus is on three separate interactions. There's a group gathered round the table of a thimble-rigger; this is a game in which you try and guess which thimble conceals the pea; it's a gambling game like the three-card trick or, in American, a shell game. In the middle is a father and son acrobat team: the boy is looking longingly at a luscious picnic being set out by a footman. On the right, a swell leans with ostentatious elegance against a carriage (the horse unseen) that contains a lovely lady, perhaps his mistress.

The racing season moves from the Derby at Epsom to Royal Ascot: and this great gathering of the upper classes takes place around the solstice. This is a traditional time for other major sporting events, all of them crowded in around the same time, all of them marking the most significant date in the year after the December solstice (otherwise known as Christmas). They traditionally include the Lord's Test match, Henley Royal Regatta and the start of Wimbledon. With commercial pressures and the competition for airtime and for live audiences, many of these have become moveable feasts: Wimbledon, once always the last week in June and the first in July, has been shifted a week later in recent years. (In 2023 the FA Cup final was held in June, after the domestic season had been pushed back to accommodate the winter World Cup, which was held in Qatar, of all places.)

But new spring festivals of sport are still being created. In 1981, Chris Brasher and John Disley, both former athletes, set up the London Marathon, which is run in April.[7] The first running had more than 7,000 entrants; in 2024 there were 54,281 starters, of whom 53,802 reached the finish, triumphantly conquering the great horizontal Everest of suburbia. It is at the same time an event for elite runners, a deeply serious run by many others seeking a lifetime-best time, and a festival for a lot more who choose to run in fancy dress, enjoying a little public attention while they raise money for good causes. The British-based charity Save the Rhino (I'm a patron) always sends out a band of runners dressed as rhinos. The original costumes weighed 10kg, though they are now down to six; it's reckoned that even the lighter versions add an hour to your time. The best run by a rhino is 4 hours 6 minutes and 35 seconds, and that was Chris Green in 2021.

Badminton Horse Trials is another spring festival and is perhaps the ultimate celebration of the horse. The sport is eventing, which is contested in three parts: dressage, cross-country and showjumping. The middle section is a run of a little over four miles over countryside

---

[7] Apart from the Covid years; it was an Oktoberfest 2020–22.

punctuated by imposing and technically challenging fences, some of them over and through a lake. Each horse and rider must take the course alone: you get no help from the herd instinct that drives the Grand National. It is a thrilling and dangerous sport, in which riders are more likely to be killed than horses, for when a horse falls the rider – riding with long stirrup leathers, unlike a Grand National jockey, who rides short – tends not to be thrown clear. When the horse lands on top of the rider it is often fatal. There were five rider deaths in the UK in a single year in 1999, including Peta Beckett, whom I knew slightly and adored.

Danger is part of the horsey sports, as anyone who has ever sat on a horse well knows. Badminton has always been a great gathering of the horsey clans of all social classes: around 100,000 attend the cross-country day to watch and talk and shop in the vast tented village selling a million items essential to the horsey life. The event occasionally attracts the attention of people in the media who are amazed by the fact that so many people like horses and choose to go to Badminton (in bad weather years) wearing wellington boots and waterproofs. How hilarious it is: people not only live in the country but they wear clothes suitable for the purpose. It all takes place over a generous tract of beautifully sculpted parkland in early May: sometimes it's sunny and warm, sometimes it's cold and rainy but it's always a great day for worshipping at the shrine of the horse – and of the spring.

Spring is the best time for cross-country riding, when the going is neither too hard nor too soft, and, if all goes well, perfect for the tendons in the forelimbs of the athletes who do most of the work. I have taken part in such events, at a much lower level than Badminton – both in terms of ability and of height of the jumps – and loved every second. I remember the terror before the start, the instantaneous switch from terror to total concentration, the entire world reduced to a tunnel three miles long and one horse wide, and the glorious high at the end: here I am, alive and whole and filled with joy, me and my horse both panting hard from a great achievement, me in the certain knowledge that I am sitting on the finest horse ever foaled and both of us together under the vast skies of spring.

Signs of spring
March 2024

1. Pair of oystercatchers fly over, calling
   Many more nettles, a good few quite tall
2. Riverside walk: Cetti's warbler song
   Male and female harriers manoeuvring together
   Colony of white dead nettles in flower
3. Norwich: green alkanet in flower
   Back home: two singing blackbirds
   Paired-up mallards
   100 fieldfare flying north (they'll end up in Scandinavia to nest)
4. London: ground ivy in flower on Highbury doorstep.
5. Still London: great tit singing from bare London planes in Gray's Inn Road
6. Back home: loud and continuous drumming, great spotted woodpecker
   Five buzzards manoeuvring, apparently two pairs and one interloper
   Budburst, sallow
7. Singing long-tailed tit
8. Lesser celandine in flower
   Many red dead nettles in flower
   Alders on Common full of catkins

11

Sweet spring

We humans see spring as a staircase of major events, each riser bringing a further advance of the year: another step towards glory. One of the most significant of these steps is the moment, one filled with delight and just a whiff of menace, when the first buzz is heard: the pioneering hum of the humble bumblebee, formerly known as humblebee and sometimes referred to as dumbledore. This first appearance is as great a miracle as anything Harry Potter's beloved headmaster ever managed. It seems too early and far too cold for a flying insect to function: but there it is, flying unsteadily but with immense purpose, seeking out the early blooms with the air of someone who could really use a good drink. I say 'it' but, of course, I mean 'she': for this is a queen bumblebee, ready to start the year, ready to found a colony, ready to live and make life.

Cold is what bumblebees are good at. They have their edge over other species because they can exploit the early spring flowers in temperatures that would kill a butterfly, so they have the earliest weeks of blooming all to themselves. They are also able to exploit higher latitudes and altitudes than their competitors. That's mostly because of their insulation: their obvious and defining furriness. They can also absorb heat with great efficiency, even from weak sunshine. Their large round bodies are better at retaining heat than a long, thin body would be: minimise the surface area to keep warm. They can generate the heat they need in their flight muscles by shivering: energy-expensive, but a sound ploy if they can fly straight to a decent flower and reload on the great energy drink of nectar. They are up and about long before the competition: the next step is to make the most of this advantage.

Only the queens fly in the early spring. All the other bumblebees are dead. The hope, the Plan A and the Plan Z of bumblebee survival, lies in the over-wintering queens, for the workers and the drones are no more.

The queen is the vehicle for the future: a fat bumbling female carrying a load of as yet unused sperm. She mated, probably with several different partners, in the previous autumn, before the great winter shutdown began. Then, as the days grew short, she found a hideaway, often a tiny hole in the ground, and there she passed the winter in the state of diapause, like the brimstone butterfly, but for a shorter time.

Once she is up and feeding well she sets about starting a colony: if she is to become an ancestor, one must become many. First she must find the right place, often an abandoned mouse nest. There she will lay the first eggs in wax cells she makes herself; the eggs, now fertilised, will hatch out female workers, for, with bees, all the workers are female. They are also infertile: they seek to propagate their genes by nurturing their siblings. This first generation is modest, usually in single figures, and the grubs are fed by the single queen who brings both nectar and pollen back to the nest. But when the workers have reached adulthood and are free-flying bumblebees in their own right, the season changes gear. The queen is now able to stay in the nest, laying eggs and tending the grubs, while the workers fetch food and attend to the hygiene of the nest, often by carting out dead bees: when a lot of animals live in very close quarters, a high standard of hygiene is essential for survival, as any city planner knows.

Bumblebees are social animals, though not on the scale of honeybees, who exist on another order of magnitude. Bumblebees are likely to deal with a colony of a couple of hundred, while for honeybees 20,000 is comfortable. That's technically a eusocial system: one in which there is usually a single breeding female, a few breeding males and a large corps of non-breeders who do the chores. Division of labour is the key to eusocial life: different individuals perform different tasks. Bumblebees are on the less complex and less crowded ends of the eusocial spectrum; at the other end termites sometimes live in colonies of a couple of million. The bumblebee nest reflects a rough and ready form of sociality: the wax cells are higgledy-piggledy rather than in the neat hexagons of honeybees.

Towards the end of the summer the colony starts producing males: the queen may do so herself, by laying eggs that she doesn't fertilise with the stored sperm. But they are more likely to come from the workers. The males' only job – their only function – is sex, to sire the next generation. At this time young queens are also produced – technically gynes – and they fly off to seek their fortunes – which means that they must also seek males. Eventually, sperm-filled, they will find a hiding place where they can wait – but not too long – for the warmth of the next spring.

There are about 250 species of bumblebee worldwide, around 20 in the UK, red-tailed and white-tailed bumblebees are both often seen in gardens. Bumblebees are all imposing insects; they need to be if they are to withstand the cold. There's a Chilean species that can be 4cm long, nicknamed flying mice. Bumblebees are mostly patterned brightly, with bands of yellow or orange:

it's a warning signal, carried by many non-related dangerous creatures. This is a sound tactic, for it conveys a message that's widely understood: you'd be well advised to keep clear. All female bumblebees can sting repeatedly, though they seldom show aggression towards humans. The tendency of dangerous creatures to look similar is called Müllerian mimicry.

Bumblebees are not great aeronauts, but they fly well enough to exploit their ecological niche. And there's no mystery as to how they do it. Science doesn't 'prove' bumblebees can't fly: it's a myth that has endured, perhaps because people take comfort in the idea that if science can't explain the flight of a bumblebee we're entitled to reject any scientific truth we find inconvenient, like climate change. But science can explain the flight of a bumblebee without much trouble: it's about wing-speed. Sure, those wings are tiny in proportion to the rest of the body, and such a design would never work on a fixed-wing aircraft. No bumblebee will ever glide. Instead, it beats its wings a phenomenal 200 times a minute. The insect is able to do this because its flight muscles aren't directly attached to the wings, so they don't have to contract 200 times a minute to make flight a possibility. Rather, it vibrates the muscle – it's like twanging an elastic band – and the immense speed of the wings makes the hum and brings us that great springtime moment. It also creates a pattern of vortices. A vortex is a term from fluid dynamics – air flows, so it's a fluid medium – and it refers to a region in which there is a flow around an axis – like a dust devil or a whirlpool or a tropical storm. On this much smaller scale, the rapidly beating wings of the bumblebee create the vortices that pull the body upwards and sustain the insect in the air as it flies.

All this is pleasingly benign. We have before us a mutually dependent relationship between the early flowering plants and the pioneering furry bees: the plants get their pollination services while feeding and sustaining their pollinators. But it pays to be suspicious when nature seems to be at its most benign: and like the BBC offering equal airtime to opposed political views, I must open the floor to the devil's chaplain, for as Darwin famously remarked: 'What a book a devil's chaplain might write on the clumsy, wasteful, blundering, low and horribly cruel works of nature.'

There's a group of bumblebee species collectively known as cuckoo bumblebees, and, like the cuckoo birds we looked at in Chapter 9, they are brood parasites. They thrive by getting others to do the work. A queen cuckoo bumblebee emerges from diapause later in the year than queens of the usual sort, so that as soon as she is awake she can invade the nest of a bumblebee when it's already a thriving concern. Her plan is to time it just right, so the colony she enters is big enough to raise the usurper's grubs, but not too big to make penetration of the hive impossible. Once there she stings the incumbent queen to death. She then lays her own eggs; the grubs will be tended and fed by the workers already in the colony, workers of a quite different species whose labour is now self-defeating.

The cuckoo queen doesn't produce her own workers, she's far too grand for that: her eggs will produce only non-working males and potential new queens. Cuckoo bumblebees look very similar to the species they parasitise: you need to be quite an expert to note their longer stings, all the better for their more aggressive lifestyle, and the lack of pollen baskets on their legs: a cuckoo doesn't need them, for she is not born to mundane tasks of fetching and carrying.

A bee is essentially a vegetarian wasp. At some stage in their evolution they took a different path. The inspiration for this transition lies in *Just So Stories*[1] territory: one possibility is that ancestral bees ate pollen-feeding insects, all covered with their food of choice, and took a liking to the food that sustained their prey. All bees feed on nectar and pollen: the first for energy and the second for protein. Pollen is essential at the larval stage of their lives, and since they can't seek it for themselves it must be provided by the adults. The great bonus of food provided by plants is that it doesn't hide or run away. When it comes to feeding on pollen and nectar, the plant is actively cooperating with its consumer.

Insects were pollinating flowering plants long before bees evolved, but with the arrival of bees the pace hotted up. Bees co-evolved with the flowers they feed from: the flowers offering floral rewards, sometimes

---

[1] *Just So Stories*, by Rudyard Kipling, first published in 1902, all of wonderfully speculative evolutionary origins – more Lamarckian than Darwinian.

in long tubes that only bees with long tongues (bumblebees, for example) could exploit. Some plant species developed spectacular ways of advertising their wares to bees, offering a flare path, sometimes only visible to humans under ultraviolet light though in plain sight for a bee. The great richness of colour and shape in wild plants owes a great deal to their evolutionary relationship with bees.

There are 16,000 known species of bee worldwide. They range in size from the tiny sweat bees that form clusters round your eyes, mouth and nostrils in some tropical countries and add an extraordinary intensity of torment on a hard day, for all that they are stingless and only a couple of millimetres long. The biggest is Wallace's giant bee, from Indonesia, which is almost 4cm long. There are around 270 species in the UK; the colder temperatures and the need to cope with the annual emergency of winter makes for less diversity than, say, tropical rainforest.

Of all those bee species, around 90 per cent are solitary. These species don't go in for colonies and the consequent division of labour. Every female is fertile, and she lays her eggs in a nest she has made herself. She makes no honey and produces no wax, but she brings food to her brood. Solitary bees are important pollinators, too.

Mason bees make nests in cracks in stones, hollow stems and holes made in wood, often by wood-boring insects. The red mason bee is pretty common in the UK: ginger with narrow black stripes; it looks like a furry wasp. The female – all females are queens in the egalitarian society of the solitary bee, or none is – starts to provision her nest site once she has found a good one. She puts together a load of nectar and pollen – a provision mass – and lays an egg of top of it. Then she seals it off with a partition of mud: which is why she's called a mason. She does this again and again until the cavity is full. After that, she plugs the entrance and moves on – maybe to make another nest. Inside, the eggs hatch into grubs, which devour the provision mass and then spin themselves cocoons; they can over-winter in this state, emerging in the spring.

The females mate as soon as they leave the nest and do so usually with their own nest-mates. But a female will generally mate more than once, so that the chances of mating with her own full brother are limited. The female eggs are laid at the back of the nest, the males to the front, so they emerge first and hang around waiting for the females; they have been observed tearing females from their cocoons in their eagerness to get on with the job.

Carpenter bees follow a similar lifestyle but a different trade: unsurprisingly they work in wood. The female makes holes in wood with her jaws, and in these she creates a series of cells, provisioning each one, laying an egg and then sealing it off with wood pulp before moving on to the next. They aren't fussy about what wood they choose, and will bore into the structural timber of buildings, causing distress to the humans who own them. They are discreet-looking creatures, lacking extravagant stripes.

It's easier to pick out the work of mining bees than the bees themselves: a little Vesuvius on an open patch of soil or the bare patch of a lawn, a small hole surrounded by spoil. The tawny mining bee is quite distinctive: a chunky thing with a thick orange coat and black face; ashy mining bees, with monochrome stripes, are more subtle. They work to the same pattern of provisioning a series of single cells.

Leafcutter bees choose holes and hollows like mason bees, but make their cells with pieces cut from leaves, glued together with saliva. If you find a series of neat semi-circular bits missing from the leaves of your roses, you have leafcutter bees around: bid them welcome, for they will do little harm to your garden: only make it better by bringing more life.

There is only one species of honeybee found in the UK – *Apis mellifera* – and probably not a single colony is truly wild. But there are honeybees all over the country and by the end of spring every year they make up a population of countless millions; some colonies will reach a peak of 50,000 individuals. The numbers fall away after this, and are at their lowest in spring, just before the first flowers are in bloom. The colony may be depleted by the hardships of winter, but it gets through: and once it has done so it can start raising the next generation of workers. It can do so because previous generations of workers spent the previous spring and summer making honey.

Honeybees are recognisably different from most other bee species in the UK, with a slim shape, and black and amber stripes on the abdomen. Don't let that slimness fool you: they are immensely powerful: few animals can match their power output rates. They are capable of carrying a load of half their own bodyweight up to 5km, though it's far more efficient to provision the hive over shorter distances, when the bees require less fuel. They carry both pollen and nectar back to the hive. They feed the pollen to the grubs: the nectar serves another purpose. Nectar is a floral payment, one that rewards the bees (and many other creatures) for their pollination services, for helping the plants to have sex. Most species just drink it, receive the energy boost and use it straightaway. But bees operate a long-term strategy: they store the nectar for future use. They do this by turning it into honey.

Nectar is up to 80 per cent water; it also contains three kinds of sugar – glucose, sucrose and fructose – along with the scent chemicals that attract the bees to the flowers in the first place. These give the honey its singularity. A bee sucks up the nectar through her hollow proboscis and holds it in the first chamber of her stomach; once it's in there an enzyme increases the acidity, and this helps to kill bacteria. She then flies back to the hive, where she will regurgitate the nectar. It is then passed from bee to bee, mouth to mouth, and this process brings down the water content. Once it's down to 18 per cent no mould or bacteria can flourish: in other words, and despite these perhaps rather daunting details of its production, honey is an immensely clean substance. The workers store it in wax chambers: a good store of honey is nothing less than the future of the colony. It's been calculated that a teaspoon of honey is the lifetime's work of a dozen bees, and even if that lifetime is only a few weeks, an awful lot of work and an awful lot of life is required to create a single moment of sweetness.

Humans value honey almost as much as the bees, and have done so for millennia. Anthropological research on a modern hunter-gatherer tribe in Africa shows that its people get as much as 15 per cent of their calories from honey. This incredibly energy-rich substance is serious brain food: honey has for centuries helped to power the organ that gave our own species our edge as we moved towards planetary domination. Sugar (as we humans mostly understand the term) was unknown outside Asia until the fifteenth century and was a luxury item until the eighteenth. For most of human existence, if you wanted the powerful energy boost that comes from sweet things, you needed honey. And as if that wasn't enough, honey had another gift for the people of the northern latitudes: booze. Britain may be beyond the range of easy grape cultivation, but honey, like almost anything else, will ferment and turn into alcohol if given half a chance. The resulting sweet and sour mess could be mixed with water at whatever concentration gave best pleasure, and drunk as mead.

The development of human civilisation marched in step with the domestication of bees: bee-keeping is by definition a dangerous job. Bees are reasonably adaptable and it is relatively easy to dictate the place a colony uses as its base. But bees didn't evolve to be the successful creatures they are by making it easy for non-bees to consume their honey.

Workers do everything the colony needs to survive, apart from reproduce. They do the housekeeping, removing dead bees and droppings, they feed the queens, the males and the grubs, they make wax and construct the cells, they collect pollen and nectar, they make honey – and they defend the hive and its treasure against invaders. They do this by stinging, a process lethal to the stinger, who is torn apart by the process, and potentially lethal to the invader, even one as big as a human. I have fled a nest of African bees, accidentally disturbed, and counted myself seriously lucky to get away with a couple of stings. I reached the vehicle at a sprinting speed that would have troubled Usain Bolt and the still greater speed of the vehicle was too much for the pursuers.

Humans used to harvest the honey by destroying the colony: there was no other option. The development of a sustainable hive was the great breakthrough in beekeeping; the removable frames that hold the combs of wax were developed in the early nineteenth century. My grandfather had three hives in his garden in the Birmingham suburb of King's Heath; I remember him in his wide hat and bee-veil, lifting the crawling and buzzing frames from the hive, and then extracting the honey from the combs with a device that spun the frames around and whizzed the honey out by centrifugal force. His honey had the delicate scent of lime flowers;

the park opposite his house had a stately line of lime trees. The poor deprived bees got through the winter on sugar syrup, a denatured and undelicious product. Some beekeepers allow their bees to keep some or all of their honey, describing the use of the winter substitute as 'like feeding your children on white bread'.

The intense social life of honeybees has been much studied, and not just for utilitarian reasons. The discovery of their extraordinary method of communication, the waggle dance, has asked complicated questions not only about bees but about the nature of language. A bee returning from a nectar-hunting expedition is able to explain the place and distance of the new trove: she communicates all this information to her sisters by dancing: repeated figures of eight and other steps that tell her sisters where to go. The information in the dance includes a calculation of the path of the sun across the sky.

The bonds between the sisterhood of hive workers are stronger than we can easily understand – and that's a genetic judgement rather than one based on abstract values. Worker bees are more closely related to their sisters than they are to their own mothers or would be to their own (hypothetical) offspring. Any parent shares 50 per cent of genes with any offspring; siblings likewise share 50 per cent of their genes. But in bee colonies the workers all have 75 per cent of their genes in common, and the grubs they raise are also their own sisters, so they all share the 75 per cent. A bee has more to gain (in terms of providing a future for the genes she carries in her body) by looking after her sisters than she ever would be by seeking to breed for herself. This helps to explain the eusocial nature of a bee colony: but it gets confusing when you learn that this system – technically haplodiploidy – isn't actually necessary for eusocial life. Termites, perhaps the most intensely social of all animals on earth, get on very well without it.

The keeping of domestic bees becomes more difficult every year. The phenomenon of colony collapse disorder was first identified in America in 2006: it is a shocking business in which the workers abandon the hive en masse, leaving behind the queen, the males, the grubs and often a fair amount of food. No single cause has been identified for this increasing problem: possibilities include pesticides, mites, fungus antibiotics and malnutrition.

Pollination brings us every third mouthful of food. We do ourselves a disservice by putting the process in peril. In recent years bees have been increasingly understood as emblems of nature conservation. They represent the crucial notion that we need to look after nature not just from the goodness of our hearts, but to ensure our own survival as a species.

Signs of spring
March 2024

9   Banks of primroses on drive to Suffolk
10   Norwich: magnolia in full bloom
11   Morning: song thrush, dunnock, great tit, chaffinch, greenfinch all in song, plus percussion from great spotted woodpecker
Wild garlic in flower
Two pairs gadwall (duck species)
12   Mallard troika over Common – one male chasing off a pair from his established breeding territory
Probably passage birds, on the way to somewhere else to breed
13   Hawthorn in leaf
Male and female harrier drop down together – nest site?
Bumblebee
14   Several daisies in bottom field
Oystercatcher pair
Blackbird song at dusk
15   Four playful curlews dive-bombing
Many more daisies
Rape fields beginning to flower
16   River: four Cetti's warblers in full song

12

Lady Chatterley's spring

Hang spring-cleaning!

Is this three-word shout the best response to spring in all literature? It's there on the first page of *The Wind in the Willows* by Kenneth Grahame, first published in 1908, and it's the soul-cry of the Mole as he realises there are better things to do on a lovely spring morning than whitewashing the ceiling. He lives in a residence deep underground, as a mole should, but 'spring was moving in the air above and in the earth below and around him, penetrating even his dark and lowly little house with its spirit of divine discontent and longing'.

And so he flings down his brush and says 'Bother!' and 'O blow!' and finally caps this already excessive language with the immortal phrase that opens this chapter. He gives up on the cleaning and gives himself over to everything else that spring offers.

This was my favourite book for several years and it remains an occasional nostalgic pleasure. And though it's full of fine things, it's the glorious beginning that makes all the rest possible. 'Something up above was calling him imperiously', so Mole goes up the tunnel to the open air. The simple straightforward joys of spring (without the cleaning) have surely never been better expressed. 'This is fine ... This is better than whitewashing!'

And the Mole walks out across the meadows in the best possible temper, revelling in being the only idle dog among all these busy citizens, and just when he thinks life could get no better, it does. He finds what he thinks is a river, but soon learns that it is *the* River. He sits and watches it, lost in an ecstasy of delight: falling in love with a place he had never seen in his life before. 'The Mole was bewitched, entranced, fascinated.' But then, impossibly, it gets better once again.

He sees an eye in a dark hole in the riverbank, and it winks at him. It turns into a face, a little brown face with whiskers. And it's the Water Rat, soon to be known as Ratty, for all that he is a vole and no close relation of *Rattus norvegicus*, the lover of rubbish dumps. It's love at first sight: or perhaps I should say bosom friendship at first sight. Rat introduces Mole to the River, and the pair set off in the Rat's rowing boat and have a pleasant picnic; Badger turns up for half a moment and Otter drops by for a chat. Rat rows Mole along the river, his new friend 'intoxicated with the sparkle, the ripple, the scents and the sounds and the sunlight'.

Here is one of the great transformation scenes. It's no superficial one, like the handsome man removing the girl's spectacles and telling her she's beautiful. Here the transformation is soul-deep: a chthonic creature of dark tunnels and confined spaces becomes – by the power of the spring – a new being entirely. He is more or less a new species: a mole who has, by an effort of will – by an inevitable process of intoxicated love – become a water vole.

The rest of the book is a reckless collection of loosely related stories. A good deal of the narrative is built round Toad, the conceited, excessive, good-hearted boaster, and the admirable, gruff, wise, no-nonsense Badger. But there are also several side stories, backwaters along the main channel of the narrative. In one of them Mole returns to his old home, overwhelmed by nostalgia, though he still goes back to the River with Rat. There's another story, this one set in late summer, in which Rat, intoxicated in his turn by the talk of travel from a ship rat, resolves to leave his beloved

River forever and roam the world. But Rat, the dreamer and writer of poetry, eventually gets over it.

One of these stories is so unlikely – and so much against the temper of the rest of the book – that it is pretty well hallucinatory: so much so that in 1967 Syd Barrett borrowed the chapter title for the first Pink Floyd album, a piece of proto-psychedelia called *The Piper at the Gates of Dawn.* It is the last day of spring, or if you prefer, the first day of summer: the solstice in which the seasons meet and merge. Mole and Ratty set off in their rowing boat in the last light of day, not all that far from midnight, in search of Otter's lost son Portly, who has been gone for days, feared drowned. They hear a strange piping, and follow it as the light of the new day is almost ready to show itself. It is a mystical experience, one quite out of keeping with a children's book about a loveable rogue: 'This is the place of my song-dream,' says Ratty. There they find Him, not named, but clearly the god Pan. And then the sun rises above the horizon and the god has vanished ... but Portly is there asleep.

It is a hymn to the last and greatest day of spring: a day that is the conclusion to the story of the seasons, as well as the mid-point and the beginning. I often skipped this chapter to get back to the adventures of Toad, but sometimes I lingered over it, and sometimes (like Ratty and Mole) I even half understood it.

Grahame writes of the River as a great narrative: when Mole first claps eyes on it 'he trotted as one trots, when very small, by the side of a man who holds one spellbound by exciting stories; and when tired at last, he sat on the bank, while the river chattered on to him, a babbling procession of the best stories in the world, sent from the heart of the earth to be told at last to the insatiable sea'.

The idea of the River as a narrative is simple and pleasing, but then we humans have always loved stories. We are a species of fabulists, and the annually told story of the seasons is a narrative we all live by. I am tempted to claim that the people who live in the seasonal lands are the most likely to create narratives and to value stories and story-telling, but that doesn't stand up for five seconds. Great novelists of the world include Gabriel García Márquez of Colombia, Jorge Luis Borges of Argentina, R. K. Narayan of India, Chinua Achebe of Nigeria, Patrick White of Australia ... and on and on. There are too many counter-arguments to make that idea feasible.

But perhaps the argument works the other way round: our innate, human love of narrative is what makes us respond so deeply to the seasonal round. All stories are about change and development: they all make a pattern from the passage of time: just like living through the seasons. Everything changes but everything stays the same.

Dr Johnson said 'the only end of writing is to enable the readers better to enjoy life or better to endure it'. Any well-told narrative will do one or the other if not both at the same time: but comedies bring us spring and tragedies winter, or their narrative equivalents. A sad tale's best for winter, as Mamillius says in *A Winter's Tale*. In *A Midsummer Night's Dream* all the couples end up reconciled and agog for love, while *Hamlet* ends in a bloodboltered shambles. Both plays depict a series of unique events which reveal the underlying and unchanging patterns that govern our existence. The distinction is nearly as old as humanity: *Oedipus Rex* ends with a hideous fate for almost everyone, while *The Odyssey* ends with the triumphant of homecoming of Odysseus. One reflects the arrival of winter, the other the arrival of spring.

Are novels of spring the best? That, of course, is a deeply personal matter, for we all have our favourites, along with the odd one or two for which we feel an aversion not all that far from hatred. But there's no doubt that a depiction of spring gets readers on your side if you can do it right.

Spring is the setting for *The Secret Garden* by Frances Hodgson Burnett, first published in book form in 1911. I knew this first as a television series of 1960, because my father, early in his career at the BBC, was working on it. I later read the book, and one scene in particular has stayed with me. The story is about Mary, a girl of ten, who is both spoiled and neglected, and now orphaned. She is living in a big house in Yorkshire, where she finds Colin, sickly, chair-bound, and as disturbed and charmless as Mary herself.

Mary finds the key to the secret garden and discovers a place that was once lovingly tended, but has been allowed to run wild. She takes it over in secret, with the help of Dickon, two years older, who speaks Yorkshire and has a marvellous understanding, not just of plants. Together they bring the smothered garden plants back to life. They take Colin out to see it – he's so intrigued that for once he can face going outside – and he likes the place. It turns out to be the garden that his late mother loved. Eventually he abandons his wheelchair and his terrors and becomes happy and healthy. So it's a story about healing. The scene I always remember is the one when Dickon shows Mary how to look after the garden: how to work out what's still living and what's dead. She asks Dickon if a plant is still alive.

> 'It's as wick as you or me,' he said; and Mary remembered that Martha had told her 'wick' meant 'alive' or 'lively'.
> 'I'm glad it's wick,' she cried out in her whisper. 'I want them all to be wick. Let us go round the garden and count how many wick ones there are.'

Dickon explains that you can tell the state of wickness by cutting into the plant, and if it's 'greenish and juicy' it's living still. Between them the children restore the garden to life, making it a secret island of beauty in a troubled world: a place of healing, where new life can be found even for hopeless cases like Mary and Colin. You may, if you cut through the undergrowth, discover traces of much older stories already discussed; the ones about the sickly king, the dying land and the quest for the Holy Grail that will cure him.

It would perhaps be overdoing things to seek traces of the Grail legend in the works of P. G. Wodehouse, but the hopes and joys of spring play a considerable part in his work. You may check the epigraph of this book to find a favourite moment, in which Bertie Wooster and Jeeves, his manservant – his gentleman's personal gentleman – discuss the weather at the beginning of *The Inimitable Jeeves*, first published in 1923. Bertie muses, as he walks off in his yellowest shoes and the Homburg:

> I don't know if you know that sort of feeling you get on these days round about the end of April and the beginning of May, when the sky's a light blue, with cotton-wool clouds, and there's a bit of a breeze blowing from the west? Kind of uplifted feeling. Romantic, if you know what I mean. I'm not much of a ladies' man, but on this particular morning it seemed to me that what I really wanted was some charming girl to buzz up and ask me to save her from assassins or something.

As readers of Wodehouse's extraordinarily extensive output well know, such moments of joy are invariably followed by all sorts of terrible and absurd complications. As Bertie says elsewhere: 'I'm not absolutely certain of the facts, but I rather fancy it's Shakespeare who says that it's always when a fellow is feeling particularly braced with things in general that Fate sneaks up behind him with the bit of lead piping.'

So poor Bertie finds himself compelled to help out his old friend Bingo Little by impersonating the romantic novelist Rosie M. Banks, and, alas, his deception is discovered. All kinds of horrors seem to be opening up before him, but, of course, Jeeves will sort things out one way or another. The servant always looks after his employer, and in the course of *The Inimitable Jeeves* he does so several times over, with the last tour de force coming in the eighteenth chapter, which is, of course, titled 'All's Well'.

Spring and the relationship between servant and employer are given a rather different emphasis in *Lady Chatterley's Lover*, which was first published (privately) in 1928. It was finally published in the UK in an unexpurgated version in 1960, after the famous obscenity trial, and to this day it's hard to disentangle the literary value of the novel from the historical one: and the meticulously described sex scenes with their elaborately casual use of once-forbidden words from the overall value of the work.

Connie – Lady Chatterley – has a paralysed and impotent husband who owns coal mines and is full of plans for modernising them and making them even more efficient. She turns to Mellors the gamekeeper, who is full of life and profoundly connected to nature. Connie had spied on him, sort of inadvertently, while he was taking a wash stripped to the hips. She thought of him later as the spring returned, 'his thin, white body, like a lonely pistil of an inviable flower!'.

The great moment takes place at last after she has been inspecting the pheasant chicks reared by Mellors as part of his duties as gamekeeper. The chicks have just hatched, it being spring, and Mellors puts one on her hand 'an atom of balancing life'. And while he is suddenly aware of 'the old flame shooting and leaping up in his loins', Connie is overcome by a deluge of tears. Mellors reaches out a hand to comfort her and they're off and running. The high spot of their subsequent romps follows a naked frolic in the rain, after which they come back to his hut and a new-lit fire and dry off on the same sheet. Mellors then goes out again and returns with an armful of flowers:

> He had brought columbines and campions and new-mown hay, and oak-tufts and honeysuckle in small bud. He fastened fluffy young oak-sprays round her breasts, sticking in tufts of bluebells and campion: and in her navel he poised a pink campion, and in her maiden-hair were forget-me-nots and woodruff.
>
> 'This is you in all your glory,' he said. 'Lady Jane at her wedding with John Thomas.'

I'm not quite sure how he got hold of new-mown hay, more of a June thing, and bluebells, a May thing, at the same moment, but this decking of Connie as a goddess of the spring is the high point of the book. After this, inevitably, the complications start to add up, and there is no Jeeves to sort things out. In the end Connie, pregnant with Mellors's child, is hoping that they will again be

All the pictures in the top row show signs of spring, roughly in the order they appear. You can find hazel catkins as early as late December

Great tits are often the first singers of the year: teach-teacher-teacher!

Springtime fit for the gods: *La Primavera* by Sandro Botticelli, completed 1482

Snowdrops are impossibly braving the chills every year

Eggs that come long before Easter: frog and spawn

Springtime joy: *Souvenir de Mauve* by Vincent Van Gogh, painted 1888

A host of golden daffodils

Lambs are a traditional part of spring: the annual sacrifice

Painted for his new nephew Vincent: *Almond Blossom* by Vincent Van Gogh, 1890

Herons are hard at it long before there are leaves on the trees

Female hares box males as a serious test of mate-worthiness

England in late spring: *The Hay Wain* by John Constable, completed 1821

A male brimstone is often the first butterfly of the year

A wood transformed: the bluebells are back

Spring comes even to cities: *Boulevard de Montmartre, Spring* by Camille Pissarro, painted 1897

Male orange-tips aren't often seen at rest

When the swallows return the pace of spring redoubles

A new rite of spring is established: *The Last Supper* by Leonardo da Vinci, completed 1498

Superb fliers: here's a dead-head hoverfly

Cuckoo! Cuckoo! This is the height of spring

A secular rite of spring: *Derby Day* by William Powell Frith, completed 1858

May blossom is out; time to cast a clout

Banded demoiselles perform springtime dances along the edge of slow-moving rivers

Spring subverted: *The First Days of Spring* by Salvador Dalí, completed 1929

together. Anthony Powell, author of the 12-volume *A Dance to the Music of Time*, suggests that a novel about their subsequent married life would be more interesting than Lawrence's account of their adulterous coupling. But *Lady Chatterley* is all about spring and nature, set against the dehumanising industrial civilisation of coal mines, machines and crippled, impotent Chatterley. Lawrence mourns the loss of nature from the lives of almost everybody. Had he seen the twenty-first century, in which a big day out usually takes people to a shopping mall and nature is something you watch on television, he could point that as prophets go, he hadn't done so badly.

Marcel Proust wrote extensively about change and decay, but he is most often associated with the phenomenon of involuntary memory: the 'Proustian experience', described in the first section of *A la recherche du temps perdu*, or *In Search of Lost Time*, published in seven volumes, most of them whoppers, between 1913 and 1927. The narrator breaks off a piece of a little sponge cake, the sort called madeleines, into his cup of elderflower tea, and the taste brings back a rush of powerful and uncontrollable memories.

And what he remembers is spring. He recalls, with immense vividness, his childhood visits to relations in the countryside at Combray at Easter time: the garden: the sound of the bell at its gate which announces the arrival of the family friend Swann: the narrator's great-aunt Léonie, who refused successively to leave her village, her house, her bedroom, and at last her bed: her servant Françoise: the narrator's beloved grandmother, who adores high culture and the outdoors: the lure of local aristocrats, the Guermantes: and the choice of two walks. The narrator and his family can choose the way that takes them past Swann's house, or the way that passes the mansion of the Guermantes; this volume of the immense work is called *Swann's Way* and a later volume is, inevitably, *The Guermantes Way*.

In this early section of the work, which is entitled simply *Combray*, there are loving descriptions of nature and the place of the village within it, the church spires forming landmarks that dance about the countryside as the narrator views them from a moving carriage. One day as he walks Swann's Way, he is enraptured by the beauty of hawthorns in full bloom – may bushes, the ones that remind you not to cast a clout until it is out – and then his attention is drawn to something still more glorious: pink hawthorns. Here, in the translation by C. K. Scott Moncrieff:

> High up on the branches, like so many of those tiny rose-trees, their pots concealed in jackets of paper lace, whose slender stems rise in a forest from the altar on the greater festivals, a thousand buds were swelling and opening, paler in colour, but each disclosing as it burst, as at the bottom of a cup of pink marble, its blood-red stain, and suggesting even more strongly than the full-blown flowers the special irresistible quality of the hawthorn tree which, wherever it budded, wherever it

was about to blossom, could bud and blossom in pink flowers alone.

The village of Combray is based on the real village of Illiers, which these days is known as Illiers-Combray. Quite something, for a real place to imitate art.

I should perhaps throw in a couple of honourable mentions before moving on to one more spring novel. Jane Austen's *Pride and Prejudice*, published in 1813, follows the rhythm of the seasons. The complex relationship between Elizabeth and Mr Darcy comes to a head in spring, when Mr Darcy proposes and is refused, leaving both parties with much to think about before they finally agree to marry the following autumn.

E. M. Forster's *A Room with a View*, published in 1908, is full of the tensions between polite and natural behaviour, and between indoor and outdoor experience. Mr Emerson observes: 'Fifty miles of Spring, and we've come to admire them. Do you suppose there's any difference between Spring in nature and Spring in man? But there we go, praising the one and condemning the other as improper, ashamed that the same works eternally through both.'

I could make a case for *Ulysses*, published in 1922, being the ultimate spring novel: after all, it is the ultimate novel of almost everything else. The action, such as it is, of James Joyce's big novel, takes place on a single day: 16 June 1904, and the early hours of the 17th, when spring has almost but not quite given way to summer. Joyce gives us no lingering descriptions of nature – for a start he was nearly blind – but we're never in any doubt that it's a lovely day. Right at the beginning his alter ego, Stephen, looks out across Dublin Bay and imagines the sea as a giant harp: 'The twining stresses, two by two. Hand plucking the harpstrings merging their twining chords. Wavewhite wedded words shimmering on the dim tide.'

The central character is Leopold Bloom: awkward and flawed but deeply kind and generous: this is essentially a book about a nice man. Like Stephen he greets a golden morning, like Stephen he has a moment of depression as the sun goes behind a cloud, like Stephen he perks up afterwards – and they set off separately and from different starting points into the long Dublin day, one that ends up with their meeting, and the establishment of a friendship, however brief, that enriches them both.

The novel's third important character is Bloom's wife, Molly, who is mostly off-stage till the very end. She seems to have spent almost the whole day in bed, the significant part of it accompanied by a first-class shit called Blazes Boylan. Her extended unpunctuated musing on sex and love and flowers concludes the book – and she is the one who talks about nature:

> I love flowers Id love to have the whole place swimming in roses God of heaven theres nothing like nature [...] he said I was a flower of the mountains yes so we are flowers all a womans body yes that was the one true thing he said in his life ...

Why did Joyce choose 16 June? It's essential for the plot that it's a nice day, so that Stephen and Bloom can spend most of it walking about Dublin, narrowly missing each other twice before they finally meet. The book would be impossible in winter. But it was on that day – 16 June 1904 – that the young James Joyce first walked out with Nora Barnacle, a girl who was working in Finn's Hotel. It was a nice walk, and at the high point Nora, as the saying goes, took him in hand. Later that year the two of them eloped to Europe; Joyce's father, on hearing Nora's surname, remarked that she'd stick to him anyway. Joyce and Nora were lifelong partners, had two children, and Nora's nature is as much a part of *Ulysses* as Joyce's intellect.

By the end of the long day that it portrays – this comes about 20 hours after the book begins – there is a certain faint air of content, even of hope, a feeling that something, even if it's not clear what, has been accomplished. Joyce is not so soft as to suggest that, from now on, all three lives will be better, the problems of the Bloom marriage healed forever, the friendship with Stephen uniting them as never before while at the same time putting this dissolute would-be writer back on the rails. But in the quiet time after Bloom has fallen asleep but before Molly has dropped off at last, the thrillingly early dawn of late spring already imminent, she concludes her own thoughts and with them, the great book of *Ulysses*:

> and then I asked him with my eyes to ask again yes and then he asked me would I yes to say yes my

mountain flower and first I put my arms around him yes and drew him down to me so he could feel my breasts all perfume yes and his heart was going like mad and yes I said yes I will Yes.

And in that passage and especially in that last much-repeated word is all of spring, yes ...

Signs of spring
March 2024

17   Antiphonal blackbirds
       Chiffchaff singing
       Four trees all in leaf, all in a line, two sallows, two weeping willows

18   River: marsh marigold in flower
       Male marsh harrier patrolling territory, displaying
       Cindy sees brimstone butterfly
       Buttercup on common
       On almost dry pool: two redshank, two oystercatcher, two teal, two shelduck, two gadwall

19   Many insects along hedge, several bumblebees
       Oystercatcher pair flying in

20   Equinox 0306
       Holkham, North Norfolk: spoonbills on nests
       Displaying lapwing
       Many singing skylarks

21   Large clump of marsh marigolds on river
       Check heronry with BTO: two nests clearly occupied

22   Displaying buzzards
       Many white dead nettles and lesser celandines
       Garlic mustard in flower
       Blackthorn blossom in spinney

13

The dark side of spring

I was sharing a small tent with my old friend Ralph in a field near Land's End. Ralph is inclined to doubt my usefulness when it comes to the practical and for that matter psychological aspects of camping and he wasn't best pleased when I woke him in the night with a startled cry and a request for the torch.

'What's the problem?'

'There's something in the tent. It scrabbled my hair.'

'Something in the tent,' he repeated with heavy patience. With a sigh that billowed the canvas he reached for his torch and switched it on. There, in the one-foot gap between our heads and the tent flap, was a hedgehog the size of a football. He acknowledged the torch, looked at us tolerantly, accepted that circumstances had changed and then, without any sense of urgency, went back out. I gave Ralph the look that Butch gives to Sundance when he shoots the snake and we went back to sleep.

It was a useful lesson about life. The fact is that it goes on even when you're not looking. Spring may be about the return of light to the seasonal lands, but an awful lot of springtime life goes on in the dark. The hedgehog depended on the increasing daylight of spring for its existence, but it had its being in spring's ever-shrinking window of darkness.

Nocturnal life can't happen without daylight. Plants (or by implication the sun) are at the base of almost every food chain and they can't operate without light. But they don't go away when night falls and they can be exploited as effectively in the times of darkness as in the light. Slugs are active at night for two good reasons: the dew makes it easier for them to move about and hardly anybody can see them. A slug in the daylight would be the easiest of easy meals for a sharp-eyed bird, but slugs operate when most birds are asleep.

But if you can find a way of penetrating the darkness, those slugs – and many other nocturnal feeders – become available. What's more, you are operating at a time when competition for food is much reduced: penetrating darkness is a specialist job. That's why the hedgehog entered our tent with such high hopes: he was looking for slugs and other creatures of the night. Slow, meticulous, inquisitive, hedgehogs hunt down prey that doesn't move much. And, of course, hedgehogs have their own defence system against attack from nocturnal predators bigger than themselves: their famous trick of curling up into a spiny ball.

In spring the darkness comes alive. It gets busier and more crowded with every passing night. There's less and less darkness, but what there is becomes more and more filled with life. We humans have always found that idea of nocturnal activity a little challenging because we are such visual creatures. Many list-making birders don't count a bird they have identified by song and call: they have to see it. We tend to think that hearing is a second-class sense, and, for us, smell is hardly a sense at all. Darkness is not our time. Chimpanzees, our closest relatives, inhabit the same sensual world that we do, so they rise when the sun does the same and sleep when it goes back down. When humans gained control of fire about a million years ago, it revolutionised our lives in many different ways: and perhaps the most important was that fire allowed us to see in the dark, to get advance warning of our enemies, human and otherwise, and to use at least some of the hours of darkness for socialising, for becoming civilised, for establishing human culture.

Have you ever walked the countryside in spring with a decent torch? One that throws a beam for a hundred yards? If so, you will have had the pleasing experience of finding a fellow mammal from eye-shine: the torchlight is reflected back at you from the eyes. If you get good at this you can recognise the species from the height of the eyes above the ground and the distance between them. But shine the same light at a fellow human (or for that matter a chimpanzee) and you don't get the same result. The eye-shine comes from an organ called the tapetum lucidum. It lies behind the retina and reflects light back onto the retina, making more light available to the photoreceptors. In other words, you can see better in low light.

Many mammals have a tapetum lucidum: catch a cat or a dog in the headlights and you get an answering glow. Many predators have them; many prey species also. Shine a light over a herd of deer huddled together at night and it looks like a small town seen from a night-flying plane. Mammals that don't have them include humans, squirrels, kangaroos and pigs.

We like the idea of 'seeing in the dark', because it seems magical. Young wolves in *The Jungle Book*[1] learn the Hunting Verse: 'Feet that make no noise, eyes that can see in the dark, ears that can hear the winds in their lairs, and sharp white teeth, all these things are the

[1] *The Jungle Book* by Rudyard Kipling, first published in 1894.

marks of our brothers except Tabaqui the jackal and the Hyaena whom we hate.' As a guide for any nocturnal predator it has a lot going for it, though the wolf also has a nose that can smell the deer on the hill. A tapetum lucidum doesn't give those who possess it the ability to see in the night as well as we see in the brightness of noon. But in the low light of night, which is not the same as the pitch darkness of a deep cave, the tapetum lucidum allows those that possess them to see a good deal better than those who don't.

Foxes are equipped with good night vision. The cubs are born in March and before spring is over they are required to do most of their foraging for themselves: hunting by night with the aid of powerful senses, including eyesight backed by a tapetum lucidum. Country foxes eat mostly rabbits and field voles, also young hares and ground-nesting birds, though they will also take earthworms and carrion. Urban foxes are half hunters and half scavengers; for them keen intelligence and a talent for improvisation are at least as important as enhanced senses.

But life begins with plants and plants aren't the static, same-state unresponsive things we humans tend to think. Many plants produce flowers that put out a scent: a come-hither for potential pollinators, inviting them in to sup on their nectar, so that the plants can have sex. Scent is not necessarily a constant thing in a flower: it can come and go, and the plant can pick and choose the time it puts out its most inviting scents. A good few flowers put out their best scent at night.

These include honeysuckle, soapwort, oxeye daisy, meadowsweet, musk mallow and hedge bedstraw. They do so for a very good reason: to avoid competing with the majority and to exploit the fliers of the spring night. Sometimes gardeners make a night garden with cultivated and exotic plants that retain their trick of nocturnal scents: adding tobacco plant, night-scented stock, evening primrose, night phlox, jasmine and wisteria.

As said earlier, we have 59 species of breeding butterflies in the UK and around 2,500 moths. Of these 800 or so are macromoths: in other words, bigger than micromoths. Almost all of them are nocturnal. Older readers will remember night journeys by car in late spring, turning into an unlit lane and seeing the twin beams light up a great snowstorm: an instant later you realise that every single flake is a moth. You can penetrate this secret world with a light trap: you can improvise one (helpful instructions on-line), or you can buy one from a specialist.[2]

I remember the first time I used mine, approaching it the following morning in mild trepidation, for fear that the task of identifying and then releasing the trapped moths in safety would be beyond me. The very first moth that I saw, perched on the outside, not even troubling to penetrate the trap's fastness and the egg boxes it contained for the safety and comfort of those it caught, was almost the size of my palm – an honorary bird – and what's more, it was beautifully coloured in subtle

---

[2] For example. nhbs.com.

designer shades of pink, crimson and green. It was unmistakably the moth on the cover of my field guide:[3] an elephant hawk moth. And it was a revelation. A further revelation came with the information that the moth was 'Common. Very widely distributed in England and Wales, Man and Ireland'. Here was something that was as common as it was beautiful and yet to me – mad for nature all my life – it was a never-seen exoticism. Now I had penetrated the night and learned at least one of its million secrets.

Many moths take advantage of the night-scented flowers: refuelling for the next bout of looking for other moths of the same species. But quite a lot of them don't bother with feeding at all: they did enough of that when they were caterpillars. (The elephant hawk moth is so called because the imposing caterpillar looks like an elephant's trunk.) Most moths are short-lived in their adult form and they take wing with a single goal: the propagation of their genes. Or to put that another way, sex. Or to be less sensational, sex and, for the female, the laying of eggs on the right food plant for the caterpillars of the species. (For the elephant hawk moth that's willowherb, fuchsia and bedstraw.) Some extend the period of mate-hunting by feeding on nectar, others don't, devoting 100 per cent of their time to the task of finding a partner. Both strategies can be winners.

---

[3] *Field Guide to the Moths of Great Britain and Ireland* by Paul Waring and Martin Townsend, illustrated by Richard Lewington.

Butterflies find each other and mate because they can see each other: they have evolved inviting colours and a flight that makes the most of them. Few creatures advertise themselves as clearly and as beautifully as a butterfly. But most moths must find each other in darkness. Life is much safer in the night; the downside is that you're not going to find a partner by fluttering your wings, however beautiful. So they do it by means of a beautiful, or at least a compellingly attractive, scent. The female puts out pheromones and the males can sense them on their feathery antennae, which are very different from the stalked, clubbed antennae of butterflies. A male can scent a female from a mile off and as soon as he has done so he sets off in her direction. This could be a mile-long flight into a headwind. Once there, he may have to fight off rival males for the privilege. In the blackness of night a male moth can find a female and know that she is beautiful from a vast distance: and then seek her out with pinpoint precision.

Other species of insects also operate at night. They are faced with the same problem: you can't see very much so you need to use other senses. A female mosquito needs a blood meal to fuel the production of eggs. There are 3,000 mosquito species worldwide, 34 of them in this country. Some get their blood from frogs, snakes and other reptiles and amphibians, others look for birds, while a fair few of them bite mammals – and, as most of us have experienced, that includes humans. They come to us in the night; one that gets inside the mosquito net can torment till dawn. So how do they find us in the dark? They detect the carbon dioxide we exhale, so you need to stop breathing for eight hours if you are to be invisible to a mosquito. They also pick up clues from body heat, sweat and skin odour.

Some insects use sound to communicate at night. Crickets are the most obvious examples: rubbing body parts together to produce that atmospheric din called stridulation. Most crickets produce their sounds by rubbing their wings together; these have an edge like a file. A few insects communicate visually and do so by making their own light. There are no fireflies in the UK but there are still glow-worms, just about. These are actually a species of beetle: the females produce the light and the males seek it. This form of bioluminescence is produced by a baffling form of chemistry, one that costs the glow-worm remarkably little in terms of energy.

Many insect species, then, are adapted for the night. Despite the recent catastrophic declines there are still more night-flying insects than you would think possible. You can see this for yourself, and the easiest way of doing so is not by looking for the insects but by becoming aware of their predators. Predators can't exist without an adequate population of their prey species: and we still have plenty of bats. There are 18 species of them in the UK. The night-flying niche is so profitable all over the world that bats have evolved into 1,400 species: a fifth of all mammal species are bats.

Bats are traditionally divided into the two sub-orders, the megachiroptera, or fruit bats who mostly don't use sonar, on account of the fact that fruit doesn't try and escape, and the microchiroptera; all the UK species fall into this category. They mostly specialise in flying insects. Don't think for a minute that this is an easy option: in fact, it's probably the hardest option of them all. A gazelle running away from a cheetah can only move in two dimensions, so interception at speed is a relatively simple matter; the cheetah success rate is getting on for 50 per cent once a chase has begun. But a flying creature moves in three dimensions, so the options for dodging are exponentially greater. It's harder to be a sparrowhawk than a cheetah: a sparrowhawk is wonderfully adapted for the pursuit and capture of flying birds and has a success rate of around 10 per cent.

Bats (mostly) make their living by chasing and catching flying creatures: they do so at night and are capable of doing it in pitch-darkness. They hibernate, emerging in spring when there are once again night-flying insects to hunt (see Chapter 15). The nearest we sight-dominated humans get to an intuitive understanding of a bat's sensual world is to say that they 'see with their ears' or build a 'sound picture' of the world around them. But it's not an image as we humans understand it or are capable of understanding it: a bat's perception of the world comes from its superb ears and from its even more superb brain, which analyses the received sounds and uses them to create a world view that humans can never share. We have radar, yes, but in order to make sense of what it reveals, we convert the return signal into a visual image, something our own brains can grasp. That's not how a bat's sonar works.

The bat's famous sonar or echolocation begins with a scream. A bat screams and listens for the echoes that come back. They use this facility for navigation, and crucially they use it for hunting. The information they get from their sonar enables them to compute the distance a flying object is from the bat, its size, shape, density and direction of travel: all essential information if they are to intercept and catch. The catching is remarkable in itself: many species catch the target — usually a moth — in their tails and sweep it into the mouth, performing a half-roll in the air while still continuing their powered flapping flight.

They make the sound with their larynx, just as we do when we scream, and mostly they emit it through their mouths; horseshoe bats and some others do so through their nose, so it's possible that the ability to echolocate evolved twice over. Most of the sounds they make are beyond human hearing. Bats hear and measure the returning echoes of these calls by way of a flap on the ear called the tragus. Most species have developed a pattern and frequency of calls that best suits their environment and choice of prey: in other words you can work out the species of bat by listening to its echolocation calls. Devices have been developed that modulate the pitch of these calls to a level that humans can actually hear, and those skilled in their use can diagnose species from the clicks and whirrs. A pipistrelle — there are three species found in the UK and they're the bats most commonly encountered — sounds like a wet slap. It's the one bat I can recognise when I use my own bat detector.

It's a well-known fact that potential prey species prefer to avoid becoming actual prey. They evolve defences, and predators must then adapt to catch up, and on and on, in what's called an evolutionary arms race. Some moth species have responded to bat predation by evolving ultrasound of their own. In some species this operates as a startler, putting bats off their line. Other moths taste foul, sometimes from toxins they sequestered from the plants they ate as caterpillars. Off-putting colours would be no use in the dark: they have developed an ultrasonic signal that advises bats not to eat them. Still other species can surround themselves with a shroud of static that jams the sonar. These defences have been found in hawk moths and tiger moths; it's been suggested that many other species have the same ability: nothing less than defence against the dark arts.

One advantage that the seasonal lands hold over those closer to the equator is the prolonged twilight: an extended period that is neither night nor day. This period of low light is a window of opportunity: barn owls exploit it with great efficiency. They prefer open country where there is more ambient light than there is among trees. In the right sort of place you will often see them in the grey hours, generally working fast, looking like great pale moths in the half-light as they work hedge-lines, ditch-lines and open country. The spring is their peak time: if all has gone well they have a brood of young owls and must take every opportunity to find food for them. They work low, listening for the sound of short-tailed field voles moving in their tunnels of grass. This is not exactly a deafening din, but barn owls can hear because they fly in almost total silence. That silent flight is an owl's USP: every bit as important as their excellent eyesight. Their silent flight means the voles can't hear them coming, but, even more importantly, it means the owls can't hear the sound of their own movement. Nothing interferes with their hearing: they can tune in to the subtle sound of voles without the white noise of their own flight getting in the way. Their ears are placed asymmetrically so they can get a cross-bearing on the sound they hear below them: they home in on that sound and then they pounce. Silently.

Nightjars take flying insects like bats, but do so by sight rather than by sonar. They are migrants, arriving in this country in April and May, when the numbers of flying insects are moving towards their peak. They, too, like the grey hours – crepuscular is the words of choice here – and they feed by making low-level runs over dusky heaths and moors. They, too, like open country, where there is more light available and less chance of bumping into trees.

The eyes of a tawny owl aren't that much better than those of the barn owl, and yet they hunt in the depths of night and usually do so in woodland. The super-sense they use for exploiting this forbidding, deep-dark habitat is memory. Brain power. You can hear a tawny owl hoot – the call that's in every graveyard scene in every horror film ever made – at any time of year, but they reach a peak in the spring, when the business of holding a territory and raising a brood becomes critical. They will call at any time of night. I often hear the call in bed, or if I get up for a midnight pee – and that midnight pee is significant, as I will show you in a moment.

How can they catch moving prey in a dark wood at the darkest hour of the day? How can they hunt without crashing into trees and injuring themselves? Because they know their stretch of country like the back of their talons. Their best weapon is their knowledge and understanding of their own place. They know every inch. They know it as well as you do your own bedroom and bathroom and corridor. You have no need to switch on the light for that necessary nocturnal journey: you can interpret scanty visual information in a meaningful way: that white patch is the stair rail, that gleam of light is reflected from the doorknob, that pale glow is journey's end.

In the same way a tawny owl knows every hunting perch, the ground beneath it and what lies between them. The bird can interpret a movement or a sound and drop silently down upon it in perfect confidence and safety. But if you blunder into the wood yourself and startle the bird, it is perfectly capable of flying slap into a tree – just as you would be capable of running into a wall if some fearsome midnight intruder panicked you on your nocturnal journey along the corridor. That's why tawnies are the most sedentary of birds: no point in moving to a new place and having to learn it from scratch. Their knowledge of their own patch is like money in the bank, and once they have established themselves in a place they won't leave it unless they are forced out.

Tawnies, like practically all nocturnal creatures, are associated with evil: with witches and malign forces, ultimately with death. That is because we humans are creatures of the light and are suspicious of every creature that is not. Cats, bats, rats, owls, spiders, toads: all these make a living at night and so are often seen as creatures of ill omen. Halloween is a feast of nocturnal animals: but what we truly fear is not cats and bats but darkness itself. Some creatures have adapted to it: and they are to be admired and celebrated rather than feared.

Human activity is associated with daytime and the light: as a result creatures that can exploit the night – even if they're not strictly nocturnal – have an advantage. It follows that these days many more creatures are inclined to operate at night, if they can. Deer of all species are better seen – at least near human habitations – in very early morning and the late evening. Otters are most active at night. There are all sorts of survival stratagems and all sorts of threats: but keeping out of the way of humanity is a very sound starting point. Every year the dark gets more and more attractive.

Signs of spring
March 2024

24   Mating marsh harriers, seen from my desk
Oystercatcher pair close to the mud path
Cetti's warbler on the marsh
25   Train Norwich to London: blossom all the way, plum and blackthorn
26   Cultivated plum and damson blossoming in garden
Cetti's warbler heard from desk
Budburst on willows along river
27   Hoverflies over lawn
Dandelion clock on Common
28   Norwich Cathedral Close – best blackbird of the year, song echoing between buildings
29   Lesser celandines and flowering garlic mustard all along the lane
Blackcap singing from the ash
30   Brimstone in the lane
Cowslips on roadside

14

Portraits of spring

I was twenty, plus, I think, four days. I had just hitchhiked to Florence, sleeping by the roadside when appropriate. The plan was to meet Jim at the Campeggio Michelangelo, a camping site just outside town, but he wasn't there. I was lost and out of sorts, not yet knowing that Jim's no-show would be the portal to life-changing adventures. So – in poor spirits but feeling

I really ought to do *something* – I went to the Uffizi Gallery. I had no idea what was inside. It just seemed the thing to do. After all, I needed to fill in the time before Jim's arrival. So I walked about a bit and visited a few rooms and looked at quite a lot of paintings and it was all sort of OK. Then I went into the next room and the world exploded.

It was as if I had never been exposed to beauty before, certainly not beauty from the hand of humanity. I knew both the paintings from reproduction, of course I did, everybody does, but there they were in their enormousness, in their nacreousness, in their gorgeousness, in their world-changing mind-altering wondrousness.

They were, of course, the two great Botticellis: *The Birth of Venus*, with the lovely naked woman rising from the sea, standing politely on her enormous scallop shell as the winds whisk her to the shore and, alongside her, the painting known as *Primavera* or *Spring*: and again and again my eyes returned to the face of Flora, to the face of Spring herself. Spring was the loveliest thing I had ever seen, the loveliest thing anyone had ever seen.

The painting is busy with enigmatic mythological figures: six females and two males plus a youngster floating in the air above the rest. There are all kinds of intriguing and complex explanations of what the picture represents, and we'll get on to them in a while, but I was lost in contemplation of Flora's face, and the beauty and fecundity that surrounded her face and her figure and her frock. So far as I was concerned, the meaning of the painting lay there: in her eyes, in the curve of her jaw, in her half-smile that invited me to step into the picture – or did it? The meaning was also in the plants: for this was an arcadia, a paradise, one that glowed with all the colours and also with a word that hadn't even been coined in 1971: biodiversity. In the impossibly rich variety of botanical life spread out before me – there are more than 500 plants in the picture – the principal figure was something far greater even than the meaning of life. She was life.

The enormous size of the painting and its fellow were compelling in themselves. They made a pair and the painter had obviously used the same paint box for both, one in which every colour had been liberally mixed with the pure light of the vernal sun. *Primavera* is more than two metres high and more than three wide: *Venus* only a little smaller: an awful lot of paint and an awful lot of sunlight. These entrancing figures are life-size or even a little larger: it was more like walking into a painting and becoming a participant than looking at one and being an observer. Anyway, it was they who were looking at me.

The two great female figures – Venus in one painting and Flora in the other – seemed to me to represent different kinds of beauty, not in physical but in moral terms. Though Flora is fully clad and Venus quite naked, it seemed – certainly to my twenty-year-old self, much taken up with such matters – that Flora was the sexier of the two. If there was something thrillingly submissive about Venus, there was something thrillingly challenging about Flora. It was not a challenge as in, OK, sonny, but you'd better be good. It was more a question of OK, step into the painting – but are you quite sure what you're letting yourself in for? Because this is bigger, deeper, richer and more packed with meaning than anything you have ever done before, anything, in fact, that you've ever dreamed of. Step in – if you really think that's wise. And it's wise, all right, but I knew then that wisdom was a rather bigger thing than I suspected.

She was 'The force that through the green fuse drives the flower':[1] everything you love and far, far more than you bargained for.

A couple of days later I gave up on Jim, left Florence and set off on the road looking for adventures. And finding them.

But I was talking about painting. So let us move on from my twenty-year-old self and all the love and wonder of those years, and talk about the painting itself: the work known as *Primavera*. If you can avert your eyes, if only for a moment, from the face of Spring – from Flora and the surrounding flora – there are other things to be considered here. Who is the woman apparently vomiting plants, for example? This, I learned later, much later, is Chloris, and she is being embraced, somewhat forcibly, by Zephyrus, the West Wind: so this painting catches the very moment of the metamorphosis of winter into spring, blown into being by the same wind that

---

[1] Dylan Thomas.

was celebrated by both Chaucer and the unnamed poet of the westron wynde.

After her subsequent marriage with Zephyrus, Chloris becomes Flora, so this is a sort of comic strip, read from right to left. In the middle, and set back a little, detached from the rest, stands a figure identified as Venus, but not the naked and youthful beauty shown in the adjacent picture. Here Venus is fully clad, surrounded by the myrtles which are sacred to her. She is modest, calm, reasonable, serene, gravely raising a hand to bless the surrounding figures in their glade. She has been compared to and even identified with Mary; her aura of untouchability and the broad hint of a halo add to this impression.

Over her head floats a blindfolded Cupid with a love-dart good to go. To the left of Venus dance three figures usually identified as the Three Graces, though they are not naked as usual, but wearing their nighties. Voluptas and Pulchritudo – pleasure and beauty – look at each other intently, wrapped up in each other and bringing their two qualities together, while the third – Castitas or Chastity – is eyeing up the armed male figure on the far left. She is the apparent target for the love-dart. She's looking rather longingly at Mercury, who is moodily poking the sky with a stick; according to some interpretations he is chasing the last cloud away before summer.

The plants themselves are packed with symbolic meaning. From the mouth of Chloris stream periwinkles, cornflowers, strawberry blossom and roses (or perhaps anemones). There are 60 flowers in Flora's dress alone, many stylised and eluding accurate identity, but they certainly include carnations, roses, cornflowers and perhaps yellow wallflowers. In her hair she wears daisies, cornflowers, strawberry blossom and perhaps yellow anemone. At her feet you can find fifty-five daisies and forty-six violets, both associated with love. There are also roses – Flora is scattering them – along with hellebore (which cures madness), blue viperine (which cures snakebite), camomile, buttercup, hyacinth, poppy, more cornflowers and strawberries, jasmine, forget-me-not, nigella, crocus, euphorbia, periwinkle and iris.

And though the allegory is all the more compelling for its uncertain meaning, and the line of figures with their interwoven storylines have delightful scope for interpretation and argument, and while the historical narrative is intriguing (it was probably painted for the wedding of Lorenzo di Pierfrancesco de' Medici to Semiramide Appiano) it's that face I still return to: Flora and her flora. Her spring in all its promise and, with it, just a hint of threat. It's not as easy as you thought it might be: but better than you ever dreamed it could be. Perhaps the truest meaning of the painting is not in the wisdom of the old but in the infatuated gaze of a twenty-year-old.

Facts are, of course, sacred, but they never tell the whole story. It was about twenty years after my Uffizi or Botticelli or Primavera or Flora epiphany in Florence, and I was in the Van Gogh Museum in Amsterdam. Naturally I was familiar with the basic facts of Van

Gogh's life: his story has become inextricable from his work, and the tale of genius and tragedy is a part of every painting that bears his name. But I didn't understand the most important aspect of the story — and of the paintings themselves, perhaps — until I was in that museum looking at that impossible detonation of colour and hope.

The revelation came not in the paintings themselves; rather, these gave a deep and essential confirmation. It was in the labels alongside them. These gave the titles of each painting and the date it was painted. And it went roughly like this, 1888. 1888. 1888. 1888. 1888. And also 1889 again and again, and again and again 1890.

It was clear that, in those two and a bit years, the number of masterpieces Van Gogh painted in a day was directly related to the time he got up in the morning. Here was perhaps the greatest discharge of artistic creativity in the history of the world: two and a bit years of genius; two and a bit years in which the world gained some of the greatest treasures in the history of the human species.

It began when Van Gogh moved to Arles in the spring of 1888. He had been living with his wonderful brother Theo in Paris for the previous two years. While he was there he made the decisive shift from the dark socially aware work he had been working on in what's now called his Dutch period, and moved towards the exuberant colours of the Impressionists, but always in his own way. It was here he painted his first sunflowers, lying on a table, with no vase. But it's all too easy to let yourself off work in a city, always easier to discuss work than do it, and besides, a diet of black coffee, absinthe and tobacco is not a long-term option.

So in February 1888 Van Gogh travelled 750 km south, moving in a few days from winter to spring: from slushy pavements, cloudy skies and grey buildings into an intoxicating environment of sun and light and colour – and blossom. He was to paint this spring again and again and perhaps the greatest tragedy of all that inescapable narrative is that the works he produced in that first encounter with the south were and are the most joyous paintings that have ever been painted.

He wrote to Theo: 'I hope to make real progress this year, which to be sure, I badly need to do. I've got a new orchard which is as good as the pink peach trees – apricot trees of a very pale pink. At the moment I'm working on some plum trees, yellowy-white with thousands of black branches. I am using up an enormous amount of canvases and paints, but I hope it's not a waste of money for all that.'[2]

Almost as soon as he arrived he was painting a sprig of almond blossoms in a tooth glass, and then he did it all over again, even better. He painted another peach tree in full bloom and then, hearing of the death of his former teacher, the Dutch realist painter Anton Mauve – a rare example of someone who gave him serious encouragement – Van Gogh picked up a brush

---

[2] *The Letters of Vincent Van Gogh*, Penguin Classics translation by Arnold Pomerans, first published in 1996.

and wrote across the foot of the painting: 'Souvenir de Mauve', in memory of Mauve. Van Gogh arranged for the completed painting to be sent to Mauve's widow; I had a print of that painting in my room in Streatham as a boy. He painted seventeen studies of blossom in that first Arles spring and each one exults in hope: a fragment of beauty in a troubled world.

It was two years later, after he had moved (via the asylum at Saint-Rémy) to Auvers, a little north of Paris, that he painted that close-up fragment of almond tree – just sky and branch and blossom – and sent it to his brother as a gift to commemorate the birth of Theo's son, his nephew, Vincent Willem van Gogh. This is one of the most famous paintings in the world: star of fridge magnet, iPad cover and T-shirt: and it's a glorious thing wherever it turns up. It's a pictorial representation of hope springing eternal.

Vincent Willem was born on 31 January 1890. On 27 July that year, his uncle Vincent shot himself with a revolver and died two days later.

In a letter to Theo some years earlier, he wrote:

> A caged bird in spring knows perfectly well that there is some way in which he should be able to serve. He is well aware that there is something to be done, but he is unable to do it. What is it? He cannot quite remember but he gets a vague inkling and says to himself: 'The others are building their nests and hatching their young and bringing

them up' and he bangs his head against the bars of the cage. But the cage does not give way and the bird is maddened by pain. What a ne'er-do-well, says another bird passing. What an idler. Yet the prisoner lives and does not die. There is no outward sign of what is going on inside him, he is doing well, he is quite cheerful in the sunshine ...

... but the season of the great migration arrives: an outbreak of melancholy. He has everything he needs, say the children who tend him in his cage – but he looks out, at the heavy, thundery sky, and in his heart of hearts he rebels against his fate. I am caged. I am caged and you say I need nothing, you idiots! I have everything I need, indeed! Oh please give me the freedom to be a bird like other birds.

And yet so many of Van Gogh's paintings, especially when he painted spring, are the most joyous things we will ever see. No doubt it's his awareness of the fragile and fleeting nature of joy that give these paintings their edge and their meaning. He didn't think life was like that: all colour and joy and hope: but he knew that – sometimes – it could be. Almost. Spring always follows winter, but every spring will eventually be followed by another winter.

What is the most famous depiction of spring by a British painter? It's one of the most famous paintings by any British artist ever:³ John Constable's *The Hay Wain* has gone in the course of 200 years — it was completed in 1821 — from revolutionary art to chocolate box. These days our eyes often skid over its sleek surface without taking too much in.

It shows a landscape in late spring: first or second week in June, judging from the elder tree in full frothing bloom in front of the house on the left, while the subject of the painting is hay-making, an activity of the high spring. The picture brings us spring just before it spills over into summer, and a major task must be completed before summer can be enjoyed. Making hay is a perilous business: you need a week of dry, sunny weather, and if you guess wrong and there's a serious downpour, your crop is ruined and you have nothing to feed your livestock over winter. First you cut your hay. This is a mixture of meadow grasses and associated plants, though not ragwort, pull that before you start cropping, because it's poisonous. You then leave the felled plants to dry in the sun, turning them a couple of times daily so the sun can do a thorough job. Once the vegetation is properly dry it will keep. It will remain edible for months: for a full year. You can store it in a barn and feed it to your livestock through the winter, when the grass is no longer growing. That not only fattens the animals you are keeping for meat and nourishes

---

³ A poll for the best paintings in Britain run by BBC Radio 4's *Today* programme in 2005 put it in second place behind Turner's *The Fighting Temeraire*.

those you are keeping for their milk; it also feeds your draft animals. Hay is also fuel for transport and agricultural work, and it will power the horse plough or the ox plough when the sowing season comes round again. If you have laid down a decent store of hay for the winter you have stolen a march on the seasons.

And you can see the hay-makers in the distance, looking to my English eyes a little like cricketers, white figures against the green. The composition is dominated by the wagon fording the stream at Flatford Mill in Suffolk, which was owned by the Constable family. The picture was actually painted in London – from a series of sketches done on the spot over the course of ten years – so this is emphatically the work of a professional engaging in an act of conscious creation, rather than that of an inspired genius who doesn't know what he's doing – which is the usual but erroneous understanding of Van Gogh.

These days it takes a small effort to see *The Hay Wain* as a painting rather than a fridge magnet or the famous box of chocolates. It seems almost too pleasant. But give it a little more time and the picture starts to find its own life again: an image of contentment rather than joy, for joy is a fierce emotion perpetually haunted by its antithesis. Here is a picture of calm optimism, one that might illustrate Alexander Pope's contention of a century earlier: not the line about hope springing eternal, but when he tells us that 'whatever is is right'. And for about another century, perhaps even a century and a half, agricultural subjects could still be painted about and written about to illustrate that contention: humans and nature in harmony creating a vista of peace.

*The Hay Wa*in didn't make much impact when it was first available to public view in London, but it was bought by a French art dealer with the improbable name of John Arrowsmith, who showed it at the Paris Salon of 1824. Here it created a sensation. All the top names raved about it: loved the living green colours that made such a contrast with the brown, murky tones associated with the acknowledged masters – colours the paintings often acquired after years of exposure to wood, coal and tobacco smoke. There was also a great admiration for the way Constable put on the paint: not painting each individual leaf, but brilliantly giving the impression – observe the *mot juste* – of a multitude of leaves with his adroit brushwork. The painting had a great influence on the Barbizon group of artists, all very keen on landscapes, and they in turn influenced the Impressionist movement. Constable has been called 'the messiah of landscape painters'.

The rise of the Impressionists involved a radical alteration to the traditional hierarchy of painting subjects. Previously the most important subjects were seen as historical, a category that included religious, classical, mythological and allegorical paintings. Portraits came second, with genre paintings – scenes of everyday life – a fairly distant third. Only after that came landscapes, with still lifes a step below that. Landscape was supposed to be the background to a classical subject, not the subject itself – but that was changing.

The revolution of the Impressionists was not just in the way they put the paint on and the way they understood light and colour. It was also about subject matter. Painting was no longer just about the ideal and the noble: it was also about the beauty you can find in the ordinary and the unapologetically bourgeois. Landscapes of ordinary places, often with ordinary people passing through them, became the subject of choice. It follows that spring was at the heart of this revolution, because that's when the ordinary is at its most beautiful. If you thumb through any book of Impressionist paintings, whether they concern the works of a single artist or many, time and again you will turn over to find a picture of spring that almost literally lights up the page.

So let's choose one to stand for them all. I have gone for Camille Pissarro's *Boulevard Montmartre, Spring*. Pissarro had an eye infection which prevented him working outside, in the manner beloved by Impressionists. But as people of great talent will, he turned the setback into a positive by completing a series of 14 paintings between February and April 1897 from an upstairs room in the Grand Hotel de Russie, which looked out over the Boulevard Montmartre.

And there in a canvas of blacks and greys he captures spring. It comes bouncing off the picture in the light of the sun and the green of the new leaves on the trees that line the street, which I think are London planes. The painting shows a line of vehicles, which looks more like a ceremonial procession than a traffic jam.

To be accurate it's a cavalcade, for all the traffic – carriages, carts, the odd omnibus – is drawn by horses. It's a picture of light and busyness and people going from place to place because they have important stuff to do: shopping, business, drinking, eating, assignations of love – you might almost caption the painting 'Hang spring cleaning!'. The green leaves and the sudden sun fill the black and grey city with light and life and love. As David Attenborough, in a balloon above the earth and in a cave deep below it, told us about the ubiquity of life on earth, so Pissarro turns away from the city he has depicted to tell us: and – even here – there is spring.

Spring is inescapable even in the cities, even in the cities of the twenty-first century. While conceptual artists seek to shock, confront and startle us into anger, horror, revulsion and perhaps even thought, so spring arrives every year at the galleries in which they exhibit. You can see the spring sun setting light to the waters of the Thames in front of Tate Modern, lifting the spirits of all those who cross the Millennium Bridge, making them look like a procession of lovelorn pilgrims.

David Hockney created a series of 116 works on his iPad during the lockdown of 2020 when he was eighty-two and he called it *The Arrival of Spring*.[4] The exaggerated colours that Hockney loves inevitably light up every one, even if the limitations of the medium make each individual work seem perhaps more simple than you would wish. But while the conceptual artists do

---

[4] The works were shown at the Royal Academy, London, the following year.

their no-doubt essential work, and seek to make final the divorce of art from craft, let us close this chapter with the concept that lies behind that Hockney lockdown project: how an artist of eighty-two produced a long series of wildly coloured images because, in a dark and fearful time, the arrival of spring once again sent his spirit soaring and the work he created as a result reminds us of the way that spring comforted and consoled us all in a time of darkness and despair.

Signs of spring
April 2024

1. May blossom
   Thirty-eight restless curlews, about to migrate north
   Green-veined white (butterfly)
   Brief lie in hammock
2. Song thrush and blackbird duetting
   Probable nest site for marsh harrier identified
   Cetti's warbler on the marsh
   Ground ivy in flower
   Wheeze-clatter song from starling
   Gnat up my nose
3. Displaying lapwings at Cantley
4. Blackcap heard from my desk
   Budburst on sycamore
   Celandine colony on common
5. Skylark over neighbour's field
   Speedwell, broom, stitchwort in flower
   Huge bank of cowslips on Norwich road
   Lucy had her first swim of the year in Hampstead Ponds
6. Peacock (butterfly)
   Cow parsley in flower
7. Forget-me-nots flowering in a field
   Singing skylark near river
   Drinks in pub garden
   Supper (brave) in our garden
8. Flowers on ash fully open
   Bird cherry in flower
   Willows in flower
   Small blue (butterfly)

15

Spring awakenings

We are used to the idea that the world wakes up in spring: as if the world was the sleeping beauty and the sun the handsome prince. It's a metaphor that makes perfect sense to us: the snows melt, the ice retreats, the warmth returns and the whole world stretches, gets out of bed and starts to dance: flowers, butterflies, birdsong, love in the air and drinks in the garden.

Every spring is like the beginning of the world as told in *The Magician's Nephew*, another tale from *The Chronicles of Narnia*. Here Aslan, having created the world, now gives it life: 'Narnia, Narnia, Narnia awake! Love. Think. Speak. Be walking trees. Be talking beasts. Be divine waters.' In the same way, if more gradually, every spring is a blessed awakening.

The idea of awakening is not just a figure of speech. It is, in the most literal way possible, precisely what happens with many animals at the beginning of spring. So come with me to Dunwich Forest in Suffolk on a bright, sunny day in mid-March, my fleece worn unzipped for the first time in months and my gloves in my pocket.

I was in an area of forest managed by the Suffolk Wildlife Trust. This was 2009, shortly after the Trust had moved in. The place was already improving before my eyes, non-native trees were slowly being taken out and natural regeneration was taking place. Undergrowth, especially bracken, was being organised in order to maximise diversity. The cut vegetation had been raked into long lines of brash, cuttings, felled bracken and branches. Many of these long, thin heaps ran alongside the access roads put in by the Forestry Commission and now much used by dog walkers. These lines are called windrows, and they were dominated by the broken browny pattern of dead bracken; an impression of reddy-brown chequered plants.

Looking is an acquired skill. You get better at it with practice and with knowledge. The best way to acquire knowledge of any kind is to be with someone who can teach. I was with John Baker of the Herpetological Conservation Trust and he was doing his best to make me look. What was obvious to him was a dizzying puzzle-picture to me. 'There! Here! Look, it's moving!'

And so it was: a brown chequer pattern moving subtly against a slightly different brown chequer pattern. It was like looking at an image slowly coming into focus: and I was looking at an adder: an adder in the process of awakening. It had been hibernating in the windrow and now it had emerged and was there on the south side soaking up the spring sun. The snake was like a mobile phone: recharging in anticipation of thrilling exchanges to come.

We have been taught to think of reptiles as cold-blooded, like amphibians and fish and unlike us. We have expanded this concept to create an idea of what a snaky personality should be: cold, sinister, unblinking, heartless and alien. But snakes operate best when their blood is hot: sometimes at temperatures higher than our own. They are not cold-blooded at all: in fact, they are ectothermic. They must get their heat from an outside source, because they can't generate it for themselves as we mammals do, the same principle that we saw with butterflies in Chapter 7 and bees in Chapter 11. All ectothermic animals need a good heat source if they are to be active and so, as soon as the adders wake up, they turn to the sun and soak up its warmth.

They have been asleep all winter – though that terminology is pretty loose. It's not sleep as we understand it: it's a near-total shutdown. We call it hibernation but that's not strictly accurate either: it's a different physiological state from that of hibernating mammals. Reptiles like snakes don't have to generate their own heat throughout the winter, as mammals must, which means that they can afford to shut down the physiological processes to an even greater extent than hibernating mammals like hedgehogs – though this comes with a greater danger of freezing, if the weather conditions are extreme and/or they have failed to find an adequate place for over-wintering. This reptilian winter torpor is called brumation.

If they survive the rigours of brumation the adders wake when warm weather returns and, even more urgently than food and drink, they need heat. They need the sun and they soak up its rays with the eagerness of a desert traveller in an oasis. Only once thoroughly awakened by the sun's rays can they start to seek out food. Adders are the only venomous species in Britain and are therefore regarded with mistrust and fear by many, even though creatures bigger than voles have little to worry about. But in the course of a two-hour stroll along the windrows of Dunwich Forest I saw two dozen awakening adders, many of them within a few yards of tracks walked at all seasons by humans and their dogs. Some of the snakes were already feeling the sun's benefit and were ready for the thrilling social life of the spring.

Once an adder's blood is up to temperature it is ready to seek out not just food but other adders, for spring is the great mating time. At this time of year two adders will come together and twine round each other in what looks like a gloriously sensual embrace. Once thus locked, they will writhe and slither against each other, until the human onlooker is convinced that this species goes right to the top of the reincarnation wish list. I have never seen adders thus involved but once in Sri Lanka I saw a couple of cobras hard at it: both six-footers standing up with heads a good three feet above the ground, twining and entwining as if they would never stop, as wild a sight as I have ever seen.

But it's not love, neither for cobras nor adders, for all that it looks like it. This is the way that males pursue their struggle for dominance and access to females. They don't go at each other with their venom-injecting fangs bared; that would be a trifle dangerous. Rather, they engage in this safe but decisive form of Indian wrestling.

Reptiles go in for this period of brumation followed by the spring awakening because British winters are too cold for active ectothermic life. Being a British reptile is a tough option: that's why we have only six species. A long period of brumation is required by the other two species of British snakes, the grass snake and the smooth snake, and also by the common lizard, sand lizard and slow worm. All six return to active life again in the spring, basking in the sun on sunny days.

The ability to shut down in adverse circumstances – to hang about not dying until things get better – gives its possessor more options. Adders have been found at 3,300 m in the Alps and they survive inside the Arctic Circle. (Mammals and birds can cope with even greater extremes, but they need a great deal more food to fuel their more demanding lifestyles.) Reptiles make a living in these very difficult environments by staying dormant – brumating – for up to 275 days in a year. They can survive in conditions that would otherwise kill them, so long as they can find a safe place to sleep away from the cold. In areas where such hideaways are scarce – no convenient windrows – they will share: more than a hundred snakes have been found in a single spot, anticipating a glorious mass awakening when the temperature rises above a critical 7.5 degrees.

Mammals and birds can survive the British winter in an active state, so long as they can find food. But a great deal of invertebrate life becomes very scarce indeed in the winter months. So does an awful lot of other kinds of food, because plants have slowed down or stopped altogether. That leaves three options. One is to change diet: blue tits and great tits eat invertebrates, especially caterpillars, in the warmer months, but switch to seeds and other plant material in the winter – and when spring comes round again they switch back. Other species go somewhere else: there are very few flying insects around in winter and swallows can feed on nothing else – so, as we've seen, they leave Britain and fly south to places where such resources abound. The other option is to sleep through it.

Torpor, or shutting down, is a tactic used by many mammals and a few birds. Hibernation is a more extreme form of this: it's generally agreed that there is a continuum of shutdown that reaches its peak in prolonged hibernation. Hummingbirds slip into a nightly torpor that involves a far greater shutting down than mere sleep, but only one species of bird goes in for something close to full hibernation. That's the common poorwill, found in British Columbia in Canada down to southern Mexico. They are night-flying hunters of flying insects, related to the European nightjars, a bird that arrives in Britain in spring after wintering in eastern and southern Africa. Some common poorwills also migrate, but many take the non-flying option and enter an extended state of torpor, hiding in crevices in rocks and waking up in the spring when there are insects on the wing again. This is roughly what Gilbert White imagined the swallows did, so he wasn't stupid at all – just wrong.

Many mammals go into a state of torpor to tide themselves over difficult times, but only three groups of them go in for the full hibernation: a sleep that lasts, with occasional interruptions, from late autumn until they wake up – perhaps emerge is a better term – when the spring comes round once again. All three groups can be found in Britain: insectivores, including hedgehogs, rodents, including dormice, and bats.

Hibernation is an extreme state. That's what makes the consequent waking up in the spring so remarkable – all the more so since such an awakening is by no means guaranteed. Hibernation in mammals is as dangerous an option as long-distance migration in birds: there is no guarantee that either option will bring you unscathed into spring. Travelling for thousands of miles has obvious perils especially in a changing world of ever-expanding human population. But playing dead for five months is not the cushy number it appears at first sight.

A mammal in a state of genuine hibernation seems dead. That's the whole point. It goes as near to death as it dares, holding on to life by a thread, attempting to get through the winter as if it wasn't physically present. You can take a hibernating mammal in your hand and you might as well be handling a dead one. Its breathing is imperceptible. It shows no response to any external stimulus. Examine it more closely and you'll find that the heart has almost stopped and the body temperature has dropped right down: the chill of not-quite death. It's still generating its own heat, but it doesn't need all that much of it to sustain life. Digestion has slowed almost to a halt. Electrical activity in the brain is down by 90 per cent.

Hibernation is not continuous. It's broken every few weeks. The animal will wake, maybe eat, sometimes from stored food, maybe drink, and probably defecate. It's been suggested that this rather perfunctory physiological activity doesn't wholly explain this brief awakening. Perhaps hibernation needs to be broken before near-death becomes actual death. It's also been suggested, paradoxically, that a hibernating animal is not actually sleeping and so gets into a state of sleep-debt: in other words, it wakes up in order to get some sleep, before once again slipping into full hibernation.

Hibernation, then, is a mysterious state. It takes place at a time when much of the world is in a kind of slumber: deciduous trees, having got rid of their leaves, shut down their photosynthesising activities; many other plants exist only as seeds or in their underground parts. Many birds have simply flown away. In secret places many mammals are as good as dead – but the whole world will come alive again with the arrival of spring. The world seems sometimes to be in a near-death state in winter: but when kissed by the spring it annually awakes.

And when a dormouse awakes it changes from a little ball of snoozing fur into a devastatingly dynamic creature, quite unlike the dormouse at the Mad Hatter's Tea Party in *Alice's Adventures in Wonderland*, who keeps going back to sleep, even though the Hatter pours hot tea on its nose and stuffs it into the teapot. Once a real dormouse is awake it's full of beans. I attended a dormouse survey at Bradfield Woods in Suffolk, where a very successful reintroduction programme[1] had been established; they were trying to count them and measure the extent of their success. This involved examining a series of benign traps, in which the dormouse could be constrained for a brief while, until it could be caught, weighed, sexed and released. The first one we tried ran straight up the handler's arm like a streak of ginger lightning, into the tree and up the branches as if it was

---

[1] Another Suffolk Wildlife Trust project.

riding an express escalator. It was never seen again, at least not that day.

Dormice are tiny things. They live in woodland canopy, they're good at hiding and are all about speed and agility. It's more or less impossible to see them under normal circumstances: if your local wood is jumping with dormice you'd never know unless you could read their signs, like the smooth rims they leave around the tops of nibbled hazelnuts. Their length without tail is 6–9cm and they weigh around 40g: there really isn't very much of them at all. They can be found all over the Old World and there are about three dozen species. The one native to Britain is the hazel dormouse; there are two non-natives, introduced species: the garden and the surprisingly named edible dormouse. Dormice were once valued as a savoury appetiser and, still more surprisingly, as a pudding, dipped in honey.

In autumn hazel dormice load up on nuts, seeds and berries, to build up fat reserves before hibernation; there's not much to a dormouse so it doesn't take much to finish them off. A good fat layer is their insurance against winter. Once loaded and as the weather turns cold, they drop down from the canopy and build themselves a nest at ground level in a well-hidden place. They curl up inside this structure, tail over face, and hibernate. They are as good at torpor as they are at frenzied activity: in any month of the year, in times of shortages and hostile conditions, they will go into torpor for a few days or even longer. They might spend as much as seven months of the year asleep.

But spring comes in the end and with it an explosion of activity. Enchantingly, the first food they take on waking up is usually spring blossoms, hawthorn for choice, also oak. They shift gradually to invertebrates, especially caterpillars, as the spring advances and there is more of such prey available. Out of sight in the canopy these tiny rodents – you could hold a couple of dozen in your cupped hands – celebrate the spring with as much liveliness as any other creature of the woods: not sleeping but living at the highest possible intensity. That's the great paradox of hibernation: it's actually all about the waking up. It's not the sleeping that matters but the twelve-month plan for staying alive and attempting to become an ancestor. They live for the spring; they sleep so they will be at their best in spring.

Hedgehogs are busy creatures. Their nightly forays after invertebrates involve a lot of searching and snacking, as well as the occasional invasion of tents. They are great snufflers, pushing their way through leaf litter, with good senses of smell and hearing for catching the creatures they disturb. They are opportunistic, and will take carrion when they find it, along with eggs and nestlings of ground-nesting birds. They are less notorious for sleepiness than dormice, but they're serious and effective hibernators. As the temperature drops and their food of choice – beetles, earthworms, caterpillars, slugs – becomes scarce, they find themselves a discreet spot, make themselves a nest of fallen leaves and retire.

Their body temperature drops from 35 degrees to around five or even lower. Their heart rate drops from

190 beats a minute to twenty. And they breathe once every couple of minutes. They wake a few times in the course of the winter, but may not even leave their nests when they do so. And then spring comes round and they are agog for food again, fuelling up after a long winter of deprivation. That's when they seek to make more hedgehogs, for in spring even hedgehogs are filled with thoughts of love. If all goes well, they will find a partner and mate — precisely in the way the old joke claims: very, very carefully.

My mother always remembered an incident of my babyhood, when I was in my pram in the garden of a friend, sitting up and looking out. My mother followed the direction of my gaze — and found a mother hedgehog walking across the lawn followed by a train of four babies. I have no personal memory of this, but — who knows? — perhaps it made me who I am.

Female bats celebrate the great awakening by becoming pregnant within a day or two — without needing the attentions of a male. For them the spring is all about giving birth and rearing young — almost always just the one, confusingly referred to as a pup. The males have no involvement at this stage of the year, foraging by themselves, and roosting alone or with a few other males. For them the time of love is autumn, when the year is spilling over into decline, the supply of flying insects is falling off and hibernation is not far away. That's when a male bat does his courting, seeking out females with a special call. Once they've mated the job is done, so far as the male is concerned. For the female it's hardly begun.

She stores the sperm in her uterus and oviduct, keeping it safe all winter. She's not pregnant: but she has the means to fall pregnant when the moment is right.

As the nights get colder, bats find safe places and go into torpor, waking up on warm nights to forage. As winter advances the periods of torpor get longer. As spring makes its annual series of advances and retreats, the reverse process takes place: more and more busy nights. With the waking comes ovulation and fertilisation by the long-stored sperm: the process is called delayed implantation. The newly pregnant females seek out maternity colonies, later find nursery roosts and towards the end of spring the pup is born. Six weeks later it will be tentatively foraging for itself. Soon enough, it's time to look for hibernation sites: places with a cool and constant temperature.

The commonest of Britain's eighteen bat species are the three species of pipistrelles — and here's a rum thing: there are hardly any known pipistrelle hibernation sites. There aren't nearly enough sites to account for the numbers of pipistrelles, so there's a mystery about one of the commonest mammals in Britain. Wherever they go, there are still plenty of them to be seen in the spring, and a bat detector will pick out the wet slap of the echolocation calls as the as-yet-unneeded males and the newly pregnant females skim through a light to scoop up a preoccupied moth with a neat waft of the tail and continue the great awakening of spring.

Other mammals are less committed to hibernation than these three groups but are still part of the continuum: badgers can pass days and weeks asleep in between bouts of foraging. Squirrels are far less active, but will rouse themselves to look for their caches of nuts. The water vole population can drop as much as 70 per cent in the hard winter – older adults and underweight, underprepared first-winter animals are the most vulnerable. Water voles spend a fair amount of the winter in bouts of torpor but come the spring they are fully active again and eager to make good the winter losses.

Frogs are amphibians and that gives them a double problem when it comes to wintering. They need to be protected from dryness as well as from the cold and look for damp places underground or beneath a rotting log. They can also over-winter in the mud at the bottom of a pond, which seems like the best plan, but it has a potential problem: if it freezes over completely, gases produced by dead leaves rotting at the bottom of the pond get trapped and that can be lethal (so if you have a garden pond, any frogs below will appreciate your breaking the ice). Frogs are active very early in the year – in the far south-west of Britain in January, and those with a keen eye will be finding frogspawn soon after. Toads leave it a little later: and on mild nights in early spring they will sometimes migrate in large numbers, moving from hibernation sites to the ponds, ditches and lakes where they breed. I have joined volunteers helping toads at places where their traditional migration routes cross roads. Once they make it, the males will attempt to mate with just about anything, including each other.

As we have seen with butterflies, insects can get through the winter in any one of the four stages of their metamorphic lives: queen bumblebees, queen wasps, queen mining bees and some hoverflies wake early as good-to-go adults. Some species stay active. At the bottom of ponds, even when these ponds are covered with ice, the larvae of dragonfly carry on as busy hunters. In spring, those that are ready emerge from the pond, climb up the stem of an emergent plant and then, in one of the great everyday miracles of nature, complete the transformation into a shimmering four-winged adult. As winter becomes spring, these underwater creatures become aeronauts on dazzling wings.

The avoidance of winter is something we humans can empathise with. We have all woken on a January morning with every part of our selves in rebellion, wanting to pull the covers back over our heads and sleep, not just until noon but at least March: to abandon all responsibilities and cares and sleep the sleep of the righteous until the days are a little longer and a little warmer and a great deal brighter. Humans can't move into true hibernation but there is evidence that winter torpor was part of life in some peasant societies of the north, in places marked by extended darkness, prolonged cold and shortage of food. In some parts of Russia families would camp down by the stove, taking it in turns to stay awake and feed it, waking only briefly each day to take on bread and water and presumably to urinate and defecate. It's possible early hominids slept away much of winter: humans are by evolution a tropical species not built for winter, and hibernation is not wired in to our genes – but in some cases humans have adopted the next best thing.

I was talking earlier about journeys to the stars, which humans might accomplish in a series of generations, in the manner of the migration of painted lady butterflies. Another option for such impossibly distant travel is a form of hibernation: to fly to some far-off planet in the way a dormouse spends the winter. It takes eight months to get to Mars under our best modern technologies: how would such unconscious astronauts cope with the great awakening?

Signs of spring
April 2024

- 9   Jackdaw chasing stoat from nest site
  Loud pair of green woodpeckers
- 10   Three Cetti's warblers in 400 yards of river
  Many more marsh marigolds
  Many sparrows in hedge in top field
- 11   Male orange-tip (butterfly)
  Budburst and flowers on several oaks
  Budburst on blackthorns
  Strong smell of water mint on marsh
  Evening, half a dozen bird species in full song at the same time
- 12   Speckled wood (butterfly)
  Herb Robert and self-seeded strawberry plant in flower
  Small white (butterfly)
  St Mark's fly
- 13   Swallow
  Singing willow warbler
  Brimstone (butterfly)
  Pub garden: small whites, orange-tips, brimstones
- 14   House martins
  Singing whitethroat
- 15   Beccles station: silver birch glade in leaf
  Cow parsley on path behind
  Patch of bluebells
  Greater celandine

16

Love in the spring

There's a strange English ritual that takes place in mid-February. It's all about joy in the rising spring and grateful thanks for love received and love given – but you wouldn't know that from the outward signs. These mostly involve men going to the local garage to fill up their cars with petrol and then entering the building to pay. They emerge with furtive, even ashamed expressions on their faces and a small bunch of red roses, for which they have paid £10. It's apparently compulsory to hold this bunch with the flowers pointing downwards.

This is, of course, St Valentine's Day, these days mostly just Valentine's Day: a celebration of the joyous identification of spring with love. None of the petrol-station males seek eye contact with another; all hold their bunches like a handbell they are trying to keep silent. And yet behind the absurdity there's something meaningful going on. It's likely these flowers will be happily received: received, indeed, with love – and why not? Spring is the season of love.

> In the spring a livelier iris changes on the burnish'd dove;
> In the spring a young man's fancy lightly turns to thoughts of love.

Bertie Wooster – see the epigraph to this book – could remember the first line. The line is known and at least half-remembered by very many people. A fair few might correctly attribute this stumbling 15-syllable phrase to the poet James Joyce always referred to as Alfred Lawn Tennyson. But I had to look it up before I knew that it comes from a narrative poem called *Locksley Hall* and that it's actually about rejection. Never mind: what matters is that the words link the two inseparables – spring and love – in a rambling phrase that snags in the memory and expresses a universal truth.

> O were my love yon Lilac fair
> Wi' purple blossoms to the spring ...

as Robert Burns wrote and perhaps sang. A festival was needed to express this, a special day that links love and spring, a day when it's accepted – or even required – that some protestation of love should be made. Perhaps such a day is particularly necessary for the English: a ritual that, for one day in the year, requires them to set aside their traditional embarrassment in the face of love.

And St Valentine's Day got the nod, perhaps because his feast day – 14 February, of course – falls at the right time of the year: the moment when we might even be persuaded to believe that winter is at last coming to an end. The date is another contender for the first day of spring, being roughly halfway between the December solstice and the March equinox, a day when the longer daylight, greater warmth and excited activity from birds is now unavoidable. Valentine's Day is traditionally said to be the day when birds start building their nests: perhaps this is code, because it is also the time of year when pigeons start frankly copulating in trees that have yet to acquire a modest screen of leaves.

But why Valentine? What has he got to do with love, or, for that matter, spring? That's not an easy question to answer. For a start there are at least three Valentines among the saints and martyrs of the early Christian church. The first is said to have ministered to Christians in third-century Rome in the face of persecution. His loving credentials are enhanced by the suggestion that he routinely performed weddings for soldiers forbidden to marry by the emperor. He was imprisoned and then executed. Naturally there are various tales attached to this bare narrative, to be believed or not according to taste. In one of them he cured the gaoler's daughter of blindness. In some versions of the tale, he wrote her a letter of farewell on the eve of his execution and signed it 'your Valentine'.

There is also Valentine of Terni. There is no record of any loving correspondence, but you can see his skull if you like. It's there in the basilica of Santa Maria in Cosmedin, in Rome – and it's crowned with flowers, a fine sermon on the limits of love, or, if you prefer, the limits of death. There are more relics of St Valentine in the Carmelite Church in Whitefriars Street, Dublin. The third Valentine was martyred in Africa.

It's possible that Valentine's Day has its roots in the Roman festival of Lupercalia, which took place on 13–15 February. It was about health and fertility: a festival of purification rather than unbridled licence. It took place under the patron deity of the month, Juno Februata, for whom the month is named; this perhaps has its origins in a Greek festival dedicated to the god Pan, who is always associated with sex, nature and music. February was the last month of the Roman year, so the festival is perhaps more a preparation for spring than a celebration of it. The festival is closely associated with wolves, and took place at the Lupercal, the cave where Romulus, the founder of Rome, and his twin brother Remus were supposedly suckled by a she-wolf. It was during the Lupercalia of 44 BC that Mark Antony, high priest of the festival, offered Julius Caesar a diadem and, with it, the right to become emperor. He refused this honour and was assassinated four weeks later.

Impossible to say if this festival of wolves led directly to the modern celebration of love on St Valentine's Day, but certainly Chaucer wrote about the day on the assumption that everyone knew what he was talking about. He wrote *The Parlement of Foules* (Chaucer was born in the early 1340s and died in 1400), which contains the lines:

> For this was on Seynt Valentynes Day
> Whan every foul cometh there to chase his mate ...

The poem recognises the tradition that on St Valentine's Day the birds all come together – to make a parliament, in short – at which they choose their partners. In Middle English there is an intriguing and perpetual confusion between brid and bird and bride: birds and young women and marriage all confused together, sometimes by accident and often on purpose, and Chaucer, like every good poet, loved a fruitful ambiguity. Young women were again birds in the 1960s before becoming chicks at the end of the decade; both locutions unacceptable today.

The cult of Valentine and his day gained traction in the era of courtly love. This was the notion that a young man could define his life by way of a profound, ennobling and usually frustrated love. Courtly love was a widely accepted convention in the Middle Ages, dating back from as early as the late eleventh century. It spilled into real life from the songs and stories of the troubadours, and was all to do with nobility, chivalry and often enough adultery, or at least adulterous longing. It was at the same time erotic and spiritual. The cultivation and pursuit of this kind of love was supposed to elevate the male lover. In the stories he often sets off to perform noble deeds in his lady's name, generally wearing some favour or love token from his lady as he does so. It was, then, meaningful and appropriate to send a love note, or, better still, a beautifully composed poem to the lady in question. It was a game and a convention, but also a matter of profound seriousness. The lady love object might well be the wife of the lord the knight served, or perhaps his equally unattainable daughter.

Courtly love could be silly, funny, witty, even slightly facetious, but it was at heart a serious business. It placed an idealised form of earthly love – erotic love – in the context of divine love. Loving and being loved by a living human had something to do with loving God and being loved by God. You could understand and reach the lofty planes of divine love by way of earthly love. The knight's reverential attitude to his own devotion allowed the object of his love to acquire a certain saintliness, even divinity. Spiritual and physical love co-existed, perhaps were not even separate things: and that is, perhaps, what lies behind the classic love tokens of St Valentine's Day. The sheepishly offered bunch of red roses doesn't just mean 'I desire you' any more than it just means 'I revere you'. It means both – and it makes a Lancelot of every giver and a Guinevere of every receiver.

This elevated theme of lofty loving has given us some of the greatest works of literature ever written. Chaucer and Petrarch are distinguished examples, but a still greater celebration of courtly love is at the heart of Dante's *The Divine Comedy*. This poem of a hundred cantos is set in spring: to be precise, on the night before Good Friday (so just before Easter) in the year 1300. The narrator, Dante himself, dreams of a journey, first through Hell and then through most of Purgatory with his wise guide Virgil. But as they come towards Paradise, Virgil, not being a Christian, can accompany him no longer, and his place is taken by Beatrice: Dante's ideal, once seen, forever loved. She leads him through the various spheres of paradise towards a final understanding of God and of life. The work ends on the line – and let's have it in Italian first, just for the love of it:

L'amor che move il sole e l'altre stelle.
Or
The love that moves the sun and other stars.

Which is a fair way beyond roses are red, violets are blue, but it's all part of the continuum.

In the conventions of courtly love, to love another human being – not just desire or admire or wish to become strategically and financially allied with – was accepted as a fine and noble thing, something that enriched all concerned. The ways of love were hard and frequently humbling, but they led to paradise. And so as spring began, you would send a message to your beloved, perhaps loving, perhaps even reproachful:

> And wilt thou leave me thus?
> Say nay, say nay for shame,
> To save thee from the blame
> Of all my grief and grame;
> And wilt thou leave me thus?
> Say nay, say nay!

This from Thomas Wyatt, who supposedly had a relationship with Anne Boleyn before she married Henry VIII, a dangerous liaison if ever there was one. He was, then, rather too late for the height of courtly love, but he wrote in the context of that tradition, producing poems about the pain of loving a distant ideal, a *princesse lointaine*. So let's pause for a moment as Wyatt remembers, in another poem, a moment of realised love: a moment of earthly paradise:

> When her loose gown from her shoulders did fall,
> And she me caught in her arms long and small,
> And therewith all sweetly did me kiss
> And softly said, 'Dear heart, how like you this?'

Every Valentine's Day should end like this. And no doubt most do.

Though perhaps that's not always such a fine thing in the long run. In *Hamlet* Ophelia sings of Valentine's Day. Her father has been murdered by Hamlet himself, and this, added to the inconstancy of Hamlet, her on-again-off-again admirer, has driven her to breakdown:

> Tomorrow is Saint Valentine's Day,
> All in the morning betime,
> And I a maid at your window,
> To be your Valentine.
> Then up he rose, and donned his clothes,
> And dupped the chamber door,
> Let in the maid, that out a maid
> Never departed more.

The custom of giving sweets and cards and flowers on St Valentine's Day grew in popularity in the eighteenth century. A collection of verse, *Gammer Gurton's Garland*, of 1784, contained the classic quatrain:

> The rose is red, the violets blue,
> The honey's sweet and so are you.
> Thou art my love and I am thine,
> I draw thee to my Valentine.

Though in fact the coupling of roses and violets can trace its origin back to Spenser and *The Faerie Queene* of 1590:

> In a fresh fountaine, far from all men's vew,
> She bath's her brest, the boyling heat to allay;

> She bath'd with roses red, and violets blew,
> And all the sweetest flowres that in the forest grew.

The custom of sending messages and gifts of love became widespread from 1840, after Rowland Hill had invented the postage stamp and it was possible to send message of love to any *princesse*, however *lointaine*, so long as you knew her address. In 1860 Cadbury's, the chocolate-makers, introduced a range called Fancy Boxes: the heart-shaped one was a must for Valentine's Day, an unambiguous message of love – which brings us back to the garage and the shifty purchase of roses red.

The further north you live in the northern hemisphere – the more acutely seasonal the rhythms of your life – the more reason there is for falling in love in spring. Research indicates altered dopamine levels with the arrival of spring: dopamine is a neurotransmitter and hormone associated with motivation, movement, learning and pleasure. But which comes first: the stimulus or the transmitter? The change or the pleasure?

Certainly the arrival of spring provides all kinds of stimulating changes. People can be outside for longer, without needing to be active to keep warm. What's more, they can start taking a few clothes off: and as more is revealed the more interesting and attractive people become – especially if you already found them interesting and attractive when fully wrapped up for winter. A parcel of delight is being unwrapped before your eyes – and with fewer clothes yourself, you too are more in the mood. Here is another form of spring awakening.

Humans do not have times of the year in which they are unable to reproduce: physiologically at least, humans of the right age are always capable of doing so. But spring is the traditional time for giving birth, for it is the stork that traditionally brings babies, and storks arrive in the spring. Until recently – and then with great help – storks hadn't bred in the UK for around 500 years, so the tradition of baby-bringing storks is likely to have been borrowed, along with Christmas trees and other ideas about childhood, from Germany. Here, in the right places, storks still nest on buildings and among people, arriving noisily and obviously in March. The annual arrival of spring babies implies conception in the high summer: and that too makes sense: fall in love in spring, consummate your love in summer. In rural communities of past times, privacy was a rare thing, especially in winter when many people must be contained in the same small dwelling, with access to a single source of warmth, going out as little as possible. But in summer, outdoor lovemaking is not only possible but desirable.

The idea of springtime love is inevitably found in films. *Easter Parade*, a film of 1948 with Fred Astaire and Judy Garland, is a glorious example. Fred, playing Don Hewes, is abandoned by his partner, Nadine, played by Ann Miller. He tries to persuade her to stay with him, and sings:[1]

---

[1] Words and music by Irving Berlin.

> The thrill that comes with spring
> When anything
> Can happen –
> That only happens with you.

But it's no good, she's off. He has a few drinks and declares defiantly that he can take any girl and make her a star. He tries to turn Hannah Brown, played by Judy Garland, into a Nadine clone and it's a disaster. So he changes tack and plays to her strengths: eventually they become a howling success – professionally at least, because that's the way Fred/Don wants it. Then they have an intimate dinner and she sings to him:

> The thrill that comes with spring
> When anything
> Can happen –
> That only happens with you.

And Fred asks: 'Why didn't you tell me I was in love with you?' Perhaps all films should be like that.

Or maybe they should be like *Notting Hill*, a film of 1999 in which Hugh Grant, as Will Thacker, a pleasant nobody running a bookshop, meets and falls hopelessly in love with a film star called Anna Scott, played by Julia Roberts, a modern *princesse lointaine*. Dalliance is followed by disaster and despair: she's gone, she's gone – what's the point of anything? It's autumn and the days of sunlight and beauty are over. Then follows a virtuoso bit of cinema in which Grant walks through the seasons, all along Portobello Road and its open-air market in Notting Hill in London, a sequence that lasts about a minute and a half while we listen to Bill Withers singing 'Ain't No Sunshine'. It seems to be one single shot, though in fact it's four shots seamlessly linked. Grant passes a heavily pregnant women, his sister with her latest love and a stall selling all the fruits of autumn; he walks on into rain and then snow, and now people are buying Christmas trees. On he walks and the weather improves, and suddenly there are spring flowers on the stalls, his sister is breaking up with the boyfriend and the woman at the beginning of the sequence now has a fine baby in her arms.

Time has passed, it's spring again: there must be a new hope, must there not? And then we learn that Anna is back in London, and we can already guess that, soon enough, all will be right with the world and we'll see Julia's smile again. Spring has taken away the world's troubles and brought back love: as it always does: as if we ever doubted it would.

Spring and love are forever united. The Beatles sang 'Here Comes the Sun' on the 1969 album *Abbey Road*. The song was written by George Harrison: and in its course Little Darling learns unequivocally that it's all right. Let's have one more song: 'All the Things You Are' by Jerome Kern, lyrics by Oscar Hammerstein II, for the 1939 musical *Very Warm for May*. Just about everyone who can sing jazz has recorded it at some time, though the best version is probably by Ella Fitzgerald:

> You are the promised kiss of springtime
> That makes the lonely winter seem long ...

But the best evocation of the true madness of love and the true madness of spring – and their inseparability – is *A Midsummer Night's Dream*. Midsummer night in the northern hemisphere is the June solstice, so in modern reckoning it's not so much the middle of summer as the end of spring: the peak of spring: the very last day and the moment of spring's supreme achievement.

It's midsummer according to the traditional reckoning that makes May Day the first day of summer and the solstice is the mid-point of the season. Fair enough: no need to be pedantic about these things, especially as this book regards spring as the period of awakening and flowering and singing and courting that takes place between the December and the June solstices.

And I have never seen the *Dream* as a play about the lazy, hazy, crazy days (and nights) of summer. Rather, it portrays the hectic madness of spring. The play is about falling madly in love, not about loving in a fully realised grown-up kind of way. We can see how grown-up love works, with the dignified affection of Theseus and Hippolyta: but once the four lovers leave the city and the civilised places of humanity, they enter the forest and all that sensible stuff is forgotten. The male lovers are both passionate for Hermia, and a moment later both equally passionate for Helena. That's spring for you: you never know when you're going to be affected by a love potion. The madness of the night, of the season, even affects the fairies, who you might have thought beyond such matters. The king and queen of the fairies are estranged after a preposterous but deeply felt row. Titania, the queen, falls in love with Bottom the weaver, a lowly fellow with a good heart. Out of pure devilment he has been given the head of an ass, but that only makes him more lovely in the eyes of the besotted queen:

> Come, sit thee down upon this flow'ry bed,
> While I thy amiable cheeks do coy,
> And stick musk roses in thy sleek smooth head,
> And kiss they fair large ears, my gentle joy,

I have always loved the way that Bottom is the only character in the wood who behaves with dignity and restraint, never for a moment taking advantage of the queen's passion for him. Eventually the night of madness comes to an end, the solstice has passed, summer and the time of fruiting and fledging and weaning has arrived, the lovers all end up with the right partner, Bottom is translated back to his familiar form, Titania loves her lord again and Puck, the maestro of the mischief of spring, is left to sum it all up:

> Jack shall have Jill;
> Nought shall go ill;
> The man shall have his mare again, and all shall
>   be well.

Of course it will: for this moment, both of enchantment and of unenchantment, is the very achievement of youth and hope and spring. And love.

Signs of spring
April 2024

- 16 Cuckoo – woken up at six by call
- 17 Cranefly
Many cuckoo pint in flower
Budburst on alders
Eddie delivered a lamb and tended hours-old piglets at Clinks Care Farm
- 18 Highland cattle returned to the next-door field
- 19 Cetti's warbler and whitethroat singing in the rain
Swallow
- 20 Glowering gorse all over the Brecks
Road before Stansted Airport full of cowslips
- 23 Road back from Stansted lined with flowering hawthorn, also broom and gorse in flower

Oological spring

We needed to use the trailer. It was full of wet straw and horse shit, all ready to be delivered to a nearby market gardener. It was early March, a cold day bright with the promise of spring. It felt good to be doing useful tasks on such a day. Cindy, my wife, adroitly backed the vehicle up to the trailer; I straddled the coupler to guide her over the last few inches – and then it happened. In my peripheral vision I saw a small brown bird fly from the middle of the offside forewheel of the trailer. I asked Cindy politely to halt, went to inspect the wheel – and saw a vista of heaven. Five heavens, in fact, five individual heavens, five blue treasures that mirrored the sky:

'Cind!'
'What's the problem?'
'There's a robin's nest in the wheel of the trailer.'

We looked at it together: a neat cup of dried grass, dead leaves and moss, lined with hair I had groomed from the horses. And in it, five eggs, coloured with an inexplicably joyous shade of blue. Each one was the most perfect thing you have ever seen, not only in its actuality, what it was, but even more so in its promise, what it could become. So long as we didn't move the damn trailer.

Well, we didn't. We made other arrangements about the muck – horses will keep on creating it – the robins raised their brood, and so far as I know their descendants are making nests in the same garden to this day; we no longer live there. Robins are famous for eccentric choices of nesting sites. They prefer low-down spots, in undergrowth, tree holes and log piles. They are, as we all know, relaxed and confident around humans; they also have no problems nesting in and around human spaces, often finding funky places to do so. Abandon some no-longer-useful object outside or in an outhouse and it becomes a potential robin nest site: bonnet of long unused car, single boot, post box, broken hurricane lamp, pocket of gardening jacket and favourite of all photographers, an old kettle.

All that is great fun, but the eggs themselves take it to another level. The eggs bring out in their finder a sense close to reverence, for they are not only beautiful but breakable. I could have crushed that nest and its contents in my hand without effort. Here was nature before me: beautiful, indomitable, almost comically fragile, and utterly in my power. Like the thrush's eggs in the Gerard Manley Hopkins poem, the eggs of the robin looked like little low heavens. Eggs are part of everybody's spring experience, even if we only see the ones made from chocolate. The renewal of spring is best expressed as an egg: beautiful in itself and more beautiful still in its meaning.

We think we know what we mean by an egg, whether it's in a robin's nest or part of an omelette, but its meaning shifts according to context. An egg can refer to a single cell or to the whole damn thing. The egg cell or ovum is the female gamete or reproductive cell. The male gamete is sperm. The ovum is usually stationary while the sperm is mobile. When they combine they form a zygote: a fertilised egg cell. Once fertilisation has happened the process of cell division can start: the miraculous process of life and growth is off and running again. That is as true for a robin as for a human. We humans are placental mammals, which means we keep our eggs inside ourselves. (Non-placental mammals lay eggs just like their and our reptilian ancestors; they are the monotremes, the platypuses and echidnas of Australia and New Guinea. Their young are not born but hatched: like all baby mammals, they get fed on milk.)

A bird's eggs form inside the female in response to hormonal changes within her, rather than as a result of copulation. In the seasonal lands this is usually a response to the changes that come with the spring, greater warmth and longer days. This egg – or more often these eggs – increase in size and begin to form a yolk before moving down a passage – the oviduct – that leads from the ovary. It's there – if the female has copulated – that the eggs will be fertilised. This system can allow a female to produce a brood with more than one father. Potential fathers often try to ensure that they are the only begetter. Dunnocks, much overlooked birds you often see creeping about at bottom of hedges, are usually regarded as dull and colourless. Heedless of our opinions they go in for flagrant infidelities, so much so that before copulating a male will attempt to remove sperm from any past rival by physically removing it, a process known as cloacal pecking.

Once the eggs have been fertilised they continue to develop, first acquiring a membrane and the albumen, the proteins in the egg white. From there liquid from within the bird's body is added to the developing egg, and it assumes its finished shape. After that the hard shell forms from calcium carbonate, also within the bird's body; this comes from food. Once the eggs are fully formed they can be laid: and out they come, blunt end first.

The egg of a bird contains a yolk; it's there to nourish the embryo as it develops, for it must do so outside the body of its mother. The eggs of placental mammals (including us humans) need no such thing; the embryo takes its nourishment directly from its mother by way of the umbilical cord. External eggs give a parent a range of options beyond the scope of a placental mammal. For example, a female codfish lays eggs in millions, which are then fertilised by a male. After that the eggs and the resulting hatchlings – fry – must fend for themselves. The parents have nothing to do with their offspring once the eggs have been laid and fertilised. The creation of millions may seem highly wasteful, because most of them will be eaten by other species – but in the course of a cod's lifetime, if one single egg gives rise to a single mature adult, one that successfully produces young of its own, then the strategy has worked.

The same strategy of many eggs and zero parental care is adopted by the British species of frogs and toads, which spawn in ponds. Frogs will do so as early as January when the weather is mild: every resulting tadpole sets off on a journey with long odds against any individual making it to adulthood. Frogs lay their eggs in clusters, toads in long strings. One of the great advances in vertebrate evolution was the development of the impermeable egg: an egg that doesn't need to be laid in water, liberating the species from the ties of water and allowing them to be wholly terrestrial.

Reptiles were the pioneers, and the six British species lay eggs that are leathery rather than brittle. They seek out warm, safe places to lay them in: a clutch of grass snake eggs hatched out in our manure heap, which had grown to a generous size while the trailer was out of action. Some reptiles go in for parental care, but none of the British sextet.

Birds operate a different strategy. Parental care is required. The eggs need looking after and so do the offspring: for weeks or months and in some species for years. This can involve both parents, sometimes just the female – and, in a few, just the male; the female lays a clutch of eggs and moves on, leaving the male to do the rest. Whatever the strategy the first task is to incubate the eggs: sitting on them and keeping them warm and safe. If they get too cold the contents die. The shells have pores so that the developing embryo can take in oxygen. An egg is a nutritious thing as most of us know from personal experience; many other species will feed on them given half a chance. We are naturally on the side of the birds and their beautiful eggs, so we tend to call such feeders thieves and robbers; might as well call blue tits mass murderers for the numbers of caterpillars they kill in the course of every spring. Egg-feeders include pine martin, polecat, stoat, weasel, rat, fox, all species of crows, including jays and magpies, gulls and hedgehogs. There's a pleasant folk tale about rats that predate a hen house: one rat will grab an egg, clutch it to his stomach and roll onto his back; a fellow rat will then seize him by the tail and drag both rat and egg out to a safe place, where they will share the meal. Alas, it's not actually true; the story tells us more about humanity's appalled fascination with rats than it does about the rats themselves.

First break the shell. That's a task of varying difficulty for both would-be predator and would-be hatchling. Baby birds manage this by way of an egg-tooth: a spike on the upper mandible of the beak, which they shed soon after hatching. The tooth — outgrowth really — allows them to batter their way into the world. The predator must bash a way in. If you find a broken eggshell you can make an intelligent guess as to whether or not it was predated. If the shell was broken outwards, it hatched; if it was broken inwards, it was predated. A hatched egg will also tend to carry traces of yolk and white, a predated egg will probably be cleaned out. You can find broken eggshells in unexpected places; I have more than once found eggshells, apparently belonging to thrushes or blackbirds, on the pavement in suburban streets. Parent birds take the eggshells from the nest for reasons of comfort and hygiene; they may dump them a fair distance from the nest site, to give no clues to potential predators of baby birds. You will sometimes find two halves of an egg together, carried out by a parent bird in a single journey.

But which bird did these pretty shells come from? It's a fascinating question, but one that moves us into dangerous territory. The time of the year is a clue: some birds are early starters. Crossbills feed on pine nuts — pesto birds — and these are available all year round. The mandibles of their beaks cross over at the tip, an ideal tool for teasing opens the scales of a pinecone and reaching the food beneath. They will lay as early as February: if it's warm enough for chicks to survive the crossbills can feed them.

Ravens are also early starters: never mind their sinister reputation or their sepulchral gronk-gronk calls, they are a touching example of lifelong fidelity and, being already paired up at the start of the season, they don't have to go through mate-hunting and courtship. Long-tailed tits start making their exquisite nests of spider's web and moss in February but may not get down to actual laying until April. Herons will move into last year's nest as early as February and be ready to lay as soon as they have made essential repairs.

And, of course, the keen-eyed and knowledgeable human can diagnose the species of the bird from the eggshell. Or from the egg itself – but again we're getting dangerous. Let's just note that blue tits lay eggs of light cream with brown speckles, while great tits' eggs are slightly larger and whiter with more speckles. Perhaps dunnocks – once cloacal pecking is over – lay the prettiest eggs, an unbroken and (of course) heavenly blue. The eggs of carrion crows, a bird never averse to stealing an egg or two, lay their own in a pleasant combination of pale bluey-green with brown and grey splodges. The eggs of hole-nesting birds tend to be plain white; there's no need for camouflage when the nest is already out of sight. These eggs are more nearly spherical than those of birds that lay their eggs in more open places; it doesn't matter if they roll a bit because they have nowhere to roll to. At the other extreme you have guillemots, cliff-nesters who lay their eggs in the open with nothing most of us would recognise as a nest, and do so in vast, noisy, highly odoriferous colonies. Their eggs are exaggeratedly tapered, almost conical, and also highly variable in colour. That means the parent birds can recognise their own eggs from all the others around it, while the sharp tapering means that the eggs are less likely to roll over the edge if they are disturbed.

So let's return to that robin's rest in the wheel. The boldness of the bird and the originality of the nest site were wonderful enough: but the beauty of the eggs themselves was unforgettable. Eggs are things you want to cherish: beautiful and vulnerable. Perhaps – dangerous territory again – we take a slightly childish delight in them: they look as if they would be pleasant to put in your mouth, like the tiny sugar-coated semi-realistic eggs we give each other for Easter, but far richer in colour. Eggs are wonderful and they enrich our lives. They are – let us accept it – desirable objects. And people have been desiring them and acquiring them for centuries.

'I openly admit that I collected birds' eggs,' said Sir David Attenborough. 'And I knew when the right moment was when you could take one and the bird would lay another, so you didn't change the population. And I learned a lot from it.' Most of what he learned, I imagine, is a passionate engagement with nature: a profoundly personal sense of involvement in the processes of the year, and with it, a very special and deeply personal interest in the spring. Chris Packham went further: 'I wouldn't reprimand a young boy that I found climbing to a nest these days, I'd give him a bunk up the tree.'

Collecting the eggs of wild birds just for the love of it has been something people – especially boys – have been doing for centuries. You find your egg and then you prepare it for your collection by piercing both ends and blowing out the contents. The shell itself will last you a lifetime. The practice of taking eggs from the nests of wild birds was made illegal in the UK under the Wildlife and Countryside Act of 1954. In *Bill Oddie's Little Black Bird Book* the author supplies a brief ornithological autobiography, which begins as follows:

> May 1947: Found an egg in a nest, put it in a match box; put match box in pocket and sat on it. The next day – identified the bits of eggs shell – hedge sparrow.[1]
>
> 1947–54: Continued to pinch birds' eggs discreetly and unforgivably, but at least became an expert on identifying the species which had laid them.

---

[1] These days more often referred to as dunnock (the cloacal peckers).

Nowadays he'd have been quite rightly fined or possible locked up. 1954: Gave up egg collecting and *instantly* became a better person.

I think the point here is that Britain has changed, along with the rest of the world. There are far more people and far fewer birds: the British bird population is down 73 million from 1971, according to the Natural History Museum, so if everyone sought a passionate engagement with nature by collecting birds' eggs we'd soon have no birds at all. All of which is fair enough: but it does mean that one more route – and by no means an unimportant one – to aforementioned passionate engagement has been blocked off. I never collected birds' eggs myself, but I did own a copy of *The Observer's Book of Birds' Eggs*, and would look over pages that showed one marvel after another, as if I was reading an inventory of the treasure house at Cair Paravel, which the four children found in the course of *The Chronicles of Narnia*.

Eggs excite the passions. So does the act of collecting almost anything: stamps, coins, guns, football programmes, medals, vinyl records, first editions, Clarice Cliff ceramics, paintings, erotica, old cars, guitars. I like to think, rather snobbishly, that I am immune to such madness, but I do have an awful lot of books and a good few bits of wildlife art. There is something about having: and if you are passionate for nature, having a bit of it makes that passion deeper and more real – more acutely *personal*. And passionate. Once you've started there comes a desire for more, as you chase some kind of completion. Think of the glory of it: a definitive collection, and it's *yours*. Helene Kröller-Müller collected modern art in the early twentieth century: her collection includes 180 drawings and 90 paintings by Vincent van Gogh – and you can see them in the Kröller-Müller Museum in the Hoge Veluwe National Park near Otterlo in the Netherlands. It's a wonderful collection and it brings knowledge and joy to millions. Like many others I have good reason to be grateful for her drive to collect.

Here's another collector. Charles Bendire was an American army major, born 1836. He loved birds' eggs and collected them obsessively. On one occasion he climbed a tree to collect an egg – in some versions of the story under enemy fire – and safely descended the tree with the egg, a large one in his mouth. It was stuck: so he prevailed on one of his men to break a tooth so that he could get the damn thing out. Other versions say that the tooth was broken accidentally during the – apparently safe – removal of the egg. The story crops up in various forms whenever egg collecting is discussed: what baffles me is that in no account can I find what species of bird had been robbed. It's the first question any proper birder or for that matter, egger would ask, and surely the one that mattered most to Bendire. Anyway, he amassed a collection of 8,000 eggs which is now in the Smithsonian in Washington DC.

No doubt the collection helped to advance scientific knowledge. At least, one hopes so. Certainly the egg collections of the past allowed one major leap forward, not only for pure knowledge but also for practical conservation. In the 1960s Derek Ratcliffe studied the eggs of peregrine falcons, comparing current eggs with those from historical collections. He was able to demonstrate that the shells of modern eggs were substantially thinner than the old ones, and that the modern thin ones were unviable, being too easy to break. The cause for thinning was the reckless use of insecticides, in particular DDT, a chemical now banned in Britain and most other places. This was one of the chemicals discussed in Rachel Carson's *Silent Spring*. More on this in Chapter 23.

Egg collectors dignified themselves with the name of oologists, much as students of crop circles call themselves cereologists. Guillemot eggs were particularly prized for their odd shape and their individuality: a drawer full of wonderfully various guillemot eggs was worth serious money; in season at Bempton Cliffs in Yorkshire local adepts known as climmers would be lowered down the cliffs, where they would take eggs and sell them to the rich collectors on the top. (The most accessible seabird colony in Britain is at Bempton Cliffs; you don't even need to leave the shore to appreciate it.) In Britain the smarter members of the oological community belonged to the Jourdain Society, which was founded jointly by Lionel Walter Rothschild, the second Baron Rothschild, famed for his carriage drawn by a team of zebras, and the Reverend Francis Jourdain. Its members carried on meeting long after egg collecting became illegal, even though their meetings were frequently raided and members were fined and imprisoned.

It was finally disbanded in 1994. The Rothschild collection now belongs to the National History Museum, which has one million legally obtained eggs.

But illegal egg-collecting goes on. A tiny community of obsessives keeps it going, the illegality and the almost universal disapproval of their activities no doubt adding to the attractions. There is a faint whiff of the paedophile ring about these people: there is a story about one collector, finally confronted by police, saying: 'Oh thank God, now I have to stop'. Not every collector feels like that: in 1985 Charles Watson's collection of 2,000 eggs was confiscated, but that didn't stop him. In all he was convicted six times and paid fines totalling thousands. He died in 2006 after falling from a larch tree which contained the nest of a protected bird.

In 2022 I paid a visit to a quarry in Trimingham in North Norfolk. Here a colony of eight bee-eaters had established themselves and were enthusiastically nesting. The site was for a few weeks busy: here were unquestionably gorgeous birds which very rarely nest in Britain. That meant the eggs themselves were of incalculable value to collectors, so the site had to be protected on a 24-hour basis. On this occasion, the birds bred successfully and if any eggers tried to stop them, they failed. I have been to many other sites where rare breeding birds are doing what they can to raise a brood – and the sheer waste of time involved in making sure that they don't get robbed by idiot humans irritates me every time. Here people who love nature in the form of birds are trying to protect nature against people who love nature in the form of eggs. An egg is part of a continuing process, one that brings us more birds. It really shouldn't be something you want to keep – certainly not if it means that there are fewer actual birds to fill the skies and lay eggs. Let's leave the last word to William Blake:

> He who binds to himself a joy
> Does the winged life destroy;
> But he who kisses the joy as it flies
> Lives in eternity's sunrise.

Signs of spring
April 2024

24	Cetti's warbler in the garden
	House martins
	Holly in flower
	Eight swallows over small patch of water
	Brief cuckoo in the evening
25	Copse full of bluebells
	Oxeye daisies, campions in flower
	Reed and sedge warbler at Cley
	Very excited redshank, paired-up avocets
26	Reed and sedge warblers on the river
	Reed bunting singing
	Full volley of cuckoo calls
27	House martins over the river
	Very many Cetti's warblers on the banks
28	Budburst ash
	Swallows over Highland cattle next door
	Singing whitethroat
	House martins flyover
29	Butterflies: small tortoiseshell, common blue, small white, peacock, orange-tip
	Common blue damselfly
	St Mark's flies back
	Swallows entering stables
	Singing sedge warbler
30	More sedge warblers
	Germander speedwell
	Distant cuckoo

18

Agricultural spring

The ploughshares bit into the earth at my feet, the handles of the plough bucked and fought in my grasp but I won, just about. Giddup, Mary, I said. Easy, Fred, easy. Was this the greatest rite of spring of them all? I kept Fred on the correct line with my left, inside rein, correcting a slight tendency to step across towards Mary; Fred, who knew his job a good deal better than

I knew mine, leaned his massive shoulders into the collar. Mary, a few years younger, followed his lead and we left a line of good clean straight furrows across the agricultural landscape of Suffolk. Straightish, anyway.

We wouldn't have won any prizes in a ploughing competition, but the three of us had unquestionably ploughed, as the corduroy lines of damp earth staring at the sky made gloriously clear. It was supposed to be just a stunt for a piece in a newspaper, but it went surprisingly deep. As I suppose it should have done. I was, after all, taking part in an experience that defines our species: I was breaking the earth. Breaking it not for what I could take out, like a wild boar, but for what I could put in, like a human. I was breaking the ground so that it might receive seeds, so that these seeds might germinate, so that from the plants that grew from them the food of the future might be harvested, processed and, when the time is right, consumed.

I am a horseman and the task of persuading two Brobdingnagian Shire horses to do as I wished was well within my experience and capabilities. It was the plough I found difficult. But after a fashion I coped: and so, like our ancestors, I was able to use the power of living non-human animals to perform a task that is crucial to humanity. The three of us did so with greater strength than I or any other human could ever possess alone. With the help of Fred and Mary I was able to slice the earth and turn it over and savour the faint but heady scent of newly turned earth. And I knew that this scent was the very beginning of civilisation.

For this was spring and there are two tasks that civilised humans must perform in spring if they are to survive the winter and get through to the spring that follows. The first is to get seeds to germinate; the second is to get baby animals born. The name for those two tasks is agriculture.

First there was fire. The control of fire changed the trajectory of human development and set us apart from our fellow animals. The second great change was agriculture. (You can argue about subsequent great steps forever, but in passing I might suggest printing, industry and computing, and, while doing so, note the ever-accelerating pace of change.)

Agriculture was invented 12,000 years ago, in several places around the world more or less simultaneously; for European civilisation it happened most significantly in the Fertile Crescent along the Nile and between the Tigris and Euphrates, as seen earlier. And that changed everything. It meant that people could now live in permanent dwellings, and could have villages, towns and eventually cities. It gave security and a future, a confidence about living into the next year. Of course all of this could only be achieved by way of unrelenting labour: when God cursed Adam after he and Eve had eaten from the forbidden tree, he said: 'In the sweat of thy face thou shalt eat bread'. The story of the expulsion from the Garden of Eden is often interpreted as a parable about agriculture: exchanging a carefree life for one of unending hard work. At least for some.

Agriculture brought people together in larger numbers than ever before. Now civilisation could be established and developed. Agriculture also gave us the idea of commodities and resources: land, food, seed and livestock. Control of these resources was not only survival: it was power. Agriculture made possible the development of elites. We might define the first elite as the people who ate their bread without sweating.

The two tasks of agriculture are to domesticate and to look after. Both plants and animals have been domesticated across the years. In the process they have been changed radically and sometimes unrecognisably. Looking after plants and animals: two aspects of the same process, a truth I learned from Fred and Mary. Mighty horses (and mighty oxen) gave humans the power to cultivate the land more effectively than they ever could before; land management by humans still feeds horses as well as humans, even if they don't eat from the same dish.

You plough the land in spring so that you can plant it. Ploughing opens the ground up so that it can receive a seed, at the same time removing, at least for now, any competing plants. The principle of arable agriculture is that the land grows only the plants that you want; the word arable comes from the act of ploughing. In the last chapter of *The Origin of Species* Charles Darwin explained the competition for light and nutrients that takes place on an entangled bank; it's the force that drives the process of natural selection. The whole point of agriculture is that this struggle for existence is not permitted to take place. Natural selection is not permitted here. We humans do the selecting. We decide which plants will grow. We pre-select the winners and – when all goes well – we fix the result by way of hard work and constant vigilance.

The first plough was a forked stick dragged through the earth by hand, the bottom part of the fork biting into the earth. It was a scratch rather than a full 180 turning of the soil, but it was a start. I have seen, many times, the use of a more sophisticated implement called the digging hoe. This is a pole with a blade on it, the blade set at 90 degrees to the shaft. It is used to this day in many places where poverty or other circumstances prevent the use of a plough. The people of the Luangwa Valley in Zambia use digging hoes because the prevalence of tsetse flies makes it hard to keep domestic animals. You must break the ground yourself, and you do so by lifting the hoe above your head – an ancient and archetypal movement caught in paintings by Millet and Van Gogh – and bringing it down into the earth, giving it acceleration with your wrists, as a golfer does with a driver. But the wielder of a hoe relaxes the wrists just before impact to avoid breaking them.

The first iron plough dates back to 475 BC in China. A scratch tool pulled by oxen was a logical development, oxen being castrated male cattle. The scratch plough was developed into the mouldboard plough, a device that reliably cuts a long slice and turns it upside down. This process conserves moisture, aerates the soil and kills competing plants – plants we began to call weeds. Enemy plants. The process of ploughing brings nutrients to the surface, and aeration allows the soil to hold more moisture.

Ploughs were developed with wheels that gave better control over direction, an advance I was very thankful for. You need to hold your plough straight, in order to maximise the total area you cultivate, getting as many furrows in as possible. That way you maximise the productivity of the land. You also need to make your turn at the end. A headland turn – lifting your plough, making a 180 turn and coming back neatly alongside your previous furrow – neither overlapping it nor leaving a gap – is the trickiest manoeuvre in ploughing, and doing it well is the heart of good cultivation. I had Fred and Mary crossing their forelegs like dressage horses to make a turn that was economical and – almost – accurate ... and I was filled with delight that was 12,000 years in the making.

The difficulty in turning a plough literally shaped the land of our ancestors. A team of four oxen is much less agile on the turn than Fred and Mary, so the fewer turns you need to make, the more efficient you are in time and motion terms. Under the manorial system of medieval England, which developed from systems installed by the Romans, the land was cultivated in strips called silleins. These were 220 yards long, a furlong, and 22 yards wide, a chain. That gives you a long, thin piece of ground and ploughing it is much quicker than it would be for the same area of land in a different shape, say, a perfect square, 70 yards on all four sides. The sillein, 220 x 22 yards, is an acre, and that is as much land as an ox plough can cultivate in a single day on medium soil. They still use furlongs on horseracing; in the Anglophone West Indies they still casually reckon distances in chains: 'Just down the street, maybe a couple of chains'. But an acre is something that goes very deep: it is a measure not so much of land as of life. An acre means a great deal more than 0.4 hectares.

In the traditional agriculture of the manorial system people mostly farmed on a three-field system: in one field rye and wheat would be planted in autumn; in another in spring peas and beans, which fix nitrogen, while the third field would be left fallow. The person who cultivated these fields had an obligation to cultivate the fields of the lord of the manor, the seigneur, and to do so with his own plough and his own oxen, while the seigneur sweated not. This wasn't precisely land ownership as we understand it now: the lord could allow the land to be used by villeins because the king said he could, and the king had his own permission from God. God ordered the seasons, God sent the spring to warm the land and God chose the men to run the world on his behalf. What could possibly go wrong?

The plague, in the form of the Black Death, tore Europe apart between 1347 and 1351, creating labour shortages and preparing the way for the Peasants' Revolt of 1381. The manorial system was breaking down. The monasteries controlled a great deal of land, and that was important to the way society and agriculture operated.

The Franciscans went so far as to say that private property was against the law of Christ.

The power of the monasteries came to an end in England when Henry VIII pulled them apart, a job he had completed by 1540. The land he seized he sold on to finance wars and other royal ambitions: by doing so he added to the power and prosperity of the landed gentry: a class whose power and prosperity come from land and its cultivation and in many cases still does. They seem to have got over the idea that private property is against the law of Christ. Their acquisition of land enabled them to exploit the seasons and the bounty of the spring more effectively than anyone else in the country.

The name of Jethro Tull echoes in many minds, partly because of the eponymous band, one of the few that have ever had a top ten hit in 5/4 time,[1] and from half-forgotten school lessons. Tull was a Berkshire farmer, but a rather singular one, not the unbarbered rustic that the sound of his name conjures up. He lived in the eighteenth century and his great achievement was to work out how better to exploit the spring. His main invention was a rotating cylinder seed drill that was drawn by horses. To children in urban classrooms this always sounded rather a hoot: what's so great about that? And this affects me how? But it meant that seeds could be planted rather than scattered, safe from birds, and in straight lines. This made it easier to tend them and to take out competing plants, and also easier

---

[1] 'Living in the Past', 1969.

to harvest them. Agriculture had entered the industrial age: and it did so before the industrial age had extended to industry. Industry began in the fields and the farms.

The population of Britain trebled between 1750 and 1850, rising to 16.6 million. This drastic change was both driven by improvements in agriculture and helped to drive them. Wet land was drained, land was reclaimed from the marshes and fens. A great deal of common land was also enclosed, in a process that was mostly to the benefit of the elite. Ownership was now the concept that dominated agricultural and economic life. As the old rhyme had it:

> The law locks up the man or woman
> Who steals the goose from off the common
> But turns the greater criminal loose
> Who steals the common from the goose.

The growing trend of globalisation meant that by 1914 half of Britain's food was imported. That was necessary to feed a population that was continuing to rise, by now close to 40 million. But the First World War made food supplies precarious. Greater self-sufficiency was required during hostilities, and that meant greater efficiency. Farmers had to look beyond modest prosperity and comfort. New methods of cultivation were coming, and these would soon make arable farming unrecognisable. The internal combustion engine meant that the power and transport no longer depended on draft animals. And we'll look at that in Chapter 20.

SPRING IS THE ONLY SEASON

In the seasonal lands most animals wild or tame are born or hatched in the spring. It's the right time to come into the world: the temperature is warmer, the weather easier and, above all, there are increasing quantities of food available. There is also more daylight, which makes it easier to see predators coming and to run away from them. In spring a parent has the best chance of raising young to adulthood: start them off when resources are increasing rather than diminishing. Aurochsen, the now-extinct wild cattle of Europe, ancestors of all our domestic breeds, dropped their calves when the weather had turned and the grass was growing again. That way the mother could feast on new grass that powered her milk production, so that her calf would have nothing but the best. In the same way wild boars in the forests still choose spring for farrowing; the sows break away from their groups and give birth to a litter and suckle them.

Aurochsen and wild boars are the same species as domestic cattle and pigs: but over the centuries they have been modified by selective breeding. Humans have selected the animals they allow to breed, choosing the lucky ones for their docility, their tolerance of confinement and alien living conditions, their fecundity, their ability to thrive on imposed diets and their yield of meat and/or milk. As a result there have been immense changes to the animals themselves: a Tamworth pig and a Jersey cow don't look much like their wild ancestors. They seem at first glance – and at second – to be members of quite different species.

AGRICULTURAL SPRING

But for all the changes that domesticity has imposed on them, our domesticated mammals are still inclined to breed at the time of year that ensures the young ones will be born in this spring. Females come into oestrus at the time of the year that will produce spring babies: sheep in the autumn (gestation five months), horses in late spring (gestation 11 months). In traditional farming there is no reason to wish this any different: in mid-June, as spring spills over into summer, you can observe a lush flood meadow full of rich grass nourishing a herd of cows, each with a calf at foot: and it seems, at least at first sight, that human ambitions are perfectly in harmony with the natural rhythms of the year.

We have chosen lambs as the symbol of the new life of the spring: piglets and calves are not without their charms, but lambs are woolly and they gambol. They are also active almost from birth, an ancient trait developed to give them a chance against wolves and lynxes. Another trait that can't be domesticated out of our chosen mammals is their tendency to be born at night: at a time when it's hardest for predators to find them. They can run away from predators when they're only a few hours old, if they see them coming, but at the moment of birth they are helpless, so darkness gives them a better chance of survival. I was once present at the birth of a foal (out of my own mare Dolores) and it took place at 3 a.m. No wolf spoiled the event.

Sheep prefer the night, too. Unlike horses and cattle, they go in for multiple births: twins are common, triplets routine and quads far from uncommon. These sometimes get into horribly complex tangles in the womb and require human intervention to sort them out and bring them all into the world in an orderly fashion. My wife Cindy did a course in lambing; this required her to deal with a freshly defrosted dead lamb in a bag. It was a lesson in how to tell by feel if the right bit of lamb is being presented in a way that will make for an easy birth. If it isn't you must push against the contractions and reorganise the presentation.

Sheep came to Britain with arriving Neolithic farmers about 6,000 years ago. Their animals probably looked rather like the uncompromisingly tough Soay breed. Sheep were one of the first mammals to be domesticated: a moment's thought explains why. They are less dangerous than cattle, more tractable than pigs and less independent than goats. Sheep seem to be halfway on our side at the start.[2] Britain already had an active wool trade when the Romans moved in in 54 BC. The Romans were keen on sheep and added their own breeds to the mix. After their departure Vikings came and added yet more strains: there are probably more sheep breeds in Britain than any other country in the world. Some are suitable for difficult terrains, some produce copious wool, others are bred for meat. Enthusiasts love the rare breeds of sheep (Soay, Derbyshire gritstone, etc.) and will explain that this breed is 'rarer than the giant

---

[2] That explains the parable about separating the sheep (good) from the goats (bad).

panda'. This is not comparing like with like: may as well say that the Bedlington terrier is rarer than the Sumatran rhinoceros. They are just dogs or just sheep: different varieties of a single species, all of them artificially bred for the pleasure of humankind. Sumatran rhinos and giant pandas are good species and irreplaceable.

The wool industry was a mighty power in British life for many years and for a good reason: it's bloody cold in the winters of the seasonal lands, and the farther north you get from the tropic of Cancer at 23.5 degrees, the more you need something to keep you warm. Woollen cloaks kept people alive. East Anglia, where I live, was the heartland of the trade: which is why the place is full of churches, built in gratitude and glory by successful wool merchants.

These days we tend to make a distinction between two kinds of agriculture: livestock and arable farming. But traditionally the two were inseparable. You couldn't run an arable farm without livestock. Livestock, in the form of oxen and horses, powered the cultivation of the land. The manure from livestock fertilised it and allowed it to produce more food. This created a problem: how do you feed them in winter, when the grass ceases to grow? (Grass starts to grow at around 8 degrees C.) The answer is hay, as already discussed in connection with Constable's *The Hay Wain*. If you cut grass and store it, it will ferment and rot; but if you dry it first it will keep throughout the winter and, what's more, it will still be nutritious. Your herbivorous livestock will eat it and survive. Taking a hay crop in late spring was essential if the farm was to survive through to the next spring, when the grass started to grow once again.

Increasingly efficient forms of crop rotation gave farmers higher arable yields. That meant more space could be allotted to livestock. As a result, the Middle Ages made meat available more often to more people than ever before. Farming for meat grew increasingly important: people were now farming not just for means of survival but for a comparative luxury. This brings problems with it: keeping animals in confined spaces is more or less a guarantee of infection. Managing this possibility is at the heart of good husbandry. In 1755 Britain coped with the problem of rinderpest[3] by slaughtering 80,000 cattle, all sick or suspected of becoming so. It was a drastic move, but it was effective. People started to build barns with high ceilings and a constant through-draught; this improved hygiene and made for greater winter survival.

Meat production became increasingly important economically. The snag was – and is – that this is not the best way to maximise the production of food. Adam Smith, the great eighteenth-century economist and philosopher, said: 'A grain-field of moderate fruitfulness produces a larger amount of food for the population than the best pasture of the same size.' So when you hear about the extraordinary efficiency of British (or

---

[3] Rinderpest, or cattle plague, was very infectious with high mortality. In 2011 the United Nations Food and Agriculture Organization declared it eliminated; the second disease to have reached this state after smallpox.

almost every other kind of agriculture) you should be aware that it is founded on the premise that humans are unable to survive without meat, not as a treat but as a daily right.

Agriculture is a volatile and ever-changing business, responding eagerly to new technologies while at the same time being traditionally reluctant to embrace new philosophies. But the idea of the traditional farm has an important place in our hearts. A farm is not just where food comes from: it's where an ideal life can be lived. The old idea of the mixed farm – arable and livestock farming operating together – reaches us on a very deep level. We love the idea of the good old farmer with his hay and his corn and his cows and his pigs and his ducks and his chickens, and part of us wants to be him. We give children toy farms to play with, plastic cows and pigs and sheep and chickens. For a while – it seemed an eternity – *Little Red Tractor* was my older son's favourite video; animated drawings based on the books by Colin Reeder, narrated by Brian Glover: 'Coom on, Little Red Tractor!' I watched Stan's adventures on his anthropomorphic machine a thousand times. I also read, again and again, the unrelated *Little Blue Tractor* from Ladybird Books; and night after night he saved the cows and the pigs and the sheep and the chickens on the night of the blizzard. 'Little Blue Tractor – thank you very much!'

The idea of the kind farmer, out in all weathers to look after his many-headed flock, is part of us, part of the way we think about the countryside. We know that it's gloriously sentimentalised, but it also represents a certain kind of truth: what we believe the countryside really should be like. But it was a truth that already looked out of date when the bombs began to fall in the Second World War: and even more so when peace came and the prize for the victory was a terrible and frightening austerity. Food! More food! We must make more food! And so a second agricultural revolution began; we'll look at that in Chapter 20.

Signs of spring
May 2024

1. Sedge warblers along riverbank; in places every 100 yards
2. Three romping hares
   Lesser whitethroat singing
   Heron chicks calling from heronry
3. Jackdaw chicks calling from dovecote
4. Many warblers along river: sedge, reed, Cetti's, one garden warbler
   Flag iris in flower
5. Five jackdaws fly out of barn – successfully fledged

19

Spring at sea

When spring arrives, all the affected parts of the world get more sun. It gets warmer and there is more light. As a result the plants grow. As spring advances the conditions for photosynthesis get better with each passing day. We all know that happens on land, for we are land-dwellers ourselves and not even the darkest and dingiest parts of our cities can escape the blooming of spring. The same thing happens at sea, though that's less obvious to us humans. The extra warmth and the extra light make the maritime plants grow. Since we're not sea slugs the process is not of direct relevance to us: but it's an annual event that feeds the endless oceans and puts food on many a table.

Every food chain starts with the sun, barring those funky exceptions like hydrothermal vents. Food chains start because plants are able to use the energy of the sun to make food, as discussed in Chapter 3. (Good word: plants are autophagous, self-feeding.) The sea is no exception: a moment's thought makes it clear that it can't be, even though it doesn't make intuitive sense to us. We are accustomed to the idea that little fish are eaten by bigger fish and these are in turn eaten by even bigger fish. Cartoons tell us the tale: a little fish about to be eaten by a medium-sized fish which is in turn about to be eaten by a real whopper. The concept was shown rather more dramatically in a hideously fascinating drawing by Pieter Bruegel the Elder in 1556, called uncompromisingly *Big Fish Eat Little Fish*. It shows a beached monster fish being opened up by humans, spilling smaller fish from every gash in its body.

But what do the *really* little fish eat? What do the littlest animals of the sea eat? The answer is plants: mostly tiny plants that together make up vast colonies of plant plankton: phytoplankton. Many of the individual species are microscopic. You might think that this stuff doesn't have much to do with you, unless you eat a lot of fish, but it's important to everything that breathes.

Phytoplankton accounts for about 1 per cent of the world's plant biomass but for more than half the photosynthesis that takes place. Since photosynthesis involves taking in carbon dioxide and pushing out oxygen this is relevant to all of us who like breathing: phytoplankton is responsible for half the earth's annual production of oxygen. It also plays a significant role in carbon sequestration. There's a good argument for claiming that phytoplankton, in all its variety, is the most important stuff for the continuation of life on earth.

And it blooms in the spring. You can see long slicks of phytoplankton if you look out at sea from a height – a decent cliff, for example – on a day with good light: it looks like a curious alteration in the colours of the ocean. And microscopic though many individual elements of phytoplankton are, you can see them from space: satellite images of phytoplankton show bluey, greeny, milky patterns on the surface that look a bit like preliminary sketches for Vincent's *The Starry Night*.

These sleek slicks of phytoplankton feed the tiniest animals of the sea: what's called zooplankton. And all at once we have a food chain. Now little fish can feed on zooplankton and in turn be fed on by larger fish, etc., etc. Though it doesn't of course always work in that neat, progressive way: the tiny crustaceans called krill – most of them smaller than your little finger – make their living by feeding on plankton and they are the food of the blue whale, the largest creature that ever existed. There are no intermediaries in this short but melodramatic food chain. While admiring the blue whale we must accept that they owe their existence to phytoplankton: no phytoplankton would mean no blue whales, hardly any life at all in the sea, and immensely reduced possibilities for life on land.

And it all doubles and redoubles in the waters of the seasonal lands when the spring comes round once again. Spring is also the time for important alterations in the dynamics and the productivity of the sea and it's called upwelling. We have spent many of the past pages of this book considering the way that the same piece of land is unrecognisably different from one season to another. But the annual transition is even more drastic in the sea. That's because the sea flows as the land does not. The contents of the same cubic area of sea can be replaced by completely different water when the spring arrives, water that comes up from the deep with far more life in it and therefore full of radically increased possibilities for even more life. Surface waters are pushed offshore by the wind and are replaced by an upwelling of cold nutrient-rich waters from below. Many species are prepared for this and ready to take advantage of this annual bonanza. The phytoplankton blooms: everything else that lives in the ocean eventually profits from this seasonal change.

The process of upwelling is an important part of the action of the Gulf Stream. In *Ulysses*, Stephen Dedalus, teased about his reluctance to wash, answers: 'All Ireland is washed by the Gulf Stream.' This is part of an oceanic movement that begins in Florida and carries warm water north, bringing a milder climate to the lands it touches. Britain is far warmer than we are entitled to expect at such northerly latitudes. London is further north than Chicago, where I once watched an American football game in temperatures that were, with wind chill thrown in, around -25 degrees C. London is also further north than Minneapolis, where the shops downtown are linked by skyways to prevent customers from being killed by the cold; further north also than Calgary, Vancouver, Winnipeg, Ottawa and Montreal. The Gulf Stream arrives first at Britain's west coast, and that explains why the west coast of Britain is milder than the east. All this has consequences for life – life that carries on out of sight of almost all humans.

The larger photosynthesising species of the ocean we usually call seaweed; in formal circumstances they are benthic macroalgae. They also play a significant part at the base of the food chain. The annual species arrive in spring and the perennial species have a new surge of growth at the same time. They come in three main types: green (around 6,200 species worldwide), brown and red (both around 1,800 species).

They are food for many species of crustaceans – shrimps, crabs and lobsters – which are themselves preyed upon in the time-honoured way. Seaweeds can, of course, grow only where there is light, in the photic zones of the ocean; those that anchor themselves to the seabed tend to be found around coasts. Creatures as large as manatees – 4m long, up to 550kg in weight – feed almost entirely on seaweeds, though they are restricted to the Gulf of Mexico, the Amazon

Basin, the Caribbean and the coast of West Africa. Not enough year-round seaweed further north.

The spring abundance of seaweeds and phytoplankton triggers increases elsewhere. That makes it a good time for marine creatures to hatch out and take advantage of the seasonal largesse. This can result in sightings of large numbers of jellyfish: sometimes in numbers that fill fishing nets and clog the cooling mechanism of coastal power stations. There is a huge range of size in these animals: from a pinhead to the lion's mane jellyfish, which can be 2m in diameter at the bell while trailing tentacles 36m long. This species is the villain in the Sherlock Holmes murder story 'The Adventure of the Lion's Mane'; the author, Sir Arthur Conan Doyle, a doctor by training, made sure that the victim had a weak heart, otherwise he might have survived. Thousands of people are stung every year by jellyfish, with results that range between mild discomfort and death. They sting to immobilise items of prey and also in self-defence. There is a move to refer to jellyfish as sea jellies, so that the term fish[1] is reserved for backboned creatures, and not for starfish, shellfish, cuttlefish and crayfish. Jellyfish have an extremely complicated life cycle that may go through as many as five stages by the time they are sexually mature adults.

---

[1] There is no single class (we belong to the class of mammals) that can be called fish; those we informally call fish belong in four separate classes: ray-finned fish, cartilaginous fish, jawless fish and lobe-finned fish.

The effects of the marine spring can be read in rock pools, though it takes a good eye and a trained mind to appreciate this to the full. (The local wildlife trusts in coastal counties usually run expeditions to rock pools when good eyes and minds can be borrowed.) I have always been fascinated by the creature called sea hares, mainly for the beauty of the name. They come to shallow waters to breed and can be found in the tidal pools when the water retreats. They are called sea hares because of their rounded shape and because they seem to have two long ears. But they are a kind of slug, with an internal shell; they can be up to 20cm long but are usually less than half that. The ears are sensory organs correctly called rhinophores. They are seaweed feeders and in spring they come into shallow waters to breed. They are hermaphrodites; each individual can play the part of both sexes and do so at the same time, for they often mate in chains, each link in that chain both male and female.

The intertidal zones are full of unexpected wonders. I remember an occasion on the beach at Flamborough Head in Yorkshire at low tide, walking across an area of what I supposed was seaweed; it was, indeed, called hornwrack. But it wasn't a species of benthic macroalgae. It was an animal, or, to be accurate, a colony of very small animals, all belonging to a species in the phylum of bryozoans, or moss animals. They are filter feeders, each member of the colony genetically identical. My companion Anthony Hurd of the Yorkshire Wildlife Trust (fully equipped with the good eyes and trained mind that are so helpful on such occasions) referred to it as 'a faunal lawn'. It seemed to me that there was an important moral difference between walking on a plant and walking on an animal.

Out of our sight the fish of the open oceans respond to the seasonal changes with complex interlocking patterns of migrations. Those studied in most depth are inevitably the fish of commercial importance: herring, cod and tuna. The adults tend to leave the spawning ground for quite different feeding grounds; it's been speculated that they move away from their own young to avoid the possibility of eating them. Cod lay eggs by the million and can't recognise their own progeny; being somewhere else when they hatch is certainly a way of avoiding filial cannibalism. In the North Sea different populations of herrings spawn at different times: within a single species there are clear diversities of migration. The Downs population of herrings spawns off the north coast of France between November and January and then moves as spring advances to feeding grounds in the middle and the north of the North Sea. Red tuna spawn in May and June in the Western Mediterranean and then move to the Arctic.

There are three basic migratory patterns in fish: we have just been looking at those that are restricted to the sea, and these are oceanodromous. But the most famous fish migration is the anadromous migration of salmon: fish that live most of their lives in the sea but return to the fresh waters in which they were hatched in order to spawn; that is to say, to lay eggs and fertilise them.

Salmon set off on their journey to the sea in spring, but their far more famous journey back takes place in late summer and autumn and their leaping of waterfalls is one of the great sights in British wildlife. I've managed to catch that, but never managed a sight of a marvel that's perhaps still greater, and that one does take place in the spring. It concerns the third type of fish migration: which is catadromous. Eels operate in the opposite way to salmon: they mostly have their being in fresh water but return to the sea to breed, travelling downstream and out across the ocean to the Sargasso Sea, an area of the Atlantic Ocean bordered by four currents: it's a liquid version of an area of land bordered by four rivers. The hatchlings go through a series of metamorphoses before heading for fresh water in early April and driving upstream, sometimes crossing the land, sometimes doing so in gatherings of millions, several miles long.

There are still vaster migrations taken by still vaster creatures. In the spring humpback whales move north. Members of the Atlantic population spend their winters in the Caribbean and off Cape Verde in Africa. This is a time of sociability, of mating and giving birth: a sort of prolonged holiday. This means that as the year turns they are seriously hungry, and so they travel north to the food-rich waters of the Arctic, brought to life again by the forces of the spring. Humpbacks are sometimes seen from the British mainland, though you tend to get better views from Scottish islands. I've seen them myself on the other side of the Atlantic, in the Bay of

Fundy in Canada: and, really, a close encounter with a great whale is as near as I have ever got to unalloyed optimism. You feel that if you can be as close as this to something as big as that there can't be much wrong with the world. It sometimes takes hours for the feeling to wear off.

Bottlenose whales also move north. They aren't enormous by whale standards, though 11m is still a decent length. But there is a mystery about them as there is about all the beaked whales. That's because they are deep-sea animals, feeding on squid, capable of prolonged submersion. They must, of course, come to the surface to breathe, but they tend to do discreetly. They remain wonderfully unknown animals.

Northern right whales also head north in the spring – those that are left. Their name tells a sad story all by itself: they were so called because they were the right whales to hunt. They might have been designed for the convenience of whaling ships: they are docile by nature, they stay close to the coast, they feed on the surface by skimming and they have a high blubber content. That has two benefits for the whaler: a great deal of oil can be harvested from their bodies and they tend to float after being harpooned. This combination of desirable attributes almost did for them: whether or not they will ever recover remains to be seen. The International Moratorium on Whaling was introduced in 1986, a comparatively recent event in the life of a long-lived species. Population estimates put their numbers at around 350.

There is, however, a straightforward and pretty accessible way of grasping the fact that the spring comes to the sea as well as to the land. It's best done from an open boat about 50 yards from the shore and it provides what is perhaps the greatest multi-sensual experience of spring that you could find anywhere on land or sea. The sight fills the eyes, the sound is a glorious cacophony and the scent of the place is like the belching of the sea monster in the Bruegel drawing.

My favourite memory of a seabird colony came when we set off from Stonehaven on the east coast of Scotland. It was mid-June, the air was still and a great wet mist had dropped down over shore and sea, reducing visibility to about 20 yards. We were looking for whales and dolphins at the time; we knew we wouldn't find any but it was perfectly possible that the cetaceans would find us: they are creatures of great intelligence and curiosity and a small chugging boat might well have piqued their interest that afternoon.

We were out of luck, but no matter. It happens all the time when you go looking for wildlife: you are trying to find one special creature but your day is made by something quite different. That's how it was on that spooky afternoon. It was as if we and we alone were in possession of a small bell of light, one that we carried with us as we made our run along the coast. On the seaward side we looked for the blow, dorsal fin and tail flukes and found none. On the seaward side we saw a city: a vast vertical city of birds.

The cliffs were high and richly ledged and every square inch that would take a bird had taken a bird. They were the auks: birds of the open ocean, miniature northern hemisphere penguins that can fly, just about.[2] That's how they get up on those dizzying cliffs. We think that the birds we call seagulls are seabirds but they're not: they're mostly birds of coasts and shorelines. But auks have almost nothing at all to do with the land. Most of the year they are out on the waves, where they eat and sleep, feeding by pursuing fish beneath the surface with long dives.

But you can't lay eggs on the sea and in spring auks must come to land so they can raise their young until they can fend for themselves on the ocean. There were three species easily in view as we chugged gently past the colony. Most of them were guillemots; we have already discussed the immense desirability of their eggs in Chapter 17. Among them were razorbills, chunkier and with bigger, rounder beaks. Foolish creatures as we are, we always like to pick a favourite and I went for black guillemots: dapper, all black but for shining white wing patches, with bright red legs matched by a red gape. On the top of the cliff – preferring burrows to the open ledge – the puffins were nesting, out of sight. But all four species flew round the boat with their effortful flight, the puffins looking like bath toys powered by a wound-up elastic band.

---

[2] The great auk, now extinct, was flightless. Last sighting 1852.

SPRING AT SEA

Here was a skyscraper community, one that rose from the sea to the point where the top beetles o'er his base into the sea, birds from a few feet above the highest lashing of the waves to the neck-cricking heights at the top – all fed by the largesse of the sea.

But we must have one more sea, one more cliff, one more bird before I end this chapter.

I was on the extraordinary island of Alderney, one of the Channel Islands, one whose coast you could walk round in four hours. The seas here are notoriously volatile. Once again it was mid-June; and I had joined a party with a job to do. This involved landing on a bit of rock that sticks out of the sea: not an easy business in a four-foot swell. The idea was to time your departure from the boat at the moment the wave peaked, which meant committing your step half a second before that. I managed this without distinction or humiliation. Once on shore I feared my nerve would not allow further progress, but I pulled myself together and climbed fifty feet or so.

Once there I found myself sitting with a few thousand gannets: birds with dagger-bills and a six-foot wingspan, all regarding me with suspicion but without active hostility. And here's the miracle: they didn't all fly off. They choose these lofty, sea-surrounded places because nothing dangerous can get them there: therefore I wasn't dangerous. It was a deeply dizzying privilege.

I was there to assist Victoria Warwick-Evans to fit satellite tags to five gannets. I was wearing a hard hat and eye-protecting goggles: if you upset a gannet your glittering eye is where the dagger-bill is most likely to end up. Vick lassoed a nearby gannet with a noose on a short length of cane and adroitly put a sock over its head. This instant darkness induced a limpness response: my task in this moment of disorientation was to clasp the wings. This I did effectively if unhandily. Information about the bird was recorded, and then the satellite tag was taped to the bird's tail: the package was far too light to inconvenience so mighty a bird. And indeed, once tagged, the bird took to the air to make a few restorative circuits of the rock. We did this four more times, after which Vick dropped down the rock to write up her notes.

I stayed at the top. There were gannets on either side of me within touching distance: my touching distance, which was pretty much the same as theirs. But we sat there together without hostility. The din was marvellous, the smell gloriously appalling and all round me the birds flew, coming and going or simply taking a turn around the rock. It was like being in the vaults of heaven surrounded by angels. True, the smell might have come from the other place, but it was paradise enow for the gannets. Here was springtime at sea: spring at its height celebrated in sight and sound and smell. I could hardly have been more privileged had I taken wing myself.

Signs of spring
May 2024

MOUNT'S BAY, CORNWALL

- 6   Three swifts
  Clifftop flowers: three-cornered leek, red campion, bluebells, bladder campion, spring squill, tormentil
- 7   Sand martins excavating nest holes
  Flowering foxgloves
  Wall (butterfly)
- 8   Speckled yellow moth (day-flying)
  Kidney vetch in flower
- 9   Hobby
  Red admiral
- 10   Boat trip: Manx shearwaters, guillemot, razorbill, puffin
- 11   Whitethroats songflight
  Smooth sheep's-bit in flower
  Kittiwake colony
- 12   Green hairstreak (butterfly)
- 13   Stonehenge: many skylarks singing

20

Agribusiness in spring

You can't understand the revolution in agriculture that took place after the Second World War unless you've eaten Spam fritters. It's a more vivid experience if you eat them as they were served to me at Sunnyhill Junior School in Streatham, south London. The fritters were accompanied by one, maybe even two domes of mashed potato, which were served with an ice cream scoop, and a single dome, similarly created, of chopped cabbage. To make the meal even more delicious a ladleful of Bisto gravy was poured over everything.

Spam was first available commercially in 1937. It was (and is) processed pork and ham that comes in a sealed tin. It's already cooked, and contains added salt, sugar and water, the whole mixture bound with potato starch and preserved with sodium nitrate; the gelatine is produced by the cooking process. Each serving contains rather more than 25 per cent fat. You create the fritters by taking the cooked meat from the tin, so you have a pink cuboid with rounded corners. You slice it and then dunk each slice in a batter of flour and water or milk, preferably bound with an egg. You then deep-fry each slice in lard. This isn't wasteful; the lard left after frying can be used again (and again). Among Sunnyhill pupils this meal was graded a mild treat.

The year I first consumed this delicacy at school was, I think, 1956. Spam was a staple of the war that had ended in 1945: it's cheap, it keeps, it can be eaten without need for cooking or fear of botulism, and it feels and tastes quite a lot like meat. Rationing was introduced into Britain in 1940, the second year of the war, and it remained in place in some form or another until July 1954, nine years after the war's end. Food was not something anybody took for granted: the long shadow of austerity fell across every one of my school dinners at Sunnyhill ... and this was a cornucopia of self-indulgence when compared with the years of total war before I was born. Eating up was a moral duty, at school ruthlessly enforced.

For food wasn't just life. It was freedom. The German blockade of shipping during the war meant that Britain could import very little food: their tactic was to starve the British into surrender. Post-war security of the nation depended on self-sufficiency in food. Grasp that and you have a 50 per cent understanding of what happened to British agriculture after the war.

To understand the other 50 per cent you must understand another point: one that goes back 12,000 years, to the dawn of agriculture. It's a matter so deeply embedded in humanity's global culture that it's probably impossible to remove – and it's our soul-deep conviction that nature is (a) infinite and (b) infinitely hostile. We have always seen nature as a bottomless well: one that will never run dry. At the same time we see nature as our enemy, eternal, immortal and unrelenting. If we wish to remain on earth as living and breathing creatures we have no option but to wage war on nature: let up for an instant and all that we have worked for will be taken away. Agriculture is about the attempt to control nature. Our ancestors faced apparently insuperable odds as they tried to do so. That ancestral understanding of nature is part of our world today, despite all the evidence to the contrary – and it was central to the formation of agricultural policy and practice after the Second World War was over.

It was essential to make agriculture more efficient than ever before: to safeguard the nation from any future attempt to starve us out, and also to feed a post-war population that would soon be growing fast. To suggest that we should worry about nature would have been ludicrous, perhaps even treasonable. Nature can look after itself: it was the plight of the British people that mattered.

Spring was never the same again.

This was made clear in the Agricultural Act of 1947, to which all political parties agreed: 'The twin pillars upon which the government's agricultural policy rests are stability and efficiency.' This was to be brought about by 'guaranteed prices and assured markets'. Prices were fixed for cereals, potatoes and sugar beet 18 months in advance; guaranteed minimum prices for fatstock (livestock that has been fattened for slaughter), milk and eggs were agreed two years ahead. This and subsequent Acts made the farmer's financial life comparatively safe. Farm incomes not only rose, they became predictable. Farmers could invest in emerging technologies without fearing it would ruin them. The most important of these was the tractor.

Petrol-powered tractors first became commercially available at the beginning of the twentieth century but their uptake was on the slow side in Britain, farmers being a traditionally minded bunch. To acquire a tractor was to take a dizzying leap into the future: a large investment with doubtful benefits. But as the machines developed and capital became available after the war, tractors became the norm. This brought about a double change to the industry. Farms no longer needed horses to drive them, so there was no longer any need to use land to grow the fodder that powered the plough. That land could now be put into the production of saleable goods. Power, in the form of fuel, could now be bought in rather than grown. Tractors not only pull, they also power complex machinery; farms could now be run with a great deal less labour. Machines are easier to manage than people: cheaper, too, and capable of working longer hours. It was soon obvious that machines were more efficient when it came to turning land into produce. In the immediate post-war period the number of farms fell by 65 per cent, as the small mixed farms of pre-war became less viable and were swallowed up by bigger concerns. There was a 77 per cent decrease in farm labour – and, meanwhile, production went up four times.

Mechanisation was just a part of this. Better science was producing different varieties of agricultural plants. Plant breeders were creating new varieties of standard crops, wheat most obviously in Britain. These resisted fungal infections and were robust enough to withstand competition from other plants: those regarded as weeds. Cereal plants were now shorter stemmed, less likely to be knocked down and lost to bad weather.

One of the key advances was winter wheat. It's actually planted in the autumn, when it germinates. It remains in the ground throughout the winter, not killed off by hard weather, ready to resume growth as soon as the weather turns. Spring is no longer the time for ploughing: that is now mostly done between September and November. This minimises soil erosion. It steals a march on agricultural weeds, for the established wheat outcompetes its rivals. It's easier to manage and yet gives a better yield. It grows earlier and so makes more efficient use of moisture in the soil. It is harvested earlier, and so is at less risk from the rains of late summer and early autumn.

The transition to winter wheat was not just an administrative convenience. It was a marker event. With the creation of winter wheat humanity scored a significant victory over the seasons. We have, in a sense, turned autumn into spring and made winter a time of fertility and growth. There are downsides to this in terms of wildlife. Before winter wheat came in the fields were mostly left as they were once the harvest had been taken: acre after acre of short stalks, cut off a few inches above the ground, along with the seeds that had fallen in the course of harvesting. These fields of stubble were an immense winter resource for many species of birds, offering both food and shelter. Winter flocks of house sparrows exploited these fields in staggering numbers; the species is now in a state of drastic decline. Winter wheat is a significant factor in the falling population of British birds.

After the war farming became increasingly a chemical process as the chemical industry shifted from military matters to agriculture. Chemicals had been used in farming long before then: the difference was not in concept but in intensity and efficiency. In ancient Egypt they burned sulphur in grain stores to poison animals that would otherwise help themselves; in nineteenth-century Britain fields were treated with copper sulphate and arsenic to fight the animals classed as pests. The Irish potato famine of 1845–52 was caused by fungal infections and there were complex attempts to prevent this, notably by the creation in 1883 of the Bordeaux Mixture, a copper-based fungicide. But after the Second World War the use of chemicals went mainstream and global.

Chemical farming has two main aims: to make the land more productive and to reduce the impact of competing organisms. The first was achieved in the early twentieth century with the development of nitrogen fertilisers. The Haber-Bosch process, which allows the fixation of nitrogen and thereby makes nitrogen available to increase the yield of the soil, has been described as the greatest technological advance of the twentieth century. It meant that the available land could feed many more people than it could before. The human population continues to grow.

The other side of the agrochemical industry might be described as the war on spring. Spring, as we have seen again and again in the course of these pages, is a time of growth. Plants grow where no plants were visible a week earlier, invertebrates appear in what had seemed a dead land, and beneath it all the soil fungi grow as threads of mycelium. The agrochemical industry wages war on all these things: herbicides kill competing plants, fungicides get rid of fungi and pesticides kill animals that might otherwise feed on the crop. With the advent of chemicals humans were able to have spring on their own terms: on farmland – in Britain in 2000 that was 18.3 million hectares or 75 per cent of all land – during the season of growth the only things that can grow are the things we have chosen to grow. Winter-sown wheat wakes up as the spring advances and grows untroubled by competitors: the cattle leave their barns and feed on a lush monoculture of ryegrass that has been nourished with fertilisers.

The combined advances of new crop varieties and agrochemicals spread to the developing nations and was known as the Green Revolution; it drove the continuing increase in the human population. It was a time when humankind was bowled over by its own brilliance. In Britain it was a thrilling aspect of the transition from wartime austerity to comparative wealth. The United States was untroubled by total war but emerged from the Great Depression to unprecedented prosperity. Those post-war years of glorious optimism are beautifully expressed by Bill Bryson in *The Life and Times of the Thunderbolt Kid*, a memoir of his childhood in Des Moines, Iowa. One sequence in particular has stayed with me.

Bryson describes the annual emergence of a city council Jeep that saturated everything it possibly could in DDT: 'A fogging machine that pumped out dense, colourful clouds of insecticide through which at least 11,000 children scampered joyously for most of the day

... nobody ever thought to stop us or to suggest that it was perhaps unwise to be scampering through choking clouds of insecticide. Possibly it was thought that a generous dusting of DDT would do us good. It was that kind of age.'

The environmental movement emerged from these changes. There is room for debate on the big date that marks its start. Contenders include 1889 and the foundation of the Plumage League by Emily Williamson of Didsbury; her reaction to the slaughter of millions of birds to create feathered hats for fashionable ladies was, by 1904, the Royal Society for the Protection of Birds. You could perhaps choose 1872, the foundation of the world's first national park, this being Yellowstone in the United States. In 1916 Charles Rothschild established the so-called Rothschild List, which contained 284 sites 'worthy of preservation'; this was the beginning of the Wildlife Trusts[1] and was a very early recognition of the fact that places in nature need protection: that nature is not, after all, infinite. In 1945 Sir Peter Scott founded the Severn Wildfowl Trust, now the Wildfowl and Wetlands Trust, which in the 1950s ran a successful campaign to prevent the extinction of the nene, or Hawaiian goose. Greenpeace was founded in 1976.

But as you consider such things, time and again you are forced to come back to the date of 1962. It marked the publication of the most important book ever written

---

[1] There's one for every county, one for Scotland and one for London.

with the word 'spring' in the title. This was, of course, *Silent Spring* by Rachel Carson.

Carson, a marine biologist by training and already a best-selling author,[2] took on the subject of the indiscriminate use of pesticides, challenging the gleeful world view of pesticides as an unalloyed good. Her mixture of top-quality research and accessible style was compelling. The title itself commanded the attention, as we saw in Chapter 5. A spring in which no bird sings: as if the gates of Hell had yawned open before us. She used the two words as a chapter heading but her literary agent suggested she use them as the title for the whole book, and they spell out the nightmare vision implicit in the text: that the synthetic pesticides we use to kill animals we don't like – mosquitoes, fire ants and so forth – kill many other species as well. She referred to pesticides as 'biocides', a term that should come back into use.

Her revelations were a breathtaking leap into modern understanding of the science we now refer to as ecology, which might be summed up as the study of the interconnectedness of absolutely everything. She pointed out that substances like DDT, which became available for civilian use in 1945, don't just take out the target species. They kill many other species as well. Bees, for example. And butterflies. What's more, the substance, once used, doesn't then go away. It remains in what we now call the ecosystem. It accumulates

---

[2] *Under the Sea Wind*, 1941.

in the bodies of insects, in the bodies of those that eat insects, and in the bodies of those that eat the insect-eaters. Birds of prey at the top of the food chain are as damaged as mosquitoes. Carson pointed out that weakened ecosystems become vulnerable to invasive species. She also made it clear that using pesticides is not a finite solution: you don't get rid of the target species even with repeated doses: rather, you create an opportunity. Some individuals in the population possess genetic advantages that allow them to survive the biocides: these breed and prosper in a world from which most of the competition has been removed. That's how resistant strains develop and an arms race with the chemists begins.

The book met with violent hostility from the chemical industry. They responded with denial, propaganda, misleading stats and ridicule, a pattern we have seen again since then: it was the way the tobacco industry dealt with the revelation that tobacco causes cancer; it's how the fossil fuel industry is dealing with the science of climate change. Robert White-Stevens, from the now defunct chemical organisation American Cyanamid Company, opposed Carson in biblical terms: 'If man were to follow the teachings of Miss Carson we would return to the dark ages and the insects and disease and vermin would once again inherit the earth.' There were many concerted attempts to discredit her work, even though it was accurately researched and peer-reviewed. But the easier tactic was to go for Carson on a personal level.

A letter to the *New Yorker* said that her work 'probably reflected her Communist sympathies' and went on to say: 'We can live without birds and animals but ... we cannot live without business.' She was a woman: she was written off as hysterical, sentimental, faddy, not a proper scientist. Some went so far as to wonder why 'a spinster worried about genetics'.

Silent Spring is one of the most important books ever written, and not just because it brought about the banning of DDT for agricultural use in America and later bans across most of the rest of the world. It also spelled out the fact that the damage humans inflict on nature isn't restricted to non-human species. By harming nature we harm ourselves. We have become our own victims. What happens to the environment affects humans – and that's because humans also live in the environment. Ever since the invention of agriculture humans have lived by the notion that nature is something separate from humans: the truth is that we are as much a part of it as mosquitoes and ants and the birds that may or may not continue to sing. If we destroy the environment we destroy ourselves.

And farming is on the front line. That sounds a little odd to modern ears: very few people work in farming these days. Farming is something we can remember from childhood, Stan and Little Red Tractor, a long way from the pressing concerns of the cities. But every person on earth is dependent on agriculture.

Livestock farming has also been revolutionised. Over the course of the twentieth century in the developed world meat has been promoted from a routine treat to a twice (or thrice) daily right, and production has kept pace with this accelerating demand. This requires ever-more intense levels of stocking. Mammals and birds are now often kept indoors, close together: perfect conditions for the spreading of infection, as we saw in Chapter 18. The problem can now be counteracted by feeding antibiotics as a prophylactic: the animals get them in their feed whether they are infected or not. It's been estimated that two-thirds of global antibiotics are used on farm animals, mostly to pre-empt infections rather than to treat them. This has massively speeded up the development of resistant strains, in the manner mentioned earlier. The agro-industrial use of antibiotics has therefore impacted on human health: antibiotics are becoming less and less effective at treating human illnesses.

The development of antibiotics that followed the discovery of the effects of Penicillium in 1928 seemed like a miracle: an instant cure for almost everything. But it was the start of another arms race: the pathogens it attacked inevitably started to develop immune strains. Overuse has made antibiotics less and less effective. It is possible – some say certain – that we are now entering a post-antibiotic age – and this is a trend that has been largely driven by farming.

Use of prophylactic antibiotics has dropped considerably in Britain and in the EU, but it's still prevalent in much of the world, especially in the United States. There is also a semi-farcical aspect of livestock farming, and that is the production of methane. Cattle emit the gas from both ends: and methane is a potent greenhouse gas. It's much more effective than carbon dioxide at retaining heat, but it doesn't stay in the atmosphere for as long – a dozen years as opposed to centuries. Which would be fine if we weren't putting more and more methane into the atmosphere as we breed more and more cattle – 940 million at the end of 2023. Agriculture is the main source of atmospheric methane, followed by the energy industry: coal, gas and biofuels. The fact that we are farting ourselves to death has to be taken seriously.

Farmers, having gone through a revolution in philosophy and practice since the Second World War, are now inclined to take an entrenched position on the new traditions they have established. But this is a generalisation, and attitudes are changing – as I hope to demonstrate in the final chapter of this book. It is, many insiders believe, a generational thing, and one that might eventually die out.

In Britain there is a traditional connection between agriculture and pleasure. People go to the countryside to enjoy a break from life in towns and cities. The country is seen as a beautiful place where you can enjoy nature. A spring walk in the countryside was regarded as one of the great treats of the twentieth century: human pleasure, human food production and wildlife all working together. Such experiences have become more and more important in an age of increasing stress, one marked by ever-increasing dependence on antidepressants – in

2022–3 86 million batches of antidepressants were prescribed to 8.6 million people by the NHS, an increase of 2 per cent over the previous year, or an additional 200,000 people. The use of antidepressants has almost doubled since 2011. The therapeutic role of the countryside is more important with every passing year, and with every passing year it gets more elusive.

The farming industry is inclined to be aggressively defensive, asking: what's your problem? Don't you eat or something? Such interrogation was turned very neatly in an exchange with the farming community by Mark Avery, former conservation director of RSPB and a lifelong campaigner for wildlife.[3] 'Actually I do eat. I might even be one of your better customers. Thanks for asking. But I also pay for farming through my taxes. That makes me an ignored stakeholder in decisions about the future of agriculture because the vested interests of farming never take much notice of those who pay the bills. And I am not just a consumer and a taxpayer. I experience the losses of wildlife in the countryside just a few minutes from my house – farming's choices have impacts on my quality of life. You don't score very highly as an industry in delivering value for money for my taxes or quality of life through your actions.' He went on to ask if UK farming was proud of its environmental record, what its plans were for

---

[3] Mark Avery is a founder member of Wild Justice, which seeks legal solutions to wildlife issues.

reducing biodiversity loss and whether it accepted that livestock farming contributed to greenhouse gases.

The Armageddon figures are depressing in the extreme: there are 73 million fewer birds in the UK since 1970; species in all taxa have declined 19 per cent on average and one in six species is facing extinction in this country. Flying insects have declined 50 per cent over the last 20 years; 80 per cent of UK butterfly species have declined since 1970. We are being pushed into a still more impoverished countryside largely because the traditionally minded farming industry hates to change. Government also tends to accept that the 1945 view of food production is still valid: ever-greater intensification is maintained by vested interest and outdated attitudes. A great deal of land is used to grow animal feed. Another important crop (for the farming industry) is sugar beet; sugar is the greatest driver of obesity; obesity costs the UK an estimated £98 billion a year. Crops are grown for biofuels rather than food. (In 2021 this amounted to 8,789 hectares in the UK but it's an issue we prefer to export: in the same year the UK imported 121 million litres from Ukraine, which required 36,000 hectares to produce it.) We can do better – and in some places we are doing so. It's more about government than farmers: the revolution that followed 1945 – an astonishing creative detonation of technology and ambition – can be followed by a revolution in which we can reclaim the countryside and by doing so reclaim the spring.

AGRIBUSINESS IN SPRING

Spring – the countryside in spring – is one of the greatest joys that life can bring us. Too much of it has been eaten away. But the realisation that by damaging the countryside we are damaging ourselves – the revelation at the heart of *Silent Spring* – is belatedly becoming the new orthodoxy.

Signs of spring
May 2024

BACK HOME

- 14 Cuckoos calling
    Many flags in flower
    Ash tree in full leaf
    Leveret
    Cuckoo flowers
- 15 Swifts
- 16 Cleavers growing well
    Common damselfly: pre-mating flight
    Reed warbler on marsh
- 17 Oxeye daisies: huge roadside bank
    Visible cuckoo
    Visible tawnies, nocturnal territorial dispute
- 18 Antiphonal Cetti's warblers in garden
    Two (poss.) hairy dragonflies
- 19 Poppies in flower
- 20 North Norfolk: peregrine on Cromer church
    Displaying goshawk
    Green alkanet patch with butterflies: seven to eight green hairstreaks, holly blue, small copper, small heath. Heard: turtle dove, Dartford warbler, woodlark
    Cley: marsh harrier food pass
- 21 Little owl chick in garden
    Flocking jackdaws – sign of autumn
    Lesser whitethroat singing again
- 22 Many more swifts
    Cuckoo calling well

21

Phenological spring

We all remember the first kiss of a love affair. Never the last. That's partly because a first kiss has a dramatic force that keeps it safe in the memory when other details have faded, and partly because we always know that the first kiss is the first. We hardly ever know that it's the last kiss when we experience it.

SPRING IS THE ONLY SEASON

First things mark out our days, weeks, years and lives. Perhaps the special joy we take in the good first comes from spring, the season of all the very best firsts; or perhaps it's the other way round and the love of a good first is in our nature and explains why spring is our very best season. As I write these words on a bright January morning I have just heard the first song thrush of the year: not in full song but a good strong version of sub-song: the bird was warming up, getting in the mood, practising rather than performing and singing its fine song of inventively repeated phrases from low down in cover rather than a high, exposed perch. Yesterday I was walking in six layers of clothing: today I sat still – if briefly – in just four as the wise thrush sang his song twice over, lest I thought he never could recapture that first fine careless rapture.

First bumblebee, first lesser celandine, first great tit song, first blackthorn blossom, first budburst, first chiffchaff, first brimstone butterfly, first blackbird song, first wild rose, first swallow ... along with the first day without a coat, the first drink outside, the first asparagus and, for some, the first kiss.

Many people are affected by the lack of light, the shortage of sun and the relentless cold of the winter months. It adds up to the syndrome called SAD: seasonal affective disorder. Perhaps we all suffer from it to a degree, whether we know it or not ... and perhaps a degree of SADness is essential if you wish to experience the joys of spring to the full.

Like most of us, I know the winter blues. Just before the solstice, a couple of weeks ago as I write these words, I had an episode of despair: brief but bewilderingly deep. It was more than enough, as I clambered out of this slough of self-pity, to have the greatest sympathy for those who feel the grip of the dark days more fully than I do. At least I have a weapon to combat the grip of the sunless times: and I find it in nature. I wish I could prescribe nature for everyone who has felt the black weight of winter too fully. It is, I know, not an effective answer to deep psychological and physiological problems, but I can say with confidence and from personal experience that an awareness of nature can at least be a factor in the battle against despair. If you are neither nature-blind nor nature-deaf; if you are nature-numerate and can count the steps of the advancing spring; if you are aware of nature and of natural changes you can't help but be aware of the retreating winter. If you can read the signs of the turning year and understand them in your mind and in your essential gut, in your heart and in your soul, then at the very least you will bring more light into your life.

Spring comes madly early to those who know how to look. Though winter in the northern hemisphere officially takes place between the December solstice and the March equinox you can read signs of spring every single day from the first day of winter to the last. Here's a recap of my records for December post-solstice 2023:

22 Buds on ash and hazel
24 Hazel catkins
28 Daisies in flower
29 Stock dove and great tit singing
30 Exotics: mauve umbellifer and periwinkle species in flower
31 More great tit song

These are not observations of great depth. There are no great rarities here: just little moments of commonplace things. Commonplace moments of joy, if you like. And they all add up to spring: even in what is still officially winter they add up to spring.

Once you've got your eye in (and your ear) you perform a trick on yourself. It becomes impossible to avoid these proliferating signs of spring. It's as if, by your own efforts, you have created spring where no spring was before. The habit of looking and listening came to me relatively late in life, but it's now deep in my nature and incapable of removal. I couldn't fail to be aware of a growth of green young nettles in the first days of January, a dandelion in flower, two male marsh harriers having a brief rivalrous grapple on the far side of the river, and that bloody marvellous song thrush.

Such vernal milestones bring about a compulsion in those who have learned to notice them. You have to tell someone. I made a recording of that song thrush – on my phone, nothing fancy – and sent it to three people who would appreciate it. Like many others I often feel an urge to write it down: as if making a note made the whole thing more real. The song thrush, the nettles, the catkins are all there in a nice new notebook/diary given to me for Christmas by my younger son.

The urge to record the seasonal changes in the world around us – especially the resurgent life of the spring – is a powerful force. There have been many notebooks in my life, some kept meticulously, some half-filled, some abandoned, some thrown away, some lying half-forgotten on the shelf where notebooks accumulate. In many of them the urge to understand the arriving spring with ever-greater intimacy is expressed by a series of scrawls in my speculative italic hand. I have written three books based on the turning of the year, the journey from season to season, and they are all, in their different ways, a celebration of spring. What better subject is there for any writer? It was, as we have seen, good enough for Marcel Proust, James Joyce and P. G. Wodehouse. This urge to notice, to celebrate by noting down, as if to make sure that the slippery spring will never get away from us, is not only a natural urge of humankind. It's also a branch of science: and the name of the science is phenology.

In the Hampshire village of Selborne there is a house called The Wakes and it celebrates two men. Both were great explorers. One went as far from Selborne as was then humanly possible, in order to seek adventure and meaning and to establish his name. The other hardly ever left the place in the entire course of a life of 73 years: and found exactly the same.

The first of these is Lawrence Oates: Captain Oates of Robert Scott's expedition to the Antarctic in 1911–12, and so a major character in a story that has become a national epic of glorious failure and futile heroism. Oates, suffering from gangrene and frostbite and desperately aware that he was holding up the expedition and compromising his colleagues' chances of survival, left the tent in a blizzard with some of the most famous last words of all time: 'I am just going outside and may be some time'. His body was never found. The expedition was beaten to the South Pole by the Norwegian Roald Amundsen. Every one of its members died.

Gilbert White was born in The Wakes in 1720 and lived there for most of his life; he died in 1793. He was the great primordial parson-naturalist; we met him earlier in this book on the subject of hibernating swallows. His life was a voyage of discovery and what he discovered was Selborne. His achievement was something close to a total understanding of place: and, with that, the way the concept of place works in nature. White was both a product of the Enlightenment and a person who was never much concerned with the resulting divorce of science from religion. He was able to ride the contradictions without dismay. He just looked and listened and thought – and wrote.

Early biologists mostly concerned themselves with dead animals: the dissection of specimens in order to understand morphological differences and degrees of relatedness. They were often concerned with the importance and usefulness to humans of the animal in question. White was different. He looked at living nature, he noted what living things did, how they interacted with each other in place and time, and how they all operated in the framework of the seasons. And he was fascinated by what they did for their own sakes, not for what they could do for us.

By doing so he was a pioneer, even an inventor, of three different sciences. The first of these is ethology, the study of animal behaviour: 'It is curious to observe with what different degrees of architectural skill Providence has endowed birds of the same genus and so nearly correspondent in their general mode of life! For while the swallows and the house-martin discover the greatest address in raising and securely fixing crusts or shells of loam as cunabula for their young, the bank-martin [sand martin] terebrates a round and regular hole in the sand or earth, which is serpentine, horizontal and about two feet deep.'

The second is ecology, the study of the interconnectedness of living things. 'Earthworms, though in appearance a small and despicable link in the chain of nature, yet, if lost, would make a lamentable chasm ... worms seem to be the great promoter of vegetation, which would proceed but lamely without them.'

The third was phenology: the study of the seasons. With his friend and colleague William Markwell from Battle in Sussex, White recorded the emergence of more than 400 species over a 25-year period, 1768 to 1793. White was not only a superb observer (without modern optics and other aids, without even easily accessible means of identification) and a meticulous record-keeper. He could also write: *The Natural History and Antiquities of Selborne* (usually just *The Natural History of Selborne*) has been in print ever since it was published in 1789 and it remains a great read to this day. The second half is increasingly devoted to seasonal observations, and begins with a list of migrants and their usual date of arrival: '19. Goat-sucker or fern-owl [nightjar], *Caprimulgus*: Beginning of May; chatters by night with a singular noise.'

At first White noted his observations in a book he called, rather quaintly 'Garden Kalendar', but from 1769 he did so on printed pages that were the gift of his friend and fellow naturalist Daines Barrington. These had columns for temperature, air pressure, the weather and so forth and paid particular attention to first flowerings and first appearances.

White did not invent the practice of recording seasonal events, but he brought a new meticulousness and a rare eye for detail. In France there are records around grape-growing that go back 500 years, revealing a pleasingly French sense of priorities. In Japan references to the appearance of cherry blossom date back to the eighth century, representing a still more pleasing revelation of Japanese priorities. There are also many folkloric references to signs of changing seasons: 'If oak comes before ash, be ready for a splash; if ash comes before oak, be ready for soak', this referring (I assume) to budburst and the likely weather that will follow.

The value in such information is over the long term. An extended period of good observation reveals changing patterns and suggests questions about why things may have changed. Robert Marsham, from the excellently named Norfolk village of Stratton Strawless, kept notes on seasonal changes from 1736, noting flowering, budburst and insect appearances. Generations of his family followed this tradition; they kept it up until the death of Mary Marsham in 1958.

It always delights me when research takes me back to the mid- and late nineteenth century, for this was the time when natural history was seen as the natural pursuit of humankind. What else would anyone do? In Rudyard Kipling's *Stalky & Co.*, the rebellious trio led by Stalky become 'Bug-Hunters', but only so they can find a safe place to smoke their pipes: members of the Natural History Society had permission to go out of bounds. 'They took no heed to flying rabbits or fluttering fritillaries and all that Turkey said of geology was utterly unquotable.'

But for less cynical types natural history was a widespread passion and keeping records of the seasons was an important part of the process. In 1891 the Royal Meteorological Society started to compile records on a national basis, gathering information from more than 600 observers, an early form of what we now call citizen science. They kept it up until 1948 – just, you might say, when such records were getting interesting. But all the same, significant changes could be read: over 58 years first flowering dates average 21 days earlier; some species as many as 34 days earlier.

Richard Fitter, an outstanding field botanist, kept details of first flowerings of 557 British species. In an article for *Science* magazine in 2002, written with his son Alastair, he noted that the average first flowering date for 385 British species had advanced 4.5 days over the previous decade, and that 150–200 species were flowering 15–20 days earlier than they did in the very recent past. Oh, and I should also mention a set of delightful records from David Grisenthwaite in Scotland, who noted the dates he cut his lawn, first cuts and last cuts since 1984. In 2004 the first cut was 13 days earlier than it had been in 1984, and the last cut 17 days later.

Here, then, is a homely kind of science that just happens to be revealing, fact by tiny fact, a great and terrible truth is being shown to us all. It is astonishing that there was no unified UK national way of recording phenological data between 1948 and 1998: missing out what might be considered the most important 50 years in the history of the earth's climate since the evolution of humankind. There has been a very decent attempt to make good since then. Nature's Calendar was established in 1998 by Tim Sparks of the Centre for Ecology & Hydrology, and since 2000 this has been run by the Woodland Trust. It has collated many historical records and has more than three million records. The website will accept your records.[1] *British Wildlife* magazine ran a piece in 2020 that compared the records of Gilbert White with these modern records. After a

---

[1] naturescalendar.woodlandtrust.org.uk

few paragraphs of necessary scientific throat-clearing on the difficulties of knowing that you are comparing like with like, and whether or not records can be considered compatible, they get down to it. And among their findings for first flowering dates, White's dates first, modern dates second:

Lesser celandine	18 March	1 March
Wood anemone	4 April	26 March
Blackthorn	23 April	17 March
Hawthorn	16 May	26 April

The attentive reader will see where all this is leading.

This discipline, as we have seen it so far, requires no more equipment than functioning eyes and ears and a nice pen. It's so straightforward – at least in its recording, analysis is a different matter entirely – that even I am capable of making a contribution. However, there is a developing branch of phenology that can only be done from space or from drones, and it's all about analysing data from airborne sensors. It's a process that elevates – quite literally – phenology from stooping over the year's first flowering bluebell to information about entire ecosystems.

It's all based on the light a plant reflects. A growing plant reflects hardly any red light at all: plants, as we have seen, power themselves by means of light, and they absorb almost all red light in the process of photosynthesis. At the same time they reflect a great deal of light in the low infrared part of the spectrum. This is beyond human perception, but we can register it with the right sensors. By measuring the two kinds of light reflected, calculations reveal how much growing is going on down below: in other words, we can compute the start, finish and length of the growing season. It is relatively straightforward, even simple to those who work with such matters, and it gives good, strong objective data. It has shown, for example, that the Amazon rainforest doesn't grow in a steady-state way, each season alike, as was always generally supposed, but has subtle shifts in the seasons in which growth is accelerated. It has also indicated in more northerly forests that there is an increase in annual productivity that can (probably) be related to an increase in temperature.

The essential truth of ecology – you might describe it as the whole point of ecology – is that it's much more complicated than you can imagine, or ever could imagine. Everything is connected to everything else and therefore everything depends on everything else. As we have seen, a great white shark is every bit as dependent on phytoplankton as a shrimp. Every ecosystem is a bewildering web of interconnectedness: and there are far more species in that web than it's possible to understand or even count. There are perhaps – estimates vary wildly – ten million species of animals on the planet. There are around 24,000 known species of insects in Britain: still far too many for a single human mind to deal with comfortably. All of ecology is a bit like that: but there are certain principles we can grasp readily enough.

We have been looking at advancing dates for early flowerings: powerful indicators of the changes in climate. The effects of climate change on ecosystems might seem at first glance to be merely interesting: perhaps even beneficial. How could anyone argue with an earlier and warmer spring? We will look further at the changes that amount to a breakdown of our climate in Chapter 23, but before that we will consider a few more of the phenological changes that have been taking places in recent decades, showing up in many different ecosystems.

Not all organisms respond equally to the same alteration in climate. As a result, species and events get out of sync with each other, and this creates the phenomenon of the phenological mismatch. Take an oak tree in lowland Britain. These days the budburst comes earlier. The caterpillars that feed on the leaves have mostly responded to this shift: they are appearing as much as two weeks earlier than they used to. However, the great tits and blue tits that feed on them have been unable to advance their nesting and egg-laying dates to accommodate this shift: only three or four days earlier. As a result, the time when tits are feeding their young – the period of peak demand – is no longer synchronised to the peak availability of caterpillars. Oak trees and tits both suffer as a result.

This shift in timing is an even greater problem for pied flycatchers. These are neat and dapper little birds, found in the wet woods on the western side of Britain. Unlike the tit species they migrate, coming up from their wintering grounds in Africa to nest every spring. Increasingly they find they are doing so after the caterpillar population has peaked.

There are many other examples being discovered as mismatch becomes a fruitful area of study. The early spider orchid is one of those classic sexual deceivers. It's found across Europe and West Asia and is a rare and sought-after plant in southern England. It operates by looking a bit like a bee – a buffish mining bee, to be precise – and smelling a lot like a female one. It is pollinated by deception: the plant's trickery entices male bees to indulge in frenzied pseudocopulation with the flower, and repeated duping allows the plants to spread their pollen to other plants of the same species. But these days female bees are emerging much earlier and males are far less likely to be distracted by the charms of the orchids. The deceivers are undone by changing circumstances.

This breakdown in synchronicity can lead to conflict with human activities. In Finland lapwings and curlews are nesting earlier: instead of nesting on fields that have recently been planted with barley, they are now doing so before the barley has been planted – and their nests get crushed when the tractors come.

In Greenland reindeer feed in winter on lichens on the coast and move inland as spring advances, and they can find what counts for lush vegetation in the far north. It's a crucial period for nutrition. But the plants they feed on are now arriving up to 26 days earlier and the reindeer's migration is out of sync.

The far north is the best place for understanding climate change and these mismatches, because the nearer you got towards either pole, the more extreme the seasonal changes are. The snowshoe hare of North America changes with the seasons: it's a golden-brown animal in the brief summer months but as winter advances it becomes white. Its survival depends on its ability to blend in with the background. But the snow is vanishing much earlier these days, leaving the white wintertime hare standing out in the emerging vegetation of the spring like a bar of soap in coal scuttle, as did the leopard (more Kipling) in *Just So Stories* – and therefore it is highly vulnerable to predators like lynx, coyote, wolf and birds of prey.

There is no disguising the truth. Not to a naturalist anyway. Politicians, fools, conspiracy theorists and leaders in the fossil fuel industry can maintain that climate change is not really happening. But anyone who can recognise a lesser celandine, a singing song thrush or a brimstone butterfly knows that there is something going on. Something is happening to our spring. The subversion of spring has begun. And the truth that is laid bare to us by those first flowerings, first hearings and first appearances is as dark and terrible as the things that indicate it are bright and beautiful.

Signs of spring
May 2024

24 Male and female harriers in the air together — so probably chicks on the ground
26 East Suffolk; singing nightingale in car park
    Back home: two lesser whitethroats singing
    Elder in flower
    Reed warbler on Common
    Bramble in flower
    Sedge warbler singing on marsh
27 Outney Common, from canoe: wild rose in bloom
    Banded demoiselles
    Deadly nightshade in flower
    Dragonfly, prob. broad-bodies chaser
28 Three swifts over the river — becoming rare birds
29 Flowers along the lane: mallow, rose, white campion
    Baby squirrel, tiny, by fallen willow
30 Cuckoo singing in the rain
31 Abundant water mint
    New-fledged magpies
    Swallows just miss my nose outside stables

22

Subversive spring

It was spring in Paris in 1913. The old order was changing, yielding place to the new, and a young composer, still only twenty, was full of brilliant ideas about spring. Not sweet and pretty and twittery, no. Here was a spring of hard and bitter agony, but what else do you expect from life? The music was first performed on 29 May. It was a celebration of high spring, at the Théâtre des Champs-Elysées and it was a riot — quite literally, in some accounts. The composer was Igor Stravinsky and the music was, of course, *The Rite of Spring*, in French *Le Sacre du printemps*, or the coronation of spring. Modernist artists made a series of revolutionary changes to all the arts they worked in, and time and time again they turned to the spring to express their revolutionary spirit and their destructive-creative ambitions. Modernism might be subtitled 'the subversion of spring'. Ideas we had accepted for generations were questioned, challenged, distorted and set on their heads: and our traditional ideas about spring took a hammering.

Sergei Diaghilev, impresario of the itinerant Ballets Russes, had commissioned Stravinsky to write the work. It was his third piece for Diaghilev, following *The Firebird* and *Petrushka*. Stravinsky's spring was not based on a vision of blossom and little lambs. In his 1936 autobiography, he said that the piece came from 'a fleeting vision ... a solemn pagan rite: sage elders, seated in a circle, watching a young girl dance herself to death. They were seeking to propitiate the gods of spring'.

A long way, then, from the sprightly dance of golden daffodils. Here instead was a ferociously different understanding of the season of new life, not jocund at all: this was spring as a violent force, rudely imposing itself on a world sinking calmly into the sleep of death. 'I was guided by no system whatsoever,' Stravinsky said. 'I had only my ear to help me.' The ballet was choreographed by Vaslav Nijinsky. His brilliance as a dancer had persuaded Diaghilev, always ready to take a punt on promising youth, that there was a choreographer of genius waiting to break out. Stravinsky did not agree, but was in no position to make a fuss. 'The poor boy knew nothing of music,' Stravinsky said. It was all part of Diaghilev's vision of the total artwork: the ultimate artistic experience: what Richard Wagner called *Gesamtkunstwerk*. Diaghilev replaced Wagnerian opera with dance and commissioned top artists to paint the backdrop; the one for the new ballet about spring was by the Russian painter Nicholas Roerich and called *The Great Sacrifice*. This immersive experience was bound together by new and challenging music: here was art coming at you in three forms at once, all threatening the conventions and moralities of the time. Nietzsche had called for a violent rebirth of modern society in his writing: here was the same message in art: a dance of life that ended in death, while the world itself was reborn.

The work was presented to a newly divided world and it exacerbated those divisions, as it was no doubt intended to. Half the audience on that first night were society people looking forward to a nice ballet with nice tunes and beautiful dancing by beautiful dancers; the other half were bohemians ready to give the most passionate applause to anything new, anything that startled. The two parties were at loggerheads from the first few bars: and it got worse. The derisive laughter at the opening phrases – played in the upper register of the bassoon – prompted Stravinsky to leave his place in the audience to watch and listen from the wings.

The piece unfolded in two parts: *The Adoration of the Earth* followed by *The Sacrifice*. Catcalls and howls of protest were countered by robust approval. The piece continued in increasing chaos, which was perhaps a legitimate response to the music – though in many accounts it was the choreography that upset people more than Stravinsky's music. The dancers performed with their toes turned in, the precise opposite to the traditions of classical ballet, and they made harsh, angular body shapes rather than lush curves. Stravinsky himself didn't care for it, complaining later[1] that the performers were 'knock-kneed and long-braided Lolitas'.

About forty people were thrown out of the theatre. There was so much din that the dancers could hardly hear the music; Nijinsky was heard shouting the cues above the hubbub. People threw stuff at the orchestra, but they carried on playing with admirable doggedness. They reached the end somehow and there were even curtain calls for the cast, the composer and the impresario from the bohemian tendency.

Naturally people queued up to say bad things. 'The work of a madman ... sheer cacophony,' said Giacomo Puccini; and it's true, it's not a lot like *La Bohème*, even if there were quite a few real bohemians in the audience. One writer suggested that *Le Sacre du printemps* should be renamed *Le Massacre du printemps*, showing that he had grasped the essential idea. Another critic wrote: 'The music ... baffles description. Practically it

---

[1] Much later. *Lolita* by Vladimir Nabokov wasn't published until 1955.

has no relation to music at all as most of us understand the word.'

A sense of smug twenty-first-century superiority over these traditionalists would be out of place. The music was startlingly new and people needed to adjust: they didn't have the equipment to appreciate it as it came fresh and raw from the orchestra. There are, for example, 444 changes in time signature in the course of the piece. It is full of violent and insistent rhythms, but you still can't tap your foot to it without fierce concentration. The section called *Glorification of the Chosen One* alone contains 49 changes of time signature in the course of 58 bars, which last a little over 90 seconds.

There were just seven performances of the ballet in that form; there was another version choreographed by Léonide Massine in 1920. It was as a concert piece that *The Rite of Spring* flourished. It was first performed as such, without distraction from Lolitas or painters, in St Petersburg in 1914 and later that same year at the Casino de Paris: after this performance Stravinsky was carried out of the theatre shoulder high. Modernism had gone mainstream.

The piece is now part of the repertoire of just about every orchestra in the world: a beloved favourite. I was part of an enraptured standing audience at the Proms, London's annual eight-week-long music festival, in the late 1960s, one that indulged in a fair amount of spontaneous dancing and a great deal of rowdy cheering at the end. A critic wrote afterwards that the promenaders seemed unaware that they had been listening to what he considered a second-class performance. No doubt he was right: though he might have considered the possibility that this was a legitimate response to a first-class piece of music. It had a huge influence on what came afterwards; Leonard Bernstein called it 'the most important piece of music of the 20th century'.

And it was about spring. It was a new and enthralling vision of the beloved season, every bit as legitimate as that of Beethoven in his Symphony No. 6, the Pastoral, in which a nightingale, a cuckoo and a quail sing out from the orchestra and prettiness is elevated to the loftiest levels of beauty. Stravinsky subverted Beethoven's vision of spring, but spring subverted is still spring: not destroyed but enhanced.

New directions in art are always shocking. That's because they are intended to shock, intended to polarise, intended to divide the crowd into philistines and true believers. Sometimes the new movement becomes orthodoxy and the fact that anyone could have ever doubted it seems risible a few decades later. There are books of quotations[2] in which various notable people repudiate, in the strongest possible terms, Impressionism, post-Impressionism, Cubism, rock and roll music, *Lady Chatterley's Lover*, *Ulysses*, The Beatles, Beethoven, Elvis – and on and on. Sometimes people can't see beyond the initial shock and fail to find the art behind it. Sometimes the artists have nothing to offer beyond

---

[2] *The Guinness Dictionary of Poisonous Quotes; The Cassell Dictionary of Regrettable Quotations.*

the initial shock: naked emperors abound in artistic innovation. But sometimes the finished work is a for-all-time 24-carat-gold masterpiece, and after-comers have the luxury of mocking those who rejected it – while often enough writing off the future greats of our own time as frauds and lunatics. The point is that the ability to shock doesn't necessarily make the artist a genius and the ability to remain unshocked doesn't necessarily make you an accurate interpreter of future greatness. What matters is the art.

Which brings us to Salvador Dalí, whose talent for bringing off an enthralling combination of shock and self-advertisement alienates people to this day – no doubt to his posthumous delight. His breakthrough picture, the one he painted just before he committed himself totally to the Surrealist movement, is called *The First Days of Spring*. There is another picture of the same year – 1929 – that might be given the same honour, entitled *The Great Masturbator*: but the spring painting has more about it – and is probably more shocking. It's shocking because it subverts spring.

Again we have a distinct shortage of primroses, daffodils, lambkins, cuckoos and nightingales. A promisingly blue sky is the backdrop to a field of grey: what looks almost like living concrete. The work mixes painting and collage, and does so with such skill that the painted imaginary objects look more real than the photograph of Dalí as a boy. This is placed right in the middle, though it's hard to focus on it for the disturbing imagery that surrounds it.

These days we all know about Freud[3] even if we have let ourselves off the task of actually reading him. (And is that Freud out there on the right of Dalí's picture, talking to a girl a year or two short of puberty?) We are familiar with Freud's idea that childhood fears and traumas lead ineluctably to adult neuroses. It's also true that Surrealist imagery is part of our heritage these days: part of pop culture, a familiar part of LP covers of the 1960s. My older son was given what looks like a fully functioning limp watch; a reference to Dalí's *The Persistence of Memory*.

All the same, even now, almost a century after it was painted, *The First Days of Spring* is still deeply disturbing: doubly so when you factor in the title. The work includes a photograph of people on a ship having a lovely time: perhaps they're the people Dalí wanted to shock. There's a gagged man leaning on a grotesque sexualised doll, a face with grasshopper attached to it, a formally dressed man mounting another formally dressed man, and a nice sort of a jug surmounted by a fish that needs a haircut. Towards the background there's a figure sitting on a chair with his back to everything. And far beyond him, tiny, almost out of sight were they not picked out by the grand grey V that leads towards the vanishing point of the exaggerated perspective, there's a man and a child hand in hand, surely a father and son. The inclusion of the photograph of the artist as a boy does not so much suggest as demand that you take a

---

[3] Sigmund Freud's *The Interpretation of Dreams* was published in 1899.

biographical approach: a son half wishing to be reconciled with his father, half wishing for his father's rejection, making this a piece about all sons and all fathers. Dalí was, indeed, thrown out of the family house later that year after boasting in an interview that it amused him to spit on the portrait of his mother.

What the hell's the picture all about, though? Freud knows. Certainly what we have before us is a powerful image of sexual anxiety and hidden desire. So where does spring come in? Dalí had just turned twenty-five: perhaps he was in the springtime of his life while his father was already deep into autumn. Or perhaps it is all about the flowering of desire as a springtime phenomenon: in spring a young man's fancy lightly turns to thoughts of hairy fish and sexy dolls. Or perhaps the point is that instead of flowering meadows Dalí must show us all that concrete. And springtime is the beloved time of year: all the more fun, then, to subvert it with the ugliness of conscious and unconscious desire. Spring, as we see it here, shows us something hateful, not just in the mind of the artist, but also in the minds of us spectators: stuff we'd much rather keep hidden, stuff that we'd much rather the artist hadn't brought to light, hypocrite spectators as we all are.

Or, to put that another way, April is the cruellest month. As arresting first lines go, this one is hard to top, referencing the opening of *The Canterbury Tales*[4] and then subverting it. Spring is the bringer of life: so if

---

[4] 'Whan that Aprille with hise shoures soote ...'

life is terrible then spring is the most terrible time of all. Life and April are both cruel. T. S. Eliot's *The Waste Land* is the great poem of modernism, and is still notorious for its difficulty. It is constantly veering off into languages other than English, apparently demanding from its readers a working knowledge of Sanskrit and an easy familiarity with Dante in the original Italian. At first innocent glance – well, as James Joyce wrote in *Finnegans Wake*: 'You is feeling like you was lost in the bush, boy?'

I read the poem as a schoolboy: Eliot's *Selected Poems* was one of the set books for A-level English. I remember the shock of the first poem in the book, *The Love Song of J. Alfred Prufrock*, and something not far from panic at the idea that I, little me of Lower Six Arts, was expected to understand it and then write about the damn thing. But we had a brilliant teacher in Pete (behind his back) Hendry, who gently allowed the poem to make a series of suggestions to us while pointing out that for each one of us it was a different poem. By the time we reached *The Waste Land* I was agog for its mysteries, for its suggestive power, for its thrilling demands on the reader, for its breathtaking display of learning, for its regular excursions into low comedy, for its enticing, seductive rhythms and its fleeting moments of total comprehension – but of what? I didn't want to solve its problems, as in cracking a code, I wanted to be a part of its mysteries.

The cruellest month! Eliot's working title for the poem was 'He Do the Police in Different Voices', which is a quotation from Dickens and at first sight a rather baffling choice. But the more you read the poem the more voices you hear, some nagging, some wistful, some offering frail wisps of hope, some comic, some tragic, voices of kings, of princes and saints and Eliot's charlady having a right old gossip down the pub. There's a European aristocrat, the prophet Ezekiel, characters from Wagner, a lover, a second-rate fortune-teller, someone who's something in the City (one who's read Dante), who seems to be addressing a murderer – and then Baudelaire pops up to add the closing line:

> You! Hypocrite lecteur! – mon semblable, – mon frère!

And that's just in the first of the five sections. As Pete walked us through the poem for the first time it seemed that it was all about the rottenness of twentieth-century society, despair at what had happened to the world. *The Waste Land*, it seemed in the eyes of a schoolboy in 1967, was an uncanny premonition (the poem was first published in 1922) of Wimpy Bars and dirty streets and Watney's Red Barrel and loss of all faith and white sliced bread (and perhaps Spam fritters): how could we have let such a promising world come to this? But despair – the real thing rather than the pose – is an elusive matter for most middle-class schoolboys. It was only with greater experience that I realised – in my mind and in my guts – that the poem is about internal as well as external horrors.

> The awful daring of a moment's surrender
> Which an age of prudence can never retract.

Eliot's marriage to Vivienne Haigh-Wood has been much written about. She was a deeply disturbed personality, and their marriage was a terrible mistake – except that as Joyce wrote in *Ulysses* (a book Eliot admired tremendously): 'The man of genius makes no mistakes. His errors are volitional and are the portals of discovery.' Eliot said himself: 'To her the marriage brought no happiness – to me it brought the state of mind out of which came *The Waste Land*.' Thus great poets write their time and it becomes all our times.

> 'My nerves are bad tonight. Yes, bad. Stay with me.
> Speak to me. Why do you never speak? Speak.
> What are you thinking of? What thinking? What?
> I never know you are thinking. Think.'
> I think we are in rats' alley
> Where the dead men lost their bones.[5]

There is despair, but there is also spring. There is even a nightingale – but it's Ovid's nightingale, a reference to a story in *Metamorphoses*. Philomela is raped by her sister's husband, the king Tereus, who then cuts

---

[5] The first four lines of this verse quoted read like a verbatim account of marital discord in action. On reading it, Vivienne wrote in the margin of the typescript 'WONDERFUL'.

her tongue out so that, like most rape victims, she will never be able to tell. But she still manages to inform her sister Procne, who sets out on a course of revenge. She serves Tereus a special meal – which turns out to be their son, cooked to a turn. In the horror that follows Tereus is turned into a hoopoe, Procne into a swallow and Philomela into a nightingale: a story that is grotesque even by Ovid's elevated standards. And yet – and yet –

> yet there the nightingale
> Filled all the desert with inviolable voice,

There are other brave hints that spring can bring brief glimpses of hope, perhaps making spring all the crueller, or perhaps a hint that a way out of the waste land exists, even if you may not be able to take it yourself. The hermit thrush, a North American species, sings in the final part, and Eliot provides an extensive ornithological note (he was a decent birdwatcher in his youth), adding helpfully: 'its "water-dripping" song is justly celebrated'. The nightingale sings again, and there are hints of beauty in a public bar, in the City church of St Magnus-the-Martyr, in the boat that responded gaily.

And in the first section there is also the hyacinth garden. Hyacinths are traditional emblems of life and rebirth, but you don't need to know that to understand the lines, a love song, bursting out almost incontinently from a poem about despair:

> You gave me hyacinths first a year ago;
> 'They called me the hyacinth girl.'
> —Yet when we came back, late, from the hyacinth
>   garden,
> Your arms full and you hair wet, I could not
> Speak, and my eyes failed, I was neither
> Living nor dead, and I knew nothing
> Looking into the heart of light, the silence.

Here is the ecstasy of love, love beyond desire. A cache of more than 1,000 letters that Eliot wrote to his American friend Emily Hale has recently come into the public domain. She was an actor and a teacher of drama and the letters reveal that she and Eliot shared a long love. Eight years after *The Waste Land* was published he told her that she, no other, was the hyacinth girl. In one of his letters to her, Eliot wrote that hope was a duty. He went so far as to underline the word: he believed that hope was a <u>duty</u>.

The poem apparently brings us nothing but a great doughy lump of despair, but it is leavened with a teaspoon of hope and that changes everything. In the end, even despair on the epic scale of *The Waste Land* is vulnerable to the power of spring and to the hope that it can't help but bring with it. Even in the desert there comes, in the end, a damp gust bringing rain.

These three great defining works of modernism, brought to us by Stravinsky, Dalí and Eliot, take spring as their theme and then subvert it, confounding our expectations. Stravinsky turns spring into a pagan ritual of brutally uncompromising life; Dalí turns spring into a cornucopia of neuroses and desire; Eliot brings us despair with its homeopathic dose of hope.

But in all these violent, difficult and dangerous interpretations of the season, we still have spring. Despite incantatory rhythms and tempi changes, despite sexy dolls and man-in-suit-on-man-in-suit sexual action, despite the cruelty of a month that breeds lilacs out of the dead land, we still have spring as it always was. In spring life returns, to understand and interpret, to enjoy or not enjoy.

But that's no longer the case.

Spring is being destroyed as we watch, destroyed as we note down the signs of the changing seasons, destroyed in a way that all the artists in creation could never hope to achieve. These days our annual rejoicing at the arrival of spring comes with a homeopathic dose of gloom. In the song of the nightingale and the hermit thrush, in the gift of hyacinths, we can all of us now find despair.

Signs of spring
June 2024

1. New-fledged jackdaws on Common
Flowering rose bush by heronry
Many speedwell
2. Spear thistle in flower
River: willow seeds floating
Hemp agrimony in flower
Busy sand martins: must be a colony quite close
Hammock tick: tree-creeper
3. Many common damselflies
Massive burdock leaves
Train to Ipswich: track lined with elder, rose and bramble flowers
River Orwell: towpath with mallow, plantain, poppy
4. Marsh harrier display flight
Reed warbler by first pond on marsh
Common spotted orchid
5. River: purple loosestrife just beginning
Banded demoiselles
Flowering water mint
6. Cuckoo calling on the wing, seen from kayak

8 Very dark male marsh harrier on ground on Common
  Many grasshoppers on path
  Much din from heronry, must be several young
  Common spotted orchid has been eaten, presumably by deer
  Banded demoiselle on marsh
  Two reed warblers by second pond
9 Two cuckoos calling
  Hobby over garden
10 Barn owl flying out of barn
  House martins over Common
  Chaffinch singing – second brood?

23

Spring in the time of climate change

My father and I thought we'd make a trip to Marazion Marsh to look for Cetti's warblers.[1] It

---

[1] Named for the eighteenth-century Italian priest and naturalist Francesco Cetti, so say *chetty*.

was May, high spring, the year, I think, 1999. Marazion Marsh lies opposite St Michael's Mount in Cornwall, and it's the most southerly RSPB reserve. It's small, 63 hectares, but holds a nice heronry and plenty of reeds. The Cettis were there because, being so far south, it was balmier than the rest of the country, and they are birds who can't abide a freeze.

My father always liked to tell the story of an encounter we had there, one I was to tell myself in *How to Be a Bad Birdwatcher*. A lady with broad shoulders, barbered hair, a forbidding manner and a milder female companion, buttonholed me and asked me if I could tell her what a Cetti sounds like. It was before the days when you could do this with an app on your phone. 'I have a mnemonic,' I said, 'but it contains an obscene word.'

She looked at me pityingly. 'I'm a medievalist.'

Understanding that as an invitation to go ahead, I said: 'Me? Cetti? If-you-don't-like-it-fuck-off.'

'Thank you very much.'

I didn't see her again, so I'll never know if it worked for her. I hope so: it certainly did for us: we found Cettis and had a damn good day, good birding followed by a good pub. A Cetti was something to boast about back then. They were first recorded in Britain in 1961 and first bred in the 1970s.

Now they breed at our place in Norfolk. They bred north of the Humber for the first time in 2006. A total of 3,450 singing males have been recorded in a single British spring. The population rose by 187 per cent between 2012 and 2020.

What are Cetti's warblers telling us?

A contribution to the *Norfolk Bird and Mammal Report 1972* noted: 'Little egret: a remarkable spring influx of at least six to the county'. In the spring of 1991 I found a little egret at Minsmere RSPB reserve in Suffolk. It was unusual enough for me to tell the warden about it; he at once set off to see it for himself; after all, this wasn't something you bump into every day. In the very early spring of 2024, again at our place, I watched two little egrets feeding and then flying off together: clearly very much wrapped up in each other. I wondered if they would breed in the local heronry. No birder would be surprised if they did.

Little egrets are small white herons. Here's Bashō on the subject:

> A bridge
> between snowy mountains
> a flock of egrets.

They are noticeable birds: the other day, I saw six from the train window between Ipswich and Manningtree. They bred in Britain for the first time in 1996; by 2015 there were more than 1,000 breeding pairs. In 25 years they have gone from nothing to abundance.

Egrets are not climate deniers. Nor are Cetti's warblers. No bird is; nor is any birder. The birds just get on with it: responding to changed circumstances. They can fly: they are nature's rapid response unit, on the leading edge of climate change. No birder can miss them, nor ignore what they mean.

Conditions in Britain used not to suit egrets and Cettis: now they do. Hard winters are killers: but these days our winters are milder. Winters are milder everywhere and in response there's a global poleward drift of birds. As the climate changes, species are moving north to take up new opportunities. In Britain new breeding species of recent years include great white egret, cattle egret, spoonbill, black-winged stilt, purple heron, little bittern and black-crowned night heron: all birds once associated with southern Europe. Next one? Favourite is glossy ibis, two failed attempts so far. Birders can see the world changing before their very binoculars. The birds are not moving because the climate might change: they are moving because it *has* changed. And they are continuing to move north because it's continuing to do so. Willow warblers were heard all over Britain 30 years ago, now they are much rarer in the south, more common the further north you travel.

The earth has an atmosphere: a layer of gases retained by gravity. It comprises 78 per cent nitrogen, 21 per cent oxygen and 1 per cent others, including 0.04 per cent carbon dioxide. Without an atmosphere there would be no life, and not just because there would be nothing to breathe. The atmosphere minimises the harmful effects of the sun, which include ultraviolent radiation, solar wind and cosmic rays. It also keeps us warm. The sun's rays hit the earth and bounce back: if all this energy went straight back into space the surface of the earth would be tens of degrees cooler. But the atmosphere contains gases that absorb and emit the heat in all directions, including downwards. These include water vapour, methane, nitrous oxide and carbon dioxide: all part of that 1 per cent. They have been termed greenhouse gases, and without them we wouldn't exist. It's also a fact that the more such gases we have in the atmosphere, the more effective they are at retaining heat. Like an extra blanket or two.

So let's go back to that world-changing event of a million years back: the control of fire. Wood is a hydrocarbon fuel; when you burn such fuels you get light and heat. It's a release of stored energy, energy that ultimately came from the sun. Once humans had heat and light at will, they – we – were able to branch off from the rest of life on earth, eventually becoming something unprecedented on earth. We became a species that could change the planet it lived on. The history of modern humanity is all about the burning of hydrocarbon fuels: the fire at the mouth of the cave, the fire that can melt metals, the steam power that drove the Industrial Revolution and the rockets that went to the moon: taking in on the way the car outside the house, the central heating, the electric lights, the cooking stove and every computer on earth, including the one on which I write these words.

Hydrocarbon fuels include wood, coal, natural gas, petrol and oil. These were all once living organisms; the last four are called fossil fuels because the organisms lived millions of years ago. When you burn any hydrocarbon fuel it emits carbon dioxide. This goes into the atmosphere, and it stays there for 300 to 1,000 years.

At the end of the nineteenth century a Swedish scientist, Svante Arrhenius, demonstrated that carbon dioxide sent into the atmosphere by human activity was changing the climate. He got the Nobel Prize in 1903, meanwhile humans carried on burning hydrocarbons. In 1938 Guy Callendar, an English steam engineer and inventor, also an amateur climatologist, released data he had collected. These took in 50 years of information from 147 weather stations around the world. He worked out that the world's temperature had gone up by 0.3 degrees over half a century and argued that the cause was cardon dioxide emissions from human activity. He thought that it was probably a good thing.

In 1958 Charles Keeling, an American scientist, collated readings taken at Mauna Loa volcano in Hawaii over five years. These proved that carbon dioxide levels in the atmosphere were rising, and his analysis showed that fossil fuels were the cause. So let me spell it out: anthropogenic climate change is something that we have known about for a long time. In 1967 computer modelling showed that if we doubled the concentration of carbon dioxide in the atmosphere, global temperature would rise by two degrees; in 1968 it was clear that the polar ice caps were melting.

We have a global emergency on our hands and we have known about it for decades. It is a clear threat to the way we live and to our continued existence on the planet – and we have done remarkably little to slow it down, still less to stop it. The problem, at least at the beginning, was that it didn't seem to be a very urgent sort of emergency. It didn't even seem to be a bad sort of emergency: blimey, bloody cold today, isn't it, I could do with some of that global warming they're talking about. Every time there's a snowstorm Donald Trump reaches for his phone to ask where the hell is global warming? 'Ice storms from Texas to Tennessee. I'm in Los Angeles and it's freezing. Global warming is a total, and expensive, hoax!'

This is a popular error: a confusion between climate, which is long-term, and weather, which is short-term. It's going to rain tomorrow is weather; in 2023 London received 647.1mm of rain – and that's climate. The fact is that the climate has changed, and continues to change. It's getting warmer.

'Hello, Simon, you don't mind me calling you Simon, do you? How are you today, Simon?' It was one of those calls you have to take for some reason, so I stuck with it, nobly refraining from saying that I would greatly prefer Dr Barnes if it's all the same to you. I told him I was well but hot; it was, after all, the summer of 2022. 'Well, Simon, we've always had heatwaves, haven't we? What about 1976?' Putting me at my ease, I suppose.

Sure, heatwaves have always been part of the pattern. But the famous summer of 1976 was, back then, a rare event, one that became part of British legend. There had been heatwaves before that, sure. But since 1976 heatwaves have increased in frequency, duration and intensity. They occurred in 1995, 1997, 2003 and

2006, as well as 2022. The maximum temperature in 1976 was 35.9 degrees and it seemed quite unbelievable at the time; in 2022 and for the first time in UK, temperatures over 40 degrees were recorded in several places, topping out at 40.3. The Met Office has UK records going back to 1884; the ten warmest years have all been since 2003. 2023 brought us the hottest June on record and the joint hottest September. These are just records for Britain: 2023 was the planet's hottest year ever recorded.

The world is getting hotter. I'm writing this on a cold day in late January, and I could do with a couple of extra degrees – hell, I would prefer another ten. And that's part of the problem for people who live in the seasonal lands, especially the more northerly ones. A little warmth, a measly two degrees doesn't seem like a problem. Bloody good thing, I'm tempted to say when I step outside and see the snowdrops cowering under the weeping willow and the hares before my window apparently running about to keep warm rather than from springtime sexual frenzies.

Hazelwood Marshes is a reserve run by Suffolk Wildlife Trust. I always liked the place: it had an understated and for that matter, under-visited beauty: freshwater marshes separated from the River Alde by a man-made river wall. There were bitterns and water rails, and it was a delight to hear their wildly different calls in spring. There was also a complex community of freshwater plants and invertebrates. But in 2013 it was forced to close for three years. I took part in the reopening[2] in the spring of 2016 – and only the sky was the same. Down below the place had changed from top to bottom. The vegetation, the invertebrates and the birds were all different: the place was now full of the sound of avocets, lapwings and redshanks. The bitterns and water rails had gone, for this was now a salt marsh, directly connected to the river and subject to the twice daily advance and retreat of the tides.

The Environment Agency had examined the river wall three years or so earlier. 'Well, we won't replace it when it's gone, but should last you another twenty years.' A few weeks after this, on 5 December 2013, a tidal surge pushed the ebb tide back up the estuary and when it reached Hazelwood it breached the river wall in three places. It did so because the sea level is rising and because extreme weather events are coming with ever greater frequency. Both are the results of the breakdown of the earth's climate.

So it's not about weather, no. It's about climate and that's a big concept, one that is not easy to grasp intuitively. A warmer climate – a warmer global climate – doesn't just mean that it's a few degrees hotter. The extra warmth is just the start. When the air is warmer more moisture evaporates, and warmer air is capable of holding onto more water vapour. But then it comes down again: so rainfall increases. When you put more energy into a system – in this case in the form of heat – it

---

[2] I did so by wrenching from the ground a sign that read 'Dangerous currents at wall breaches – no access at any time'.

gets more energetic: as a result the frequency and extent of storms also increases. The Met Office tracks the UK storm season from September through to August: the season 2023–4 brought us storms named Agnes, Babet, Ciarán, Debi, Elin, Fergus, Gerrit, Henk, Isha and Jocelyn – all by January. Kathleen followed in April and, in late August, Lilian. The closest rival to this year, and the only previous season with so many storms, was 2016, which finished with storm Katie. The warmer oceans around the equator create more frequent and more violent tropical storms, hurricanes and typhoons.

The level of the sea is rising. There are two reasons for this: as the polar ice caps melt there is more water in liquid form in the oceans. And, more significantly, water, like many other substances, expands with the heat: the oceans take up more room than they used to, causing ever more damage to islands and coasts and compromising the future of entire island nations. The warmer oceans absorb less carbon and so become more acidic, and this affects fish populations, which in turn affects the human populations that eat them. The flooding that comes from increased rainfall. This is exacerbated by upstream deforestation: trees are cut down to create more agricultural land, because there are more and more people to feed. This releases water quickly rather than holding on to it. Major flooding events are now part of planetary routine: between 2010 and 2019 weather-related events displaced 23 million people every year.[3]

---

[3] Figures from the United Nations.

And despite all this extra water the added warmth also creates drought in other places, drying up water sources. The problem walks hand in hand with increasing desertification: less room for wildlife, less room for agriculture. With drought comes the dramatic problem of wildfires. The displacement of human populations and other problems caused by climate change are an increasing threat to global health: the World Health Organisation calculates that climate events are currently causing 250,000 additional deaths every year, from under-nutrition, malaria, diarrhoea and heatstroke.

The people who cause most of the problems – the people who live in the developed world – are comparatively immune. That's why climate change is still seen widely in these places as a future problem, one for other people to worry about, one that might not even happen – even though the temperature has risen 1.1 degrees since 1900 and will reach 1.5 degrees in a few decades. Every indication is that it will continue rising after that.

Climate change is indeed an inconvenient truth, and humans have a long history of knowing what to do with inconvenient truths. We either ignore them or deny them. Classic example: heliocentrism. The notion that the earth goes round the sun – i.e. that the earth is not the centre of the universe – was proposed in the sixteenth century by Nicolaus Copernicus – and his proposition was rejected. How could we humans be something peripheral? The later astronomer Galileo Galilei did further work on heliocentrism: the Catholic

Church said it was heresy and all publications on that subject were placed on the index of forbidden books.

Many people furiously rejected Darwin's theory of evolution; and, for that matter, many still do. A recent poll found that 25 per cent of people in Britain don't accept it. It's also true that many who do accept evolution cling to a misunderstanding of it: one that makes humanity the crown and the purpose of the process: evolution as a march of progress leading inevitably to glorious old us.[4] Other examples of rejected scientific truths include continental drift, basic hygiene, Freud and the subconscious, germ theory and the origin of life.

Misinformation is wonderfully easily available: one click and the earth is flat again. What does science know? There is a treasured belief that, according to science, a bumblebee can't fly. Alas, science is perfectly capable of explaining the aerodynamics of bumblebees – it's to do with leading edge vortices and the extraordinary rapidity of the wingbeat. The bumblebee theory is merely the classic expression of science denial. True, science doesn't know everything, but then it has never claimed to. All the same, there's a widespread view that scientists are not to be trusted: gods who have failed. But science is not a religion and infallibility is not part of its creed. Science is about seeking truth and

---

[4] Evolution is not driven by goals, it is not teleological. Nor is it about progress. It is about survival: you, dear reader, are as fully evolved as mistle thrush or a tapeworm.

advancing knowledge: there's nothing wrong in being wrong, only in falsifying your data.

But if you falsify your data in a form that people want, you're going to find plenty of takers. The tobacco companies hit back against reports that tobacco is damaging to heath with all kinds of confusion and misinformation. These days we can all wonder at the advert that told us: 'More doctors smoke Camel than any other cigarette'. That same technique has been followed by the big oil companies. Propaganda, misinformation and lobbying have all been used to soften and discredit climate science. Example: an advertorial placed in many major newspapers in the United States was headlined: 'Who told you the earth was warming, Chicken Little?' Oil companies were funding climate change denial until 2018.

Increasingly, this denial has become polarised. There was a time when environmental concern was an all-party matter. A survey in 2023 by the Wildlife Trusts showed that people who support wildlife charities are evenly split politically. In 2005 David Cameron, as Conservative prime minister, announced that he was going to lead 'the greenest government ever'. His successors Theresa May and Boris Johnson were both comparatively bold in climate matters.

But in recent years the emphasis has shifted. Environmental disdain has become part of the hard-right package. It's become a badge of toughness. At the Conservative party conference in 2023 a new phrase swept through the bars and lobbies and caucuses: 'net zero zealots'.[5] Those who wanted to make climate – i.e. the future of the planet – a serious issue were despised as softies. It really was and is as childish as that: macho posturing by both sexes.

The history of tobacco denial has fascinating parallels with climate denial. The difference is that one individual's actions can change things dramatically for the individual concerned: you can give up smoking. That doesn't work with the climate. But similarities can be found in both the denial and the addiction: that is to say, our addiction to oil. Convincing the world that climate breakdown isn't happening – that it's perfectly OK to carry on just as we are – is as hard a task as persuading James Bond to smoke one more Morland Special (the cigarette with three gold rings) after a moment of special tension. The world's addiction to meat is just as intense and widespread as our addiction to oil, and, as we have seen in Chapter 21, this puts methane, another significant greenhouse gas, into the atmosphere.

COP 28 in 2023, the United Nations Climate Change Conference, was held in the UAE, without a hint of irony. It was attended by many lobbyists from the oil industry. The event's president, Dr Sultan Al Jaber, told the world that there was 'no science' behind plans to phase out fossil fuels in order to restrict temperature to 1.5 degrees. There was, however, some progress to celebrate: the conference ended with agreement – perhaps

---

[5] Net zero is a wished-for future state in which the amount of carbon released is equal to the amount sequestered.

inevitably delayed by objections from Saudi Arabia – that there would be a global move away from use of carbon energy 'in a just, orderly and equitable fashion' in order to reach net zero by 2050. This was, in a quiet way, revolutionary: it was the first time there had been global agreement on the fact that anthropogenic carbon emission was one of the factors driving climate change. It might seem rather late in the day to come to such an agreement, but that at least is better than further denial. There was also widespread agreement that each country should triple its commitment to renewable sources of energy – wind, water, sunlight, etc. However, China and India refused to be part of this, preferring to rely instead on their resources of coal.

Politicians on the far right are denying that climate change has any relevance to us, telling us, for example, that immigration is 'an existential threat' to our way of life and that this is the matter that should be occupying our minds. It's good, effective populist politics, tried and tested across the centuries: give the people a soft target, an out-group to blame for all woes. We would all prefer not to be told that climate change is already compromising the existence and the future of everything that lives on the planet, and that it might be an idea to take that seriously.

At this point the thought occurs to me that you might, dear reader, be finding this the least amusing chapter in the book. It was certainly the least fun to research and write. And to make this slightly worse, the change in our climate is something we can experience with immense vividness every spring, if we can only tune into nature. You'll recall that I went to Trimingham in North Norfolk in the high spring of 2022, because there were eight European bee-eaters there.[6] They breed mostly in southern Europe and West Asia, spending their winters farther south. On their northerly return flight they sometimes overshoot and turn up in England; gone on holiday by mistake, in fact. I remember seeing one from the top deck of a horse in the mid-nineties. A pair bred in Sussex in 1955, the first recorded instance. Trimingham was their sixth recorded attempt at breeding since 2002. I watched four of them perched on the wires, hawking after flying insects with that élan that only a bee-eater can muster. It was a moment of perfect delight: you didn't have to be a committed birdwatcher to share it either.

But it was a beauty shot through with horror. These wonderful birds were a message of destruction and despair as well as one of wonder and glory. It seemed then that the cruellest thing of all was that the human-generated crisis of climate breakdown has robbed us humans of the innocent soul-deep joy that we take in the coming of spring. Spring is not silent, not yet. But the sound it makes is now a warning. The joyful shout of the Cetti's warbler is a klaxon warning us of the terrible things that have happened and the terrible truth that there are worse to come.

---

[6] There are 27 species worldwide in this almost absurdly gorgeous family.

SPRING IN THE TIME OF CLIMATE CHANGE

The Greek word for home is *oikos* and is the root of economy and ecology. They should be sister sciences: instead, they are in bitter opposition. As a direct result, we are busy destroying our home. Climate breakdown is an unfolding disaster, and the worst is yet to come. On 1 February 2023 I found a daffodil – a fully open trumpet, a blazing yellow – on the lane that leads to our house. Should I rejoice? Or recoil in horror, as if I had opened the fridge and found a corpse inside? It seems that we humans are destroying the spring. In the long list of human crimes, this might be the worst of all.

Signs of spring
June 2024

11	Common meadow rue in flower, with thick-legged flower beetle
	Many new reeds
12	Cuckoo in garden
13	Three male cuckoos, one female responding
	River: pair of swans with five cygnets
14	Goldcrest singing
	Beccles station: buddleia in flower
15	Skylark singing over neighbour's field
17	Steart Marshes, Somerset: meadow brown (butterfly)
	Broad-bodied chaser (dragonfly)
	Many singing skylarks
	Sea star and sea lavender in flower on saltmarsh
	Little ringed plover and avocet making second breeding attempt
18	First sunny day for some time: outbreak of birdsong including Cetti's warbler, blackbird, blackcap and song thrush
19	Meadow brown
	Ragwort in flower
	Small copper (butterfly)
20	Two common spotted orchids in full bloom
	Clump of hemp agrimony about to flower
	Song thrush still singing hard at the moment of the solstice
21:51	Solstice
22:03	Male cuckoo calls once. Female responds instantly

23.5

Spring comes to Holkham

At six minutes past three in the morning on 20 March 2024, the earth was precisely at the midpoint of its biannual wobble. All over the world the time of daylight was as long as the time of darkness. It was the equinox, equilux if you prefer. From that point, every day in the northern hemisphere had a little more light than the one before, until we reached the solstice at ten to nine in the evening on 20 June.

More or less exactly nine hours after the point of equinox – so a little past noon – I was leaning comfortably against a 4x4 with binoculars in my hand. I seem to have spent an awful lot of my life in precisely that position, but this time I wasn't looking out over a nature reserve or the African savannah. I was looking at a field. A perfectly ordinary field on a perfectly ordinary farm in North Norfolk. There was a green fuzz of growing wheat. I have looked over a million fields very similar to this and sensed the dark cloud of depression.

Not today. The field dipped down, rather sharply for Norfolk, and I could see eight roe deer drifting unhurriedly away. Half a dozen hares were romping with March enthusiasm. And above my head skylarks sang: so many it was as hard to separate them as it is hard to separate individual voices in a choir singing the B Minor Mass. I could clearly see four very close, rising together, challenging each other for rights over this bit of airspace and the excellent breeding territory that lay beneath. It would be claimed by the mightiest singer of the quartet.

My old friend Jake Fiennes was talking about hedges, a fairly frequent event, it has to be said. 'I haven't cut these hedges for four years,' he said. 'That's saved us ten grand – and it's made more space for nature. Now we're getting blackcap and lesser whitethroat nesting here. We had one pair of yellowhammers, now we've got ten.'

The field was an awkward shape, but Jake had rationalised it, meaning that it takes much less time and much less fuel to cultivate it: six annual days' work instead of nine. The awkward bits have simply come out of production, which brings money in when allied to a government scheme. The edges of the field had been tilled but not planted: in a few weeks they would be red with poppies and blue with cornflowers, leaping up from treasure long stored in the seedbank.

This was Great Farm: ten fields and a comfortable 100 hectares: a classic small family farm, and it has been run as such by previous tenants since the eighteenth century. In recent years it had been farmed with all the rigours of post-war intensity, ploughed up to the hedges, lavishly treated with chemicals, the hedges annually flailed – all in the belief that there is no other way. It was Spam fritter mentality in action: a process driven by the post-war desperation to maximise the productivity of the land. But since Jake has had a say in the running, it has become more efficient, more productive, more profitable – and at the same time nature has been let back in.

Great Farm is one of 48 farms on the Holkham estate, which is owned by the eighth Earl of Leicester, who once – 'call me Tom' – kindly gave me a kitchen lunch before showing me round. Since then Jake has become Tom's conservation manager, and an estate that has prided itself on its progressive nature since the first earl in the eighteenth century has advanced still further. And it's an extraordinary place. The Palladian house is surrounded by classic parkland, its lawns mowed by a herd of 600 fallow deer, with wilder woodland beyond. The long and dead-straight South Avenue is a celebration of the well-mannered nature goddess beloved by eighteenth-century squires. Outside there is farmland, taking the estate up to 25,000 acres, and this includes England's largest privately owned National Nature Reserve at 9,600 acres. In an unusual arrangement this is managed by the estate, in consultation with Natural England. The reserve includes saltmarsh, sand dunes, woodland, grazing marsh and a foreshore of such staggering immensity that it's only narrowly beaten by the immensity of the Norfolk sky. It has a million human visitors a year, along with 300,000 dogs and a few thousand horses.

The nature reserve is my natural habitat, of course, and there, just as the spring was getting into its stride – even giving us a few hints of post-equinox sun – it was a treat to see displaying lapwing and fidgety brent geese, almost ready to set off for their breeding grounds in northern Siberia. All around I could feel the restless urge for change, the same urge that drew the Mole from his hole, abandoning the whitewash pail for adventure. Hang spring cleaning! I even had a look at the spoonbill colony: big untidy nests clumped unhandily over well-whitewashed branches. This was the first successful spoonbill colony in this country, established in 1999, and the earliest birds of this year's lot were already hard at it: immaculate white feathers now stained with the sharp yellow of their breeding plumage, balancing in the trees on those complicated nests, carrying sticks to make them bigger and still more untidy in their extraordinary soup-ladle bills.

But it wasn't the spoonbills that stayed with me, nor the fallow deer nor the brents nor the avenue nor the excellent pub lunch at the Hero nor the dunes nor even that impossible beach. It was the skylarks: so many I stopped wondering why the accepted collective noun is an exaltation of larks. Here were larks ascending, blithe spirits beyond easy counting, larks who poured and pelted music – all in the context not of a nature reserve but of a perfectly ordinary farm managed for profit and productivity.

Jake is not one for telling people what to do, mainly because it doesn't work. His aim is to conquer hearts and minds: to get the farmers he works with to see the point and manage their land with nature in mind, in the certain knowledge that this is something that enriches us all – and not just humanity. Funnily enough, the most sceptical person involved in the Great Farm transformation was the tractor man; perhaps he felt that his driving skills were being disrespected by taking away those awkward corners. But this was now his favourite field: 'There's always something to look at.' These days working on a farm is often a lonely business, with frighteningly long working hours and much stress from unreliable weather. The suicide rate among farming people is dismayingly high.[1] Here was someone whose working day has been enriched.

---

[1] In 2022–3 there were 36 reported suicides among British farming people.

Jake is involved in many committees and is constantly in touch with government. His aim is to change farming: that is to say, to change the way we manage 75 per cent of Britain. He does that by talking, lobbying, emails by the billion, sitting in meetings, making presentations, networking, writing an excellent and important book[2] and, of course, by example. 'I haven't done anything special on Great Farm,' he said. 'Nothing difficult. Anyone can do this.'

Earlier that morning we had driven past farms in the hands of various tenants, many with brutalised, useless hedges, ploughed to the margins in the traditional way. Moving from these places to Great Farm is like the before and after pictures in an old advertisement: treat your fields with Fiennes's Elixir and they, too, will look like this!

In some ways it's going back: back to the nature-rich countryside we started to abandon in 1945, back to the time when Gerard Manley Hopkins walked through the agricultural countryside and wrote about the ascending lark and his rash-fresh re-winded new-skeinèd score. But it's also a potential route to the future, one that is ours if we care to accept it: one in which nature is not confined to dwindling, desperate last-stand zoo-like islands but as a valued, important and inevitable part of our lives.

We are not bound forever to bad choices. We are perfectly capable of making good ones. We can make good

---

[2] *Land Healer* by Jake Fiennes published in 2022.

choices about the way we manage our countryside, our cities and our climate. And as I leaned against Jake's mud-encrusted 4x4 on what was officially the first day of spring, I had to accept that our current course of pell-mell helter-skelter self-destruction is not inevitable.

T. S. Eliot said that hope was a <u>duty</u>: and it's a duty we owe to our great-grandchildren: in the hope that they will bless our memory rather than curse it. Hope remains an option: of course it does, for every year we have spring. We have a <u>duty</u>: one that comes in 23.5 different forms: a duty to the wobbling earth, to the miracle of photosynthesis, to the rituals of Easter, to the ancient myths of rebirth that helped to form us, to the nightingale, to Wordsworth's daffodils, to the first brimstone butterfly, to the firecrackers of Lamma Island, to the returning swallows, to the first cricket match of the year, to the bumbling bees, to Lady Chatterley, to the moths of the black skies, to Botticelli's Flora, to the awaking hedgehog, to lovers everywhere, to eggs that look little low heavens, to the farmers who shaped the land, to the angelic gannets, to the farmers who make room for nature, to Gilbert White and Selborne, to T. S. Eliot and the hyacinth girl, to those who work to lessen the impacts of the changing climate – and, of course, in the end, to the skylarks. I may have said this before, but –

Hope springs eternal in the human breast.

ACKNOWLEDGEMENTS

Thanks to everyone who has participated, willingly or not, in a million conversations about spring and its meaning over the last couple of years.

Cindy and Ralph made me to look at plants. My sisters Rachel and Julia helped me to remember childhood in Streatham. John recalled our sporting life on Streatham Common. Celia taught me about bees. Thanks to Dom Theobald and Rachel Barnes for advice on painting. Many thanks to Jake Fiennes for showing me round Holkham; his wonderful work there allowed me to finish this book on a good note.

Thanks as always to Cindy, Joseph and Eddie for support, good vibes, patience and understanding. Special thanks to Cindy (cindyleewright.com) for the line drawings.

At Bloomsbury: many thanks to Ian Marshall, who took this project on with dauntless courage. Also to Francisco Vilhena, Amy Whitaker and Brittani Davies. Thanks to Richard Collins for an editing job that combined hawk-like eyes with sympathy and understanding, Louise Tucker for the thankless and

ACKNOWLEDGEMENTS

essential job of proofreading and David Atkinson for the index.

At Georgina Capel Associates, thanks to Irene Baldoni, and as ever, to George, who makes it possible for me to write books.

INDEX

Acanthasitti 81
Achebe, Chinua 203
Acheson, Nick 89
Achilles 71
aconites 92
Adams, Douglas ix
adders 253–6
Adonis 64–5, 68, 72
Agricultural Act (1947) 336
agriculture 60–1, 63, 103, 301–16, 333–49
   Canaanite festivals 141
   Green Revolution 340
   chemical farming 338–40
   manorial system 306–7
   mechanisation 336–7
   prophylactic antibiotic use 345–6
   and suicide 407
Al Jaber, Sultan 398
alder 16, 20, 92, 163, 165, 182, 284
Alderney 329
alexanders 146
'All the Things You Are' 281–2
American Cyanamid 343
Amundsen, Roald 356
Andress, Ursula 169
androgen 79
anemones 65, 237–8, 361

angiosperms 31–2
animal sacrifices 46–7
antidepressants 346–7
Aphrodite 64–5
Appiano, Semiramide 238
Archelaus 51
Aristotle 156
Arrhenius, Svente 390
Arthur, King 57, 59
ash 16, 20, 36, 232, 249, 300, 349, 354, 358
Asimov, Isaac 12
Astaire, Fred 279
Aswan Dam 60
Attenborough, Sir David 17–18, 247, 293
Attis 65–6
auks 328
aurochsen 310
Austen, Jane, *Pride and Prejudice* 211
Avengers films 71
Avery, Mark 347
avocets 299, 393, 402

Bacchanalia 67
Bach, J. S. 12, 62
badgers 201, 264
Badminton Horse Trials 179–81
Baker, John 253

INDEX

Baldr 66
Ballad of Finnegan's Wake 55–6
Ballets Russes 368
banded demoiselles 366, 382–3
Barbizon group 245
Barnacle, Nora 213
Barnes Common 89
Barrett, Syd 202
Barrington, Daines 358
bar-tailed godwits 162
Bashō 145, 387
bats xii, 33, 51, 111, 165, 225–9, 231, 257
    pregnancy 262–3
Baudelaire, Charles 377
Beatles, the 281, 372
Beckett, Peta 180
Bede 50
Bedlington terriers 313
bee-eaters 298, 400
bee orchids 34
bees xii, 33, 35, 38, 111, 183–98, 214, 253, 342, 352, 364, 396, 409
    African bees 195
    bee-keeping 194–7
    bumblebee flight 187–8
    carpenter bees 191
    co-evolution 189–90
    colony collapse disorder 197
    colony genetics 196–7
    cuckoo bumblebees 188–9
    honeybees 192–7
    honeybees' waggle dance 196
    leafcutter bees 192
    mason bees 190–1
    mimicry 187–8
    mining bees 192, 265, 364
    pseudocopulation 364
    solitary bees 190
    species numbers 186, 190
    Wallace's giant bee 190
Beethoven, Ludwig van 372
Beijing Olympics 135n
Belize 116
Bempton Cliffs 297
Bendire, Charles 296
Beowulf 71
Berlin, Irving 279n
biofuels 346, 348
bioluminescence 225
bird cherry 249
bird populations, declining 295
bird ringing 157–8
birds' eggs 287–99
bird's-foot trefoil 121
birdsong 76–91, 252
    and gender 90–1
Birdwatching with Your Eyes Closed 159
bitterns 388, 392–3
Black Death 307
blackbirds 20, 86–7, 90–1, 95, 151n, 165, 181, 198, 214, 232, 248, 291, 352, 402
blackcaps 20, 89, 91, 159, 232, 249, 402, 404
black-headed gulls 130, 155
blackthorn 35, 113, 215, 232, 266, 352, 361
black-winged stilts 388
Blake, William 105, 126, 299
blue tits 36, 256, 290, 292, 363
blue viperine 238
bluebells 28, 208, 267, 299, 331, 361
Boat Race 174
Boleyn, Anne 276

INDEX

Bordeaux Mixture 339
Borges, Jorge Luis 203
Borneo 18–19
Botticelli, Sandro, *Primavera* and *The Birth of Venus* 234–8, 409
bracken 252
Bradfield Woods 259
brambles 366, 382
Brasher, Chris 179
brimstone butterflies 114, 117–19, 121–2, 185, 214, 232, 267, 352, 365, 409
British Trust for Ornithology (BTO) 163–4, 215
British Wildlife magazine 360
broom 249, 284
Browning, Robert 108
Bruegel, Pieter, the Elder 318, 327
brumation 254–6
Bryson, Bill 340
buckthorn, alder and purging 121
buddleia 125, 401
bulbs 27–8, 34
burdock 382
Burnett, Frances Hodgson, *The Secret Garden* 204–5
Burns, Robert 271
buttercups 214, 238
butterflies ix, xii, 113–29, 222, 224, 252–3, 342
　life cycles 117–20, 265
　male combats 126–7
　migrations 124–6
　population decline 127, 348
　see also individual species
buzzards 73, 92, 182, 215

cabbages 121
Cadbury's 278
Camberwell beauty butterflies 123
Cameron, David 397
camomile 238
campions 208, 299, 331, 366
Canaanite agricultural festivals 141
Captain America films 71–2
carnations 238
carrots 29
Carson, Rachel, *Silent Spring* 75–6, 297, 342–4, 349
cattle 305, 310–12, 314, 340, 346
celandines 249, 267
　lesser celandines 182, 215, 232, 352, 361, 365
Centre for Ecology & Hydrology 360
Cetti, Francesco 385n
Cetti's warblers 20, 159, 181, 198, 232, 248, 266, 284, 299–300, 316, 349, 385–8, 400, 402
chaffinches 130, 147, 198, 383
Chaucer, Geoffrey 273, 275
　The Canterbury Tales 97–8, 375
cheetahs 226
chickweed 29
chiffchaffs 88–9, 113, 151, 158–9, 214, 352
chimpanzees 219–20
Chinese New Year 131–6
Chinese water deer 73
Chloris 236–7
chlorophyll 23
Christmas trees 279, 281
cinnabar moths 114
Clare, John 107, 122
cleavers 349

INDEX

climate change 187, 343, 363, 365, 385–401
climmers 297
clouded yellow butterflies 123
cobras 255
cod 324
columbines 208
comma butterflies 119, 121
common blue butterflies 121, 300
common meadow rue 401
common poorwills 257
conifers 24–5
Constable, John, *The Hay Wain* 243–5, 313
continental drift 396
COP 28, 398–9
Copernicus, Nicolaus 395
cornflowers 237–8, 405
cotoneaster 114
courtly love 273–6
cow parsley 26–7, 249, 267
Coward, Noël 106
cowslips 232, 249, 284
crabs 321
craneflies 284
cranes 155–6
cricket 168–71, 174
crickets 225
crocuses 147, 238
crossbills 291–2
crows 290, 292
cuckoo pint (arum lily) 34, 107, 110, 122, 165, 284
cuckoos 81–2, 110, 162–5, 169, 188, 284, 299–300, 349–50, 366, 372, 373, 382–3, 401–2
    Indian cuckoo 133
curlews 198, 248, 364
cyanobacteria 22

daffodils 27–8, 48, 94–6, 103–5, 110, 122, 368, 373, 401, 409
daisies 16, 198, 238, 354
    oxeye daisies 222, 299, 349
Dalí, Salvador 373–5, 380–1
damselflies 300, 349, 382
    see also banded demoiselles
damson blossom 232
dandelions 232, 354
Dante 275, 376–7
Dartford warblers 159, 350
Darwin, Charles 31, 85, 188, 304, 396
daylight saving 9
DDT 297, 340–2, 344
de' Medici, Lorenzo di Pierfrancesco 238
deadly nightshade 366
Derby, the 177–8
Descent of Inanna 64
desert rhinos 19
deserts 18–19, 21
Diaghilev, Sergei 368–9
diapause 118, 120
Dickens, Charles 377
Dickinson, Emily 123
Dionysus 67
Disley, John 179
distillation 9
dormancy 31, 256
dormice 257, 260–1
Doyle, Sir Arthur Conan 322
dragonflies 160, 265, 349, 366, 401
Dunlop, John 176
Dunnet Head x
dunnocks 73, 86–7, 91–2, 110, 130, 146, 164, 198, 288, 292, 294n

INDEX

Dunsterville, J. C. 52
Dunwich Forest 252, 254

earth
  atmosphere 388–9
  orbit and rotation 3–7, 15, 22, 403
earthworms 357
Easter 38–42, 44–6, 48–52, 133, 139, 141, 168, 174, 209, 275, 293, 409
Easter bunny 42, 49, 52
Easter eggs 44–5, 48–9, 293
Easter Parade 279–80
eels 325
eggs 42–4
  hard-boiled 143
  see also Easter eggs
egrets 36, 54, 73, 111, 147, 387–8
Eid 141
elder xiii, 243, 366, 368, 382
elderflower tea 209
elephant hawk moths 114, 223
Eliot, T. S. 10, 409
The Waste Land 58n, 376–81
Enlightenment 102, 104
Environment Agency 393
Eostre 50
Epic of Gilgamesh 64, 71
Equator 5
equinoxes 6–7, 27, 37, 39, 42, 45, 141, 156, 177, 214, 271, 353, 403–4, 406
euphorbia 238
Euphrates, River 60, 303
evening primrose 222
evolution (natural selection) 12, 32, 85, 189–90, 228, 265–6, 289, 304–5, 360, 396

FA Cup 173–4, 179
fallow deer 407
Fantastic Four 71
Fertile Crescent 60, 303
fieldfares 20, 181
Fiennes, Jake 404–5, 407–9
Finland 364
Finnegan, Tim 55–6, 67
First World War 309
Fitter, Richard 360
Fitzgerald, Ella 281
Flamborough Head 323
floods 394
Flora 234–8, 409
food chains 318
football 171–4
Forestry Commission 252
forget-me-nots 208, 238, 249
Forster, E. M., *A Room with a View* 211
foxes 221, 290
foxgloves 29, 331
Franciscans 308
Frazer, Sir James 59–60
French Revolution 105
Freud, Sigmund 374–5, 396
Frith, William Powell 178
frogs 133, 224, 264, 289
fuchsia 223

gadwalls 20, 198, 214
Galileo 395
Gammer Gurton's Garland 277
gannets 329–30, 409
García Márquez, Gabriel 203
Garden of Eden 108, 303
garden tiger moths 114–15
garden warblers 316
gardens 100–1

INDEX

Garland, Judy 279–80
garlic mustard 121, 215, 232
geese 20, 154, 406
    bar-headed geese 162
    Egyptian geese 146, 165
germ theory 396
germination 7
Glencoyne Bay 96
globalisation 309
Glover, Brian 315
gnats 92, 147, 165, 248
Gobi Desert 21
goldcrests 165, 401
goldfinches 165
Good Friday 40, 275
gorse 284
goshawks 350
Grahame, Kenneth, *The Wind in the Willows* 199–203
Grand National 174–5, 177, 180
Grant, Hugh 280–1
grass snakes 255
grasshopper 382
gravity 2–3
great crested grebes 110
Great Depression 340
Great Farm 405–8
Great Oxidation Event 23
great tits 16, 36, 54, 87–8, 92, 147, 182, 198, 256, 292, 352, 354, 363
green alkanet 181, 350
green hairstreak butterflies 331, 350
Green, Chris 179
Green Man 62–3
greenfinches 130, 198
Greenland 364
Greenpeace 341

green-veined white butterflies 248
Grimm, Jacob and Wilhelm 68–9
Grisenthwaite, David 360
ground elder 110
ground ivy 110, 182, 248
guillemots 293, 297, 328, 331
Gulf Stream 320

Haber-Bosch process 339
Hadley Wood 89
Haigh-Wood, Vivienne 378
haikus 144–6
Hale, Emily 380
Hammerstein, Oscar 281
Hampstead Heath 105
Hampstead Ponds 249
hanami 144
Handel's *Messiah* 41
hares 49–54, 111, 130, 221, 316, 349, 392, 404
    snowshoe hares 365
Harrison, George 281
Hathaway, Anne 65
hawthorn 198, 210, 261, 284, 361
hazel 16, 54, 354
hazelnuts 260
Hazelwood Marshes 392–3
heatwaves 391–2
hedge bedstraw 222–3
hedgehogs 218–19, 254, 257, 261–2, 290, 409
heliocentrism 395–6
Helios 13
helium 11
hellebore 238
hemp agrimony 382, 402
Hendry, Pete 376–7
Henley Royal Regatta 178
Henry VIII, King 98, 276, 308

INDEX

Herb Robert 267
'Here Comes the Sun' 281
hermit thrushes 379, 381
herons xiii, 20, 80, 130, 146–7, 165, 215, 292, 316, 383, 386–8
Herpetological Conservation Trust 253
herrings 324
hibernation 24, 118, 152, 157–8, 226, 253–4, 256–66, 356
Hickling Broad 128
Highland cattle 284, 300
Hill, Rowland 278
Hiranyakashipu 137–8
hoarfrost 19
hobbies 159–60, 331, 383
Hockney, David, *The Arrival of Spring* 247–8
Holi festival 136–9, 143
Holkham estate 215, 405–6
holly 121, 299
holly blue butterflies 121, 350
Holy Grail 58–9, 205–6
Holy Saturday 40
Holy Trinity 52
Homer
  The Iliad 71, 156
  The Odyssey 204
hominid evolution 265–6
honey 193–5
honeysuckle 208, 222
Hong Kong 132–3, 135
Hopkins, Gerard Manley 88n, 107–8, 287, 408
horse racing 174–8
horse riding 180–1
Horus 62
Hou Yi 13

house martins 155, 267, 299–300, 383
hoverflies 232, 265
How to Be a Bad Birdwatcher 135, 386
Howde, Philip 128
Hughes, Ted, 'Swifts' 109–10, 160
Huitzilopochtli 13
human population, growth of 100–1, 103, 309
hummingbirds 257
Hurd, Anthony 323
hyacinths 238, 379–81, 409
hydrocarbon fuels 389–90
hydrogen 11, 22–3

Impressionists 239, 245–6, 372
Inanna 63–4
Industrial Revolution 103–4, 389
intercalation 139–40
International Moratorium on Whaling 326
iris flags 20, 27, 238, 316, 349
Irish potato famine 339
Iron Man 71–2
Isis 61–2
Islamic calendar 139–40
Issa 144
Izanami 66–7

jackdaws 266, 316, 350, 382
Japanese flowering cherry 20–1, 143–4, 146, 358
jasmine 222, 238
jays 290
jellyfish 322
Jeremiah 155
Jersey cows 310

INDEX

Jesus Christ 47–8, 58, 142–3, 308
'John Barleycorn' 56–7, 67
Johnson, Boris 397
Johnson, Samuel 203
jonquils 147
Jordan, River 141n
Jourdain, Rev. Francis 297
Jourdain Society 297
Joyce, James 270, 355
    Finnegans Wake 56, 72, 376
    Ulysses ix, 12, 65, 211–14, 320, 372, 378
Julius Caesar 273
Jung, Carl 60
juniper 24
Juno Februata 272

kangaroos 220
Keats, John
    'La Belle Dame Sans Merci' 76
    'Ode to a Nightingale' 105
Keeling, Charles 390
Kern, Jerome 281
kestrels 91, 122
kidney vetch 331
Kipling, Rudyard 52, 189n, 359, 365, 359, 365
    The Jungle Book 220–1
kittiwakes 331
Klütz 157
Krishna 136–8
Kröller-Müller, Helene 296

lacewings 147
lady's smock 121
ladybirds 165
Lamb of God 47–8
lambs 42, 45–6, 284, 311–12
Lamma Island 132–4, 136, 409

Lancelot and Guinevere 275
Lantern Festival 135
lapwings 53–4, 215, 248, 364, 393, 406
large white butterflies 121–2
Last Supper 58
Lawrence, D. H. 109
Lady Chatterley's Lover 207–9, 372, 409
leap years 139
Lehrer, Tom 47
Leiston 146
Lent 39–40, 44, 139, 141
Lent lilies 27
Leonardo da Vinci 142
Lepidoptera 115–16
Lewis, C. S., *Chronicles of Narnia* 57, 70, 252, 295
light traps 222
lilacs 271, 381
Lindo, David 151n
lions 170–1
Little Red Tractor 315, 344
little ringed plovers 402
Lizard Point x, 8
lizards 33, 255
lobsters 321
Loki 66
London Bridge 9–10
London Marathon 179
London plane trees 20, 182, 246
long-tailed tits 182, 292
Lord's test match 178
Louis XIV, King of France 44
Luangwa Valley 305
lunisolar calendars 133, 139–40
Lupercalia 272–3
lycorine 28
lynxes 311, 365

magnolia 147, 198
magpies 290, 366
mallards 20, 91, 181, 198
mallows 146, 222, 366, 382
Malory, Sir Thomas 58
manatees 321–2
Manz shearwaters 331
Marazion Marsh 385–6
Mark Antony 273
Markwell, William 357
Marrakesh 140
Mars 15
marsh harriers 36, 146–7, 181,
    198, 214, 232, 248, 350, 354,
    366, 382
marsh marigolds 214–15, 266
marsh tits 54
Marsham, Mary 359
Marsham, Robert 359
Marvell, Andrew, 'The
    Garden' 101
Massine, Léonide 371
Mauna Loa volcano 390
Maundy Thursday 40
mauve umbellifers 354
Mauve, Anton 240–1
May, Theresa 397
may blossom 248
May Day 177, 282
meadow brown butterflies 401–2
meadowsweet 20, 222
Mercury 5, 12
Mesopotamia 13, 44, 60, 63
Met Office 392, 394
methane 346
Middle English 273
migration
    birds 150–64, 242, 257, 363–4
    butterflies 124–6, 266

fish 324–5
toads 264
Zugunruhe 157
milk parsley 128
Millet, Jean-François 305
Milton, John, *Paradise Lost* 67–8
Minsmere RSPB reserve 387
mistle thrushes 396n
mistletoe 66
monarch butterflies 125–6
Morris, William 20
Moses 142
mosquitoes 224–5, 344
moths 32, 114–16, 222–4, 227–8,
    263, 331, 409
    see also individual species
Mount Everest 162
Müllerian mimicry 187
Mumbai 136, 139
muntjac 54, 72
Murtagh, John 167–9, 174
musk mallow 222

Nabokov, Vladimir 370n
Namib Desert 19
Narayan, R. K. 203
Natural England 406
Natural History Museum 295, 298
natural selection, *see* evolution
Nature's Calendar 360
Naumann, Johann Andreas 157
nectar 33–4, 118–21, 126, 184–5,
    189, 191, 193, 195–6,
    221, 223
nene (Hawaiian goose) 341
net zero 397–8
nettles 26, 36, 110, 121, 125,
    127, 354–5
    dead nettles 147, 181–2, 215

INDEX

Newbolt, Sir Henry 169n
Nian 134
Nietzsche, Friedrich 369
nigella 238
night-flying insects 224–6
night phlox 222
night-scented plants 221–3
nightingales 89–90, 105, 366, 372–3, 378–9, 381, 409
nightjars 229, 257, 358
Nijinsky, Vaslav 368, 370
Nile, River 60–2, 303
Norfolk Bird and Mammal Report 387
Norfolk Broads xii, 16, 127–9, 162–3
North Sea 324
Norwich Cathedral 62, 232
Notting Hill 280–1
Nowruz festival 143
nuclear fusion 11
nuclear warfare 14

oak 29, 208, 261, 266, 358, 363
Oates, Lawrence 356
Observer's Book of Birds' Eggs 295
octopuses 170
Oddie, Bill 294–5
Oedipus 138, 204
Oedipus Rex 204
oestrogen 79
oikos 401
Oldfield, Mike, *Tubular Bells* 87
orange-tip butterflies 120–1, 266–7, 300
orchids 30n
Orwell, River 382
Oscines 81–2
Osiris 61–2, 72

ospreys 159
Outney Common 366
Ovid, *Metamorphoses* xi, 13, 378–9
owls 228–31
   barn owls 151n, 228–9, 383
   little owls 350
   tawny owls 165, 229–31, 349
oystercatchers xiii, 146–7, 165, 181, 198, 214, 232

Packham, Chris 294
painted lady butterflies 121, 125–6, 266
Pan 272
Pan pipes 81
partridges 52–3
Paschal Lamb 141
passerines 80–1
Passover 39, 46, 50, 139, 141–2
Patagonia 21
peacock butterflies 119, 121, 249, 300
peak sunlight 8
Peasants' Revolt 307
Pelé 95, 97
penicillin 345
peregrine falcons 297, 350
periwinkles 16, 237–8, 354
Petrarch 275
Phaeton 13–14
pheromones 224
photosynthesis 22–5, 27, 30, 45, 259, 317, 319, 321, 361, 409
Phylloscopus warblers 151
phytoplankton 318–20, 322, 362
pied flycatchers 363–4
pigs 220, 284, 310–12, 315
pine martens 290

INDEX

Pink Floyd 202
Pissarro, Camille, *Montmartre, Spring* 246–7
plantains 382
Plato, *The Republic* 79
Pliny the Elder 51
ploughs, development of 305–6
plum blossom 130, 232, 240
Plumage League 341
polecats 290
pollen 31–4, 107, 185, 189, 191, 193, 195, 364
pollinators 32–4
Pope, Alexander 101–2, 105, 109, 129, 244
poppies 30, 145, 238, 349, 382, 405
Powell, Anthony 209
Presley, Elvis 372
primroses 35, 94, 111, 198, 222, 373
Proust, Marcel 355; *À la recherche du temps perdu*, 209–11
Proxima Centauri 12
Puccini, Giacomo 370
puffins 328, 331
purple loosestrife 382

Quetzalcoatl 66
Quran 140

Ra 13
rabbits 49–50, 52–3, 221, 359
Radha 137–8
ragwort 243, 402
rainbows 130
rainforests ix, 18–19, 21, 163, 190, 362
Ramadan 139–41
rape fields 198

Ratcliffe Derek 297
rats 201, 231, 290–1
Raveningham estate 54, 111
ravens 292
razorbills 328, 331
red admiral butterflies 121, 124–5, 331
red kites 72, 92
red tuna 324
redshanks 214, 299, 393
reed buntings 299
reed warblers 20, 159, 164, 299, 316, 349, 366, 382–3
Reeder, Colin 315
reeds 401
reindeer 364
rhizomes 26–7
Richard II, King 97
rinderpest 314
Roberts, Julia 280–1
Robin Hood 62
robins 20, 82–3, 86, 91, 122, 151, 286–7, 293
Romans 64, 67, 306, 312
Romanticism 94, 104–9
Romulus and Remus 272
rooks 130
rosemary 146
roses 122, 192, 212, 237–8, 270, 274–5, 277–8, 283
Rothschild, Charles 341
Rothschild, Lionel Walter 297
Rothschild List 341
rowing 174
Royal Meteorological Society 359
Royal Society for the Protection of Birds (RSPB) 170, 341, 347, 386–7
ryegrass 340

Saga, Emperor 144
St Magnus-the-Martyr church 379
St Mark's flies 267, 300
St Peter's church, Streatham 38–41, 56
sakura 144
sallows 110, 182, 214
salmon 325
Samson 138
sand martins 155, 158, 331, 357, 382
Sargasso Sea 325
Save the Rhino 179
Scots pine 24
Scott, Sir Peter 341
Scott, Robert Falcon 356
Scott Moncrieff, C. K. 210
sea hares 323
sea lavenders 402
sea levels, rising 394
sea slugs 318
sea stars 402
seabird colonies 327–8
seasonal affected disorder (SAD) 9, 352–3
seaweeds 321–3
Secombe, Harry xii
Second World War 71, 128, 316, 333, 335, 339, 346
sedge warblers 20, 89, 159, 299–300, 316, 366
seed drill, invention of 308
seeds 30–1
Selborne 151, 355–8, 409
Severn Wildfowl Trust 341
sexual selection 85
Shakespeare, William 206
   As You Like It xi
   Hamlet 204

The Merchant of Venice 138
A Midsummer Night's Dream 204, 282–3
Sonnets 99–100
Venus and Adonis 65
A Winter's Tale 204
Sham el Nessim 143
sheep 311–13
shelducks 214
Shelley, Mary 106
Shelley, Percy Bysshe, 'To a Skylark' 106
Shetland Isles 8
Shire horses 302
shrimps 321, 362
Shrove Tuesday 44
silleins 306–7
silver birch 267
silver Y moths 114
six-spot burnet 114
skylarks 88, 90, 106, 146, 215, 249, 331, 401–2, 404, 407, 409
Sleeping Beauty 69
slow worms 255
slugs 218–19, 261
   sea slugs and sea hares 318, 323
small blue butterflies 249
small copper butterflies 350, 402
small heath butterflies 350
small tortoiseshell butterflies 119, 121, 300
small white butterflies 121–2, 267, 300
smallpox 314n
Smith, Adam 314n
smooth sheep's bit 331
snakes 224, 253–6, 290
Snow White 68–9

snowdrops 34, 92, 111, 147, 392
soapwort 222
Sól 13
solar monotheism 13
solar system 10
solstices x, xii, 5–6, 8, 16, 21–2, 42, 86, 113, 133, 158, 178, 202, 271, 282–3, 353, 402, 404
song thrushes xiii, 36, 87, 92, 108–9, 130, 147, 198, 248, 287, 291, 352, 354–5, 365, 402
Songkran festival 143
Sophocles 79
South China Morning Post 132
Southwold 106
Spam fritters 333–4
Sparks, Tim 360
sparrowhawks 226
sparrows 266, 294, 338
spear thistles 382
speckled wood butterflies 118, 267
speedwell 249, 300, 382
Spenser, Edmund, *The Faerie Queene* 277–8
spider orchids 364
Spiderman 71
spiders 155, 231
  webs 292
spoonbills 215, 388, 406–7
spotted orchids 383, 402
spring squill 331
squirrels 73, 220, 264, 366
starlings 248
Steart Marshes 401
stock doves 16, 54, 354
stolons 26–7
stonechats 72

storks 155, 157, 279
storms, named 394
Stratton Strawless 359
Stravinsky, Igor, *The Rite of Spring* 368–72, 380
strawberry blossom 237–8, 267
Strumpshaw Fen 128
Suffolk Wildlife Trust 252, 259n, 392
sugar beet 348
Sumatran rhinoceros 313
sun 10–15, 21–2
sun myths 13–14
sundowners 8
sunflowers 239
Superman 71
Surya 13
swallows 91, 149–55, 157, 160, 256–7, 267, 284, 299–300, 352, 356–7, 366, 379, 409
swallowtails 127–9
swans 73, 122, 130, 154, 401
swifts 12, 109–10, 155, 160–1, 331, 349–50, 366
syrinx 81

Tammuz 63–4, 68
tapetum lucidum 220–1
tennis 172–3
Tennyson, Alfred Lord, *Locksley Hall* 270
Teotihuacán 143
terns 161
Tezcatlipoca 13
thick-legged flower beetles 401
Thompson, Frances 169n
Three Graces 237
three-cornered leeks 331
Tigris, River 60, 303

INDEX

toads 51, 146, 201–2, 231, 264, 289
toadstools 22
tobacco industry 397
tobacco plants 222
Tolstoy, Leo, *Resurrection* 41
tormentil 331
torpor 254, 256–7, 260, 263–5
tree-creepers 382
Trimingham 298, 400
Tropic of Cancer ix, 5, 60, 313
Tropic of Capricorn ix, 5
Troublesome Whisky 41
Trump, Donald 391
tsetse flies 305
Tull, Jethro 308
Turner, J. M. W., *The Fighting Temeraire* 243n
turtle doves 155, 350
twilight 8
Tyranni 81

Ukraine 348
umbellifers 16
universe, expanding 12
Uranus 5

Valentine's Day 269–78
Van Gogh, Vincent 238–42, 296, 305, 319
Venus 12
Very Warm for May 281
Vikings 312
violets 238, 275, 277–8
Virgil 275
Virgin Mary 51
Vishnu 137–8
voles 221, 229, 254
  water voles 201, 264

Wagner, Richard 369
wall butterflies 331
wallflowers 238
warblers, *see individual species*
Waring, Paul, and Martin Townsend, *Field Guide to Moths* 223n
Warwick-Evans, Victoria 329–30
wasps 189, 191, 265
water mint 20, 266, 366, 382
water rails 392–3
Watson, Charles 298
Waugh, Evelyn, *Brideshead Revisited* 53
Weis-Fogh clap-and-fling 125
Weston, Jesse 57
'Westron wynde' 98–9
whales ix, 22, 319–20, 325–7
wheatears 158
whisk(e)y 9, 41, 55–7
White, Gilbert 151–2, 159, 257, 356–8, 360–1, 409
White, Patrick 203
White-Stevens, Robert 343
whitethroats 20, 267, 284, 300, 316, 331, 350, 366, 404
wild boars 28, 65, 310
wild garlic 198
Wild Justice 347n
wild plum blossom 35
Wildfowl and Wetlands Trust 341
Wildlife and Countryside Act (1954) 294
wildlife charities 397
Wildlife Trusts 341, 397
Williamson, Emily 341
willow warblers 89–90, 151, 267, 388
willowherb 223

INDEX

willows 20, 92, 110, 147, 214, 232, 249, 366, 382, 392
Wimbledon 172–3, 178–9
windrows 252–4, 256
winter wheat 337–8, 340
wisteria 222
witchcraft 51
Withers, Bill 281
Wodehouse, P. G. 174n, 355
   The Inimitable Jeeves 206–7
wolves 220–1, 272–3, 311, 365
wood pigeons 36, 54, 130, 271
wood warblers 151, 159
Woodland Trust 360
woodlarks 86, 350
woodpeckers 54, 72, 87, 92, 111, 182, 198, 266

wool industry 313
Wordsworth, Dorothy 96
Wordsworth, William 94–6, 103, 105, 123, 409
wrens 16, 81, 82n, 86, 91, 110, 130, 146
Wyatt, Thomas 276

Yare, River 110
yellowhammers 404
yew 24
Yorkshire Wildlife Trust 323
Yoxford 16
Yung Shue Wan 132, 135

Zephyrus 236–7
Zoroastrianism 143

IMAGE CREDITS

Hazel catkins: Sandra Standbridge/Getty Images; Singing great tit: Zoe Allen/Getty Images; *Primavera*, Sandro Botticelli (1445–1510), La Primavera (Spring), c.1478. Tempera on panel. Uffizzi, Florence. Picture credit: Corbis via Getty Images; Snowdrops: Christina Bollen/Alamy Stock Photo; Frogspawn: Ed Brown Wildlife/Alamy Stock Photo; Vincent Van Gogh (1853–1890), *Pink Peach Trees 'Souvenir de Mauve'*, c.30 March 1888. Oil on canvas. Kröller-Müller Museum. Picture credit: © Collection Kröller-Müller Museum, Otterlo, the Netherlands. Photo: Rik Klein Gotink; Daffodils: Geoff Smith/Alamy Stock Photo; Lamb: Joanathan Neale/Alamy Stock Photo; Vincent Van Gogh (1853–1890), *Almond Blossom*, February 1890. Oil on canvas. Van Gogh Museum, Amsterdam. Picture credit: Bridgeman Images/The Van Gogh Museum, Amsterdam (Vincent Van Gogh Foundation); Grey heron: godrick/Getty Images; Boxing hares: Nick Hurst/Getty Images Plus; John Constable (1776–1837), *The Hay Wain*, 1821. Oil on canvas. The National Gallery, London. Picture credit: Alamy; Brimstone: Dirk von Mallinckrodt/Getty Images; Bluebell wood: Graham Custance

IMAGE CREDITS

Photography/Getty Images; Camille Pissarro (1830–1903), *Boulevard Montmartre, Spring*, 1897. Oil on canvas. Private Collection. Picture credit: Alamy; Orange tip butterfly: David Tipling/Universal Images Group via Getty Images; Swallows in flight: Carl Morrow/Alamy Stock Photo; Leonardo Da Vinci, *The Last Supper*: Alamy Stock Photo; Hoverfly: Arterra/Getty Images; Cuckoo: Nature Photographers Ltd/Alamy Stock Photo; William Powell Frith (1819–1909), *The Derby Day*, 1856–8. Oil paint on canvas. Tate Britain, London. Picture credit: Photo Tate; Hawthorn in blossom: Chris Robbins/Alamy Stock Photo; Banded demoiselle: Premium Stock Photography/Alamy Stock Photo; Salvador Dalí (1904–1989), *The First Day of Spring*, 1929. Oil and collage on panel. Salvador Dalí Museum, St Petersburg, Florida. Picture credit: Bridgeman Images/ Superstock © Salvador Dalí, Fundació Gala-Salvador Dalí, DACS 2024.

A NOTE ON THE AUTHOR

Simon Barnes is a writer and journalist who was the chief sportswriter and wildlife columnist for *The Times* until 2014, having worked for the paper for 30 years. He is the author of many wild volumes, including the bestselling *Bad Birdwatcher* trilogy, *Rewild Yourself* and, most recently, *How to be a Bad Botanist*. He is a trustee of Conservation South Luangwa and patron of Save the Rhino. In 2014, he was awarded the Rothschild Medal for services to conservation. He lives in Norfolk with his family, where he manages several acres for wildlife.

A NOTE ON THE TYPE

The text of this book is set in Fournier. Fournier is derived from the *romain du roi*, which was created towards the end of the seventeenth century from designs made by a committee of the Académie of Sciences for the exclusive use of the Imprimerie Royale. The original Fournier types were cut by the famous Paris founder Pierre Simon Fournier in about 1742. These types were some of the most influential designs of the eight and are counted among the earliest examples of the 'transitional' style of typeface. This Monotype version dates from 1924. Fournier is a light, clear face whose distinctive features are capital letters that are quite tall and bold in relation to the lower-case letters, and *decorative italics, which show the influence of the calligraphy of Fournier's time.*